Change within Tradition
among
Jewish Women
in
Libya
❖

Change within Tradition among Jewish Women in Libya

❖

Rachel Simon

A Samuel and Althea Stroum Book

UNIVERSITY OF WASHINGTON PRESS
SEATTLE & LONDON

This book is published with the assistance of a grant from the
Stroum Book Fund, established through the generosity of
Samuel and Althea Stroum.

LIBRARY OF CONGRESS CATALOGING-IN-PUBLICATION DATA
Simon, Rachel
Change within tradition among Jewish women in Libya / Rachel
Simon.
p.   cm.
"A Samuel and Althea Stroum book."
Includes bibliographical references and index.
ISBN 0-295-97167-3 (alk. paper)
1. Jews—Libya—History—19th century. 2. Jews—Libya—History—
20th century. 3. Women, Jewish—Libya. 4. Libya—Ethnic relations. I.
Title.
DS135.L44S56 1992
305.48'89240612'09034—dc20   91-35675
                                                                CIP

The paper used in this publication meets the minimum requirements
of American National Standard for Information Sciences—
Permanence of Paper for Printed Library Materials, ANSI Z39.48-1984.
∞

❖ CONTENTS ❖

Abbreviations / vi

Acknowledgments / vii

Map of Libya / 2

Introduction / 3

1 Status within the Family and the Community / 21

2 Family Life / 45

3 Work / 84

4 Educational Opportunities / 108

5 Participation in Public Life / 154

Conclusion / 204

Bibliography / 209

Index / 213

ADEI	Associazione Donne Ebree d'Italia
AIU	Alliance Israélite Universelle, Paris
AJDC	American Joint Distribution Committee
ASD	Archivio Storico e Diplomatico, Rome
BMA	British Military Administration
CAHJP	Central Archives for the History of the Jewish People, Jerusalem
CZA	Central Zionist Archives, Jerusalem
ENIO	Ecole Normale Israélite Orientale
GIT	Gioventù Israelitica Tripolitana
JNF	Jewish National Fund
MAL	Military Administration Lira
PRO	Public Record Office, London
SEF	Società Ebraica Femminile
WIZO	Women's International Zionist Organization

❖ ACKNOWLEDGMENTS ❖

I would like to thank the staffs of the following archives and libraries, where most of the research for this study was conducted: Archivio Storico e Diplomatico, Rome; Ben Zvi Institute, Jerusalem; Central Archives for the History of the Jewish People, Jerusalem; Central Zionist Archives, Jerusalem; National and University Library, Jerusalem; Princeton University Library, Princeton, New Jersey; Public Record Office, London; and University of Washington Libraries, Seattle, Washington. The study was written in part while I was a Stroum Fellow for Advanced Research in Jewish Studies in the Jewish Studies Program, the Henry M. Jackson School of International Studies, University of Washington, Seattle. I would like to thank the Jewish Studies Program and the Middle East Center at the University of Washington for their support during my stay in Seattle. Thanks also to the University of Washington Press, and especially to Pamela J. Bruton for the thorough editing. Last but not least, special thanks to my family for their support during the various phases of this study.

*Change within Tradition
among
Jewish Women
in
Libya*

❖

MEDITERRANEAN SEA

TUNISIA

Tripoli
Zu'ara • Zanzur • Tajura
Zawiya • Amrus
'Aziziya • Khoms
Tarhuna • Mislata • Zliten
Nalut • Yefren • Gharyan • Misrata
Jado • Beni Walid
Mizda
Sedada • Sirt
Bu'ayrat al-Hasun

Gulf of Sidra

Derna

Barce

Benghazi
Soluq

Tubruq
Port Bardia

Zuwaytina
Ajdabiya

Derg
Ghadames

T R I P O L I T A N I A

ALGERIA

F E Z Z A N

L I B Y A

C Y R E N A I C A

EGYPT

200 miles

250 kilometers

Introduction

❖

B y the end of the nineteenth century, the societies of the Middle
East and North Africa, along with other members of the world
community, had witnessed far-reaching changes triggered by political,
economic, social, and cultural developments. This study focuses on
those changes influencing Jewish women in Libya during the late nineteenth century until the mass emigration of Jews from Libya in the mid-
twentieth century. It examines how changes in Libyan society as a
whole (including foreign interventions) affected Libyan Jewish women
and analyzes the developments in their status, family life, work, education, and participation in public life. It also examines how the developments in each of these spheres influenced one another and how changes
were woven into the traditional way of life and thought.

THE JEWISH PRESENCE IN LIBYA

With the departure of more than 4,000 Jews from Libya in the summer
of 1967, a virtual end was put to the ancient Jewish presence in the
region. The hasty mass evacuation of Jews from Libya in 1967 was
triggered by the anti-Jewish riots in Tripoli during the Arab-Israeli Six-

Day War of June 1967. This wave of Jewish emigration from Libya was preceded by that of 1949–51, which carried more than 30,000 Libyan Jews to Israel, following the establishment of the state of Israel (May 1948) and in anticipation of Libyan independence (December 1951).[1]

Prior to this, there was little voluntary population movement among the Libyan Jews: they experienced no significant permanent migration waves, and the size and spread of their settlements were conditioned primarily by external factors, such as economic hardships and security problems. Roman retaliation following the revolt against Trajan in Cyrenaica (115–17 CE), the Arab penetration starting in the mid-seventh century, and continuous rebellions of the indigenous population against the central regime, which often resulted in mass deportations—all these as well as environmental and economic factors contributed to the decreasing numbers of Libyan Jews and their isolation from the rest of the Jewish world. When the Ottomans occupied Tripoli in 1551, there were hardly any urban Jews in Libya. In the following years, Jews from the Tripolitanian hinterland gradually moved to the Mediterranean coastal towns and brought with them numerous manners and customs that were influenced by those of the non-Jewish majority.

From the sixteenth century on, the indigenous Libyan Jews were occasionally supplemented by Jews from Europe, mainly from Spain and Italy. Following the expulsion of Jews from Spain in the late fifteenth century, some Sephardic Jews settled in Libya. Despite their small numbers, their cultural influence on the local Jews was great due to the high scholarly level of some of these immigrants (especially of Rabbi Shim'on Lavi) compared with that of most of the Libyan Jews. Furthermore, Lavi's Kabbala studies endeared him to the indigenous population, among whom mysticism was very widespread. Mainly from the seventeenth century onward, Italian and some other European Jewish individuals settled in Libya to take advantage of business opportunities or the permission for Jewish men in Islamic countries to marry a

1. For further information on the Jews of Libya, see R. De Felice, *Jews in an Arab Land: Libya, 1835–1970* (Austin: University of Texas Press, 1985); M. Ha-Cohen, *Higgid Mordecai* (Jerusalem: Ben-Zvi Institute, 1978) (for a partial English translation and commentary, see H. E. Goldberg, *The Book of Mordechai: A Study of the Jews of Libya* [Philadelphia: Institute for the Study of Human Issues, 1980]; the references are to the complete Hebrew original unless otherwise stated); H. Z. Hirschberg, *A History of the Jews in North Africa* (Leiden: E. J. Brill, 1981), 2:147–87; R. Simon, "Yehudey Luv yeha-Sevivah ha-Nokhrit be-Shaley ha-Tequfah ha-'Uthmanit," *Pe'amim* 3 (1979): 5–36; F. Zuarez et al., eds., *Yahadut Luv* (Tel-Aviv: Va'ad Qehilot Luv be-Yisra'el, 1982).

second wife if the first one bore them no sons. Jewish communities made a special effort to ransom Jewish victims of piracy. Some of these former captives also settled in Libya.

The differing origins of the Libyan Jews did not cause a split in the community, as was the case in some other North African regions (the most striking example was that of Tunis). Apparently this was because of the relatively small number of European Jews in Libya and because they usually intermarried with the indigenous Jews. The different origins were, however, reflected in the socioeconomic structure of the community, as well as in the political status and the cultural outlook of certain groups of Jews. Due to their involvement in international trade and finance, the Jews who came from Europe were usually the wealthiest in the community. This strengthened their social position in the community and their political status and relations with the authorities. Furthermore, because of the social and cultural connections that these traders had with Europe, they tended more than the indigenous Jews to follow European customs and were also more exposed to European cultural and ideological influence. This difference assumed major importance toward the end of the nineteenth century with the increase of European penetration of Libya. Furthermore, in the Ottoman Empire, Jews who came from Europe usually kept their foreign citizenship in order to benefit from the Capitulations Agreements (see next section). These agreements allowed them to be protected by their respective European consuls and governments and also partly exempted them from taxation. Because of their economic and political reliance on Europe and their identification with many European political and cultural trends, those Jews in Libya who originated in Europe often served during the late Ottoman period as a channel for European influence and advocated European ideas and modes of behavior.

There are no official population data for Libya during most of the Ottoman period (1551–1911). At the end of the period, there were about 20,000 Jews in Libya (among some million or more Muslims), and their numbers passed 35,000 (among approximately three million Muslims and Christians) in the late 1940s, prior to the mass Jewish emigration to Israel and Italy (see table 1). Most of the Libyan Jews lived in the urban coastal centers, but quite a few were settled in rural areas on the Mediterranean coast and in the Tripolitanian hinterland. Almost two thirds of the Jews lived in Tripoli, the capital of the western province of Tripolitania. Their proportion in Tripoli gradually decreased from

Table 1. The Jewish Population in Libya

	1906	1936	1945	1948	1954
Tripolitania					
Tripoli	12,000	17,196	19,330	21,000	3,580
Zu'ara	40	736	814	794	—
Zawiya	450	566	776	676	—
'Amrus	1,000	1,313	1,563	1,240	—
Zliten	450	607	788	604	—
Zanzur	60	117	119[a]	—	—
Khoms	400	745	901	902	—
Misrata	600	838	1,125	912	16
Tajura	200	174	223	202	—
Mislata	400	404	418	410	—
Tarhuna	n.a.	95	185	191	—
Urfella	60	58	84	85	—
Sirt	50	341	114	180	—
Gharyan	800	419	502	464	—
Yefren	1,000	375	390	391	—
Other	n.a.	42	51	—	
Total	[17,510]	24,026	27,383	28,051	3,596
Cyrenaica					
Benghazi	2,000	3,098	n.a	3,700	260
Derna	150	322	n.a	⎫	—
Tubruq	n.a.	240	n.a	800[b]	—
Other	n.a.	505	n.a	⎭	—
Total	[2,150]	4,165	4,500	4,500	260
Total	[19,660]	28,191	31, 883	32,551	3,856

SOURCES: For 1906: "Die Zahl der Juden in Tripolis," *Zeitschrift für Demographie und Statistik der Juden* 2 (1906): 176; Ha-Cohen, *Higgid Mordecai*, p. 339. For 1936: Istituto generale di statistica (Italy), *VIII Censimento generale della populazione*, vol. 5 (Rome, 1939): 80–85 (quoted in part in De Felice, *Jews in an Arab Land*, p. 347). For 1945: De Felice, *Jews in an Arab Land*, p. 362, quoting from BMA, "Annual Report by the Chief Civil Administrator on the BMA of Tripolitania for the Period 1st January 1945 to 31st December 1945," p. 53. For 1948: H. Abravanel, "Shenat Ḥayim le-OSE bi-Ṭripoli (17.3.49–16.3.50)," *Yalquṭ ha-Mizraḥ ha-Tikhon* 2 (1950): 85–87 (quoted in part in De Felice, *Jews in an Arab Land*, p. 379). Additional information was derived from correspondence from Libya.

NOTE: n.a. indicates no information was available, and the totals given in brackets are estimates. A dash indicates that there was no Jewish population. This table does not include Jews who were not Ottoman subjects or those who were not Libyan citizens.

[a]My estimate to arrive at given total. These are Jews who left Zanzur following the 1945 riots.

[b]There were 800 Jews outside Benghazi in Cyrenaica, but we do not know their distribution.

about a third to about a quarter of the total population following the transfer from Ottoman to Italian rule. Large Jewish communities also existed in Benghazi, the capital of the eastern province of Cyrenaica, in towns and large villages near Tripoli ('Amrus, known also as Sūq al-Jum'ah), on the eastern Tripolitanian coast (Misrata and Khoms), on the western Tripolitanian coast (Zu'ara and Zawiya), and in the Tripolitanian hinterland (Gharyan and Yefren). Following the mass Jewish emigration from Libya in 1949–51, Jewish communities remained in Libya only in Tripoli and Benghazi. Most of the remaining Jews left after the Six-Day War (June 1967) and the Libyan revolution led by Mu'ammar al-Qadhdhāfī (September 1969).

These demographic factors had significant implications for the characteristics of the Jewish communities of Libya. Despite intercommunal Jewish contacts and constant domestic migration (mostly from the rural hinterland to the coastal urban centers), the communities differed in their ways of life. This refers both to their socioeconomic structure as well as to their cultural character and their political organization. As a result of their lengthy isolation from other Jewish centers and their extended coexistence with Arab and Berber Muslims, the Jews of Libya were strongly influenced by the manners, customs, regulations, and beliefs of the surrounding Muslim majority. This influence differed according to region. In the Tripolitanian mountains the Berber Muslim influence was paramount and relatively homogeneous, and in the coastal regions Arab Muslim influence was mixed with Ottoman and growing European components, especially in Tripoli and its vicinity.

During the nineteenth and twentieth centuries, there were changes in Jewish settlement and residential modes in Libya, and these, too, affected social behavior. Throughout most of the Ottoman period, in each town or village the majority of the Jews lived separately from the gentile population in a special quarter (*ḥārah*) or street. Beginning in the late nineteenth century, however, thanks to improved security and the desire for better living conditions, Jews started to move out of the old Jewish quarters to new, mixed neighborhoods. Furthermore, in the new towns founded during this period, Jews settled among the gentiles (mainly Muslims) from the very beginning. This process was facilitated by government incentives to settlers in these newly developing regions. In addition, Jewish entrepreneurs who started new businesses along the eastern Tripolitanian coast were interested in hiring fellow Jews. The departure from segregated quarters somewhat decreased the continuation of traditional modes of behavior, eased involvement with the non-Jewish world, and further increased the imitation of foreign manners and customs.

As a result of all these factors, Libyan Jewry was quite heterogeneous in composition and character. There were urban and rural elements and the very rich and the extremely poor. Some communities were very isolated, and others had extensive connections with world Jewry and with the gentile world inside and outside Libya, but every community had some connection with gentiles. Identifications were made with different political powers. All this had an impact on Jewish cultural, social, and economic life in Libya and, as such, also on the status of Jewish women.

FOCI OF INSPIRATION AND IMITATION FOR THE JEWS

Since the mid-sixteenth century, Libya has experienced the rule of various regimes, which have differed as to their origin, religion, overall policies, and attitude toward the population at large and toward the Jewish minority. These different outlooks affected relations between the Jews and the authorities and the gentile society. This, in turn, also influenced the position of women.

During most of the Ottoman period, the daily life of the Libyan Jews was highly influenced by their Muslim environment, which gave local flavor and interpretation to Jewish law, tradition, and customs. This resulted not only from the fact that the majority of the population were Muslims but also from state policy. The Ottoman Empire, being a Muslim state, had a clearly defined attitude toward monotheistic non-Muslims, referred to as the People of the Book (Ahl al-Kitāb), both inside and outside its boundaries. Those monotheistic non-Muslims who accepted Muslim authority within the Realm of Islam (Dār al-Islām) were regarded as Protected People (Ahl al-Dhimmah), whose life, property, beliefs, and freedom of worship were guaranteed by the ruler, but who had to obey certain discriminatory regulations regarding their public appearance and behavior, conditions of worship, and taxation. Those monotheistic non-Muslims who did not accept Muslim rule belonged to the Realm of War (Dār al-Ḥarb) and were subject to warfare until surrender. There were, however, times when the Muslim state realized that this goal had to be temporarily postponed due to the balance of power between it and its enemies. In those cases, the two parties signed treaties, which were regarded by the Muslim authorities only as temporary cease-fire agreements. These treaties included permission for citizens of the non-Muslim state to visit the Ottoman Empire for political, religious, or economic reasons. Due to the international situation starting in the sixteenth century, the Ottoman Empire and European states entered into separate and constantly updated pacts known as the Capitulations Agreements. These gave the citizens of the European signatory states exterritorial status in the Ottoman Empire, which included immunity from Ottoman law, consular protection, and almost complete tax exemption. These agreements gradually facilitated the European penetration of the Ottoman Empire and made European activities there almost immune from Ottoman intervention.[2]

European Christians in Libya were, however, concentrated in closed neighborhoods in Tripoli and Benghazi and had little contact with the society at large. Thus, although there were some European Jews and Christians in Libya, the Muslim influence was paramount because the majority of the population as well as the authorities were Muslims. Consequently, both the daily influence of the neighborhood and the supreme authority stemmed from similar cultural roots. Although many differences existed between Arab, Berber, and Turkish traditions, Islam served as a unifying factor, bridging numerous regional, tribal, and national characteristics.

During the second half of the nineteenth century, changes in Ottoman policy and administration, as well as the increasing presence and activity of European agents in the Ottoman Empire as a whole, modified the nature of Muslim influence. As a result of the nineteenth-century reforms (Tanzimat) in the Ottoman Empire, numerous members of the administration and the army became Westernized in various degrees. This development spurred further ideological and structural changes in the empire. Despite its remoteness and traditional population, Libya was relatively strongly influenced by these reform trends because the region served as an "Ottoman Siberia," to which numerous political exiles and prisoners were sent. Many of these people were highly qualified administrators and officers whose outlook was Westernized, liberal-minded, and constitutionalist. Due to the scarcity of quali-

---

2. On the People of the Book, see *Encyclopaedia of Islam,* new ed. (Leiden: E. J. Brill, 1960–), s.v. "Ahl al-Kitāb"; on the Protected People, see ibid., s.v. "Dhimma"; on the Capitulations Agreements, see ibid., s.v. "Imtiyāzāt."

fied personnel in Libya, the local authorities allowed a large number of these individuals to serve in the provincial administration and the army. Some even reached very senior positions and wanted to use their status and the state apparatus to implement their ideas.

By that time, although the Ottoman Empire continued to regard itself as the leading Islamic state, many of its functionaries were less-observant Muslims, and Islam was no longer their sole or even main guiding force. As a result, the model that the Ottoman establishment in Libya set for Libyan society started to change during the second half of the nineteenth century, and this caused a split between the Ottoman establishment and a large part of the indigenous Muslim population. Although the latter did not have a unified identity and opposed any foreign control (even that of a neighboring tribe), Islam served as a loose bond between the conflicting elements, including the tribes and the authorities. Consequently, the reforming ideas of Ottoman officials usually did not find favor among the Muslim majority. However, they did find some support among the minorities, including the Jews, because of the equality that they promised to the population as a whole, regardless of religious affiliation.

This period also witnessed an increased European penetration of the Ottoman Empire, including Libya. This was basically politically motivated, but it was accomplished largely by privately initiated cultural and economic enterprises, which gradually became strongly connected with the state. Since the Ottoman regime was aware of the expansionist policies of many European powers, it tried to circumvent their activities in the empire. For that reason, overt political activity of foreign powers in Ottoman domains was not tolerated, and the purchase of real estate by foreigners was forbidden. As a result, the sole opening for foreign involvement and influence, apart from direct pressure on the central government in Istanbul, was through cultural and economic activities. In Libya, this kind of involvement was conducted mainly by Italy, with France and the other European powers playing only secondary roles. As it eventually turned out, the main tool and target of the European penetration was the Jewish community.

The Italian penetration of Libya was ideologically motivated and government sponsored, yet much of it was conducted by private and public (nongovernmental) entities. The latter were, however, often morally and even financially supported by the state. Following the final unification of Italy in 1861, Italian politicians, statesmen, and ideologues wanted to make Italy a world power and advocated the building of an Italian empire. These people regarded the former Roman Empire as the natural sphere of Italian expansion. Due, however, to direct European rule or interests in most of this region, Libya remained one of the very few possible territories for future Italian colonialism from the European point of view. One of the major Italian operations in Libya was the establishment of an educational network with the opening of a boys school in Tripoli in 1876. This network spread Italian culture and inculcated political ideas, resulting in the appearance of overt Italian political propaganda in the printed media, especially following the relaxation of the Press Law after the Young Turks Revolution of 1908. Italian economic activities culminated in the opening of a branch of the Banco di Roma in Tripoli in 1907, which acted as a covert government agency for economic expansion.

The Jews who had economic and social contacts with Europe preferred to send their children to the Italian schools. Furthermore, since those Jews knew European and local languages and were well acquainted with the local customs and conditions, they were the natural intermediaries between the Italians and the indigenous population and the authorities. This brought Libyan Jewish youth and adults alike into closer contact with Italians. As a result, the spread of Italian culture, the increased Italian economic influence, and the growing presence of Italian educators, businessmen, and diplomats with their families gradually served to shift the focus of cultural and social inspiration and imitation from the Arab-Ottoman Muslim to the Italian-European model among certain groups within the Jewish community, mainly in Tripoli.

Another source of European influence in Ottoman Libya, though on a more limited scale, was France. This was achieved through a Paris-based Jewish organization, the Alliance Israélite Universelle (AIU, established in 1860).[3] The aim of the AIU was to improve the political, social, economic, and cultural conditions of the Jews worldwide. The AIU acted through regional committees and educational institutions, which were under the authority of the AIU center in Paris. The AIU founded a committee in Tripoli in the late 1860s, from which local Jews sought

---

3. For a general survey of the AIU's activities worldwide, see N. Leven, *Cinquante ans d'histoire: L'Alliance Israélite Universelle, 1860–1910* (Paris: Librairie F. Alcan, 1920); A. Chouraqui, *L'Alliance Israélite Universelle et la renaissance juive contemporaine, 1860–1960* (Paris: Presses Universitaires de France, 1965). For more details on its activities in Libya, see below, especially chaps. 3 and 4.

help following political harassment or economic difficulties. The influence of the AIU in Libya increased when it launched its educational activities there in 1890. The AIU direct operation was limited to Tripoli and was aimed primarily at the Jews. The AIU, through its committee and schools, tried to introduce modern European and Jewish ideas to the Libyan Jews by way of cultural and social activities. As a result, the AIU's influence spread beyond its student body and their immediate families, although remaining basically within the Jewish community. In contrast to the pupils in the Italian schools, who were mostly from the richer families and had strong connections with Europe, the pupils in the AIU institutions were mostly from the lower classes. Consequently, the patterns of the spread of Italian and French influence within the Jewish community were somewhat different. In addition, the Ottoman authorities did not suspect that the AIU's operation, unlike the Italian activities, was a guise for political expansionist ambitions, and as a result, the AIU could act in a more friendly and cooperative atmosphere. The Italians, on the other hand, operated mainly among wealthy Jews, many of whom were Italian subjects. The latter were often under Italian consular pressure to use only Italian educational facilities, and the political imperialist goals of the whole operation were clear to everyone.

Italian and French influence was especially felt in Tripoli, and mainly among the Jews, because the Muslim authorities and population regarded the European penetration as subversive and aiming at political, cultural, religious, and economic subjugation. The Jews, on the other hand, regarded this penetration as beneficial, because it provided them with improved professional skills and political protection, in addition to being a source for general education and welfare. At the beginning, these operations attracted mainly upper-class and upper-middle-class Jews with European citizenship. Because the availability of political protection and vocational training came at a time of continuous economic crisis, gradually indigenous Jews of a lower socioeconomic status were also drawn into the sphere of foreign influence. These Jews were more traditional in their outlook, were more influenced by the Muslim neighborhood, and regarded the authorities with awe. As a result of these developments, on the eve of the Italian invasion of Libya, a growing number of Jews in the region regarded Europe, mainly as represented by the local Italian and French institutions, as their external model of inspiration and imitation.

Awareness within the Libyan Jewish community of modern trends in the Jewish world grew during this period and was enhanced by the interest that some international Jewish organizations (e.g., the AIU, the Jewish Territorial Organization, and the Anglo-Jewish Association) took in Jewish communities that were in need of political, economic, and cultural support. Simultaneously, there were some indigenous Jews, mainly in Tripoli and Benghazi (most of whom were European citizens), who initiated contacts with modern Jewish organizations. As a result of these tendencies, Jewish periodicals in Hebrew reached Libya from Europe and Palestine and started to publish news items from Libya, thus including the Jews of Libya in the general arena of Jewish events. In addition, contacts with the Zionist organization were established in 1900 through local initiative, but they were interrupted soon after due to slow and tepid reaction from the center in Vienna.

Although these contacts were limited in number, they were conducted by influential members of the growing Westernized component of the community, whose importance increased further under Italian rule. This expanding group was more and more inclined to be regarded as truly Westernized, in both thought and practice. As a result of its contacts with Europe, this group was also exposed to the improved status of women there and the strengthening of their cultural, socioeconomic, and political roles. Although these innovations, and especially those related to women, were slow to infiltrate into Libyan Jewry, there were some noted beginnings, especially in the large urban centers.

The tendency among the Jewish community of Libya to focus on Europe, and mainly on Italy, as the center of inspiration grew once Libya came under Italian rule (1911–43).[4] The attitude of the Italian regime toward the indigenous population of Libya was quite different from that of the Ottoman authorities. The religious (Islamic) bond between the regime and the majority of the population and the policy of viewing non-Muslims as tolerated but discriminated minorities no longer existed. The Italian regime did not distinguish between its subjects on the basis of religion, but according to their loyalty and contribution to the state. This attitude altered the status of the various components of the population and, by equalizing their point of departure, in fact raised the position of the Jews and lowered that of the Muslims.

Not only were the administration and the army primarily Italian, but

4. On the Italian colonization, see C. G. Segrè, *Fourth Shore: The Italian Colonization of Libya* (Chicago: University of Chicago Press, 1974).

Italian education became the core of the state educational system. In addition, some 50,000 Italians settled in Libya, most of them in the major cities, administrative centers, and agricultural colonies, which were set up in regions that were evacuated by Muslims. (Muslims often fled when the Italians conquered a place, and also the Italians evicted Muslims, mainly from rich agricultural areas.) Consequently, the daily contact between Jews and Italians increased. The Jews maintained their traditional practice of being loyal to the regime. They were, however, in a perplexing position caused by the struggle between the Italian regime and the Muslim majority in Libya. This conflict was based on the different origin and religion of the authorities compared with those of most of the local population, and it culminated in the Muslim anti-Italian militant resistance, which was completely crushed only in the early 1930s. The Libyan Jews were in a delicate situation. Being identified too strongly with the hated regime would have ruined their relations with the Muslims, among whom many Jews continued to live and do business. The Italians, on their part, were also careful not to be viewed as particularly in favor of the Jews, in order not to further alienate and infuriate the Muslims. Although the latter had gradually been subdued under Italian rule, they were still accustomed to regarding all non-Muslims as inferiors. To accept a Christian European regime enforced upon them by military power was bad enough for the Muslims, but to swallow a Jewish ascendancy over them was intolerable. As a result of these developments and dilemmas, there was a growing Italianization of the Libyan Jews, especially in the major cities, but many Jews tried to continue their cordial relations with the Muslims and to perpetuate their Jewish traditions and customs.

The Italian period also witnessed growing contacts between the Jews of Libya and the Zionist movement. These ties were especially strong with the Italian Zionist branch, to which the Libyan Zionists were subordinate. Close relations were also established with the Zionist settlers in Palestine. These contacts brought forth new political ideas and social concepts aimed at restructuring Jewish society and creating a "new Jew." This development included the idea that the status and role of women should be equal to those of men. Although the number of registered Zionists in Libya during the 1930s was low and did not exceed 300, the cultural influence of Zionism on the Libyan Jews was far greater, especially in the coastal towns. One of the important tools for spreading Zionism was offering courses in the Hebrew language and incorporating instruction in modern social and political ideas. These ideas were also introduced through the press, which entered Libya in growing numbers. All sorts of publications became more available, both foreign and those printed (in growing numbers) in Libya.

As a result of these developments, most Jewish boys received both Italian and traditional Jewish education. Since, however, the Jewish community did not provide education for girls until the early 1940s, only urban Jewish girls were formally educated. They received European (mainly Italian and French) and Hebrew education, both of which were in essence modern and Western. Italian and Zionist cultural, political, and social ideas had their greatest impact on the Libyan Jews (including women) in the big cities. In the countryside, this influence was weaker and barely reached Jewish women.

During World War II Libyan Jewry was confronted with the hideous side of Western Christian civilization. Starting in late 1938, anti-Semitic racial legislation was introduced in Italy and was in force also in Libya. Jews were barred from state and public enterprises and institutions, including education, and many of them were put in concentration or labor camps and even deported from the country.[5]

As a result of the large-scale transfer of Jewish men to concentration and labor camps during the war, many adult males were absent for lengthy periods of time from their families. Consequently, growing economic and social responsibilities were entrusted to women. Furthermore, the spread of epidemics in the camp of Cyrenaican evacuees increased the importance and numbers of Jewish female inmates who were specially trained in camp to serve as nurses. Thus, similarly to previous periods of crisis, although the Jewish community as a whole suffered greatly, this situation necessitated the combined efforts of all the remaining capable members of the community. Although we do not know exactly how many women took advantage of these opportunities, the existing evidence suggests that during and after World War II growing numbers of Jewish women went to work outside their homes and gained more responsibility inside and outside their homes. The Jews distinguished between the distorted and degenerate developments in Fascist and Nazi domains and the enlightened, humane ideas of the West. Furthermore, they realized that the turn to the former is possible

5. On the Jewish community of Libya during World War II, see R. Simon, "Yehudey Luv ʿal Saf Shoʾah," *Peʿamim* 28 (1986): 44–77.

even among those who advocate the latter. Consequently, although many Libyan Jews continued to believe in cultural and social Westernization, their admiration of Europe waned, and they began to search for a better combination of Jewish and Western values.

Together with this process, the Libyan Jews, starting with those in Cyrenaica, came into closer contact with the "new Jew," as personified by the Palestinian Jews in the British army, when the latter gradually occupied Libya during 1942–43 and brought about the retreat of the Italians and the Germans to Tunisia. The British Military Administration (BMA) lasted in Libya until the establishment of an independent Arab state in late 1951. The BMA regarded itself as a temporary rule until the United Nations reached a decision regarding the political future of Libya. Consequently, the BMA did not want to initiate any policy changes in Libya. Because many of the BMA's members had served in or were from Arab countries, and because of external developments and the return of numerous political exiles to Libya, Arab nationalism increased in Libya. As time went on, the British wanted to develop various institutions in preparation for the future political entity. They decided that these bodies should be based on the majority population but would serve all the indigenous inhabitants, including the Jews. This policy was strongly opposed by the Jews, who had gradually distanced themselves from Muslim society and increased their identification with Zionism.

The Palestinian Jewish soldiers met a frightened community, which was eager for protection, understanding, material help, and spiritual support. As a result, the cultural, social, and political influence of the Jewish soldiers over their Libyan coreligionists was great, especially in Cyrenaica, whose Jews suffered the most inside Libya during the war. The main achievement of the Palestinian Jewish soldiers with regard to Libyan Jewry was the restructuring of large parts of the educational system on the model of the Hebrew educational network in Palestine. Simultaneously, Palestinian Jewish soldiers and emissaries helped to form Jewish youth movements in Libya, which were also based on the Palestinian model. In addition to the educational and vocational aspects of these enterprises, they had important political, cultural, and social impacts on the community at large because of their emphasis on political Zionism and social change—including changes in the position of women.

The focusing of the Libyan Jews on their Palestinian brethren as their center of inspiration was sharpened by the establishment of the state of Israel (1948) and the permission of the BMA for Israeli representatives to coordinate the free emigration of Jews from Libya to Israel (1949–51). These emissaries did not spend all their time in administrative work but made it a point to visit local Jewish communities, talk with them, and teach them. As a result, they further imbued in them Israeli political and social concepts. It was, however, made absolutely clear to the Israeli authorities that nonreligious emissaries would not be welcomed by the Libyan community, because the latter, despite its growing Westernization, remained a strictly religiously observant one.

As a result of the worsening economic conditions during this period, the reliance of the Jewish community on external support grew. The events of the war had greatly harmed Europe, and consequently, beginning in the early 1940s, the main source of Jewish aid was the American Joint Distribution Committee (AJDC). The AJDC was active in Libya both as an individual organization and also as the main financial source for other groups, such as the Jewish Agency for Palestine and the AIU. Although several of the AJDC functionaries in Libya were indigenous Jews, the senior officials were from Europe. Furthermore, the policies of the organization were shaped by Western Jewish ideas. As a result, the AJDC, too, had a certain influence over the shaping of behavior patterns among the Jews of Libya, including the status of Libyan Jewish women.[6]

The distancing of the Jews of Libya from Muslim influence was not only due to the strengthening of Western, European, and Zionist influences. There was never much respect among Libyan Jews for the indigenous Muslims and Islamic scholarship. The Muslim influence over the Jews was consequently limited to daily customs and prejudices, including the worship of saints, but did not extend to more profound cultural issues. The Jews hardly ever sent their chidren to Muslim schools and strongly refused to do so even when the BMA wanted all indigenous children to attend the Arab school system. Furthermore, Jews hardly ever participated in the emerging Libyan Arab national movement and politics, and the few exceptions were mainly to safeguard the position of Jews in the emerging independent Libyan state. This avoidance resulted

6. On the AJDC in general, see *Encyclopaedia Judaica* (Jerusalem: Keter Publishing House, 1973), s.v. "American Jewish Joint Distribution Committee"; O. Handlin, *A Continuing Task: American Joint Distribution Committee, 1914–1964* (New York: Random House, 1964).

not only from the traditional low esteem that the Libyan Jews felt toward their Muslim neighbors but also from the continuous Jewish migration from the countryside to the Mediterranean coast, from rural to urban centers, and from living near Muslims to living near Italians. As a result, fewer Jews had to be submissive to Muslims to win their protection.

The anti-Jewish riots of 4–7 November 1945 by Muslims in coastal Tripolitania were a watershed in Jewish-Muslim relations in Libya,[7] similar to the effect of World War II on Jewish-Italian relations. The Jews lost confidence in both gentile groups, but there were some significant differences between the two cases. Even though the Jews became more critical in their acceptance of things Western and their trust in Italy was shattered, this did not mean a complete rupture between Libyan Jews and Europe. During and after the war, the Jews of Libya distinguished between the Italians as a people and the atrocities of the war that were perpetrated by the collaboration between the Fascist and Nazi regimes. Jewish-Muslim relations in Libya, on the other hand, were based upon Muslim supremacy and mutual adaptation of customs as a result of a lengthy coexistence, but without any Jewish attempt at spiritual growth through this channel. Even before the riots, the Jews knew that Muslim protection was based on interdependence—the need of the Muslim society for services that only the Jews provided. Furthermore, the Jews had experienced numerous small-scale Muslim attacks for economic and religious reasons over the years. Thus, the Libyan Jews increasingly distanced themselves from Muslim influence due to physical detachment, horrible memories, and a background of rooted cultural disrespect. As a result, once the state of Israel was established and the prospects of Arab independence in Libya became a reality, about 90 percent of the Libyan Jews chose to emigrate to Israel.

EFFECTS OF SOCIETAL CHANGE ON JEWISH WOMEN

While adhering to Jewish law and traditions, the Libyan Jews changed their external focus of inspiration during the nineteenth and twentieth centuries and moved gradually from the Muslim realm (in its Arab, Berber, and Ottoman forms), through the European-Italian sphere, to the modern Westernized Jewish-Israeli orbit. The acquisition of new

7. Zuarez et al., *Yahadut Luv*, pp. 207–27.

ideas and customs depended on spiritual, physical, and socioeconomic factors, but not every Libyan Jew accepted all the innovations. Furthermore, those concepts regarding the status of women were among the ones that were the most difficult for many to adopt. Consequently, even though there were changes in the cultural, social, and economic behavior of the Libyan Jews, these changes were slower to affect the status of Jewish women than that of Jewish men.

Jewish tradition and law, coupled with the conditions in which the Jews had lived among the nations, greatly influenced the status of Jewish women. In Libya, the lengthy existence under the realm of Islam with varied degrees of external influences added local, Muslim, and Western coloring to the basic Jewish attitudes toward women.[8] Jewish life in Libya underwent constant modifications with regard to its political, economic, cultural, and social outlook. Every change had further implications on the other ingredients of society. Consequently, the status of Jewish women in Libya was affected by a wide variety of changes, especially beginning in the second half of the nineteenth century.

The authorities were not the only source from which the population received different messages regarding proper behavior, including that toward women. Economic conditions also had an important effect. During the nineteenth century Libya witnessed severe economic crises that forced drastic changes in economic structure and behavior. These developments, in turn, had further repercussions not only on the selection of professions and trades but also on the identity of the people who performed them. Economic necessity was most instrumental in shaping women's status, and the process did not end with the work women performed. Work was also connected with authority, self-reliance, responsibility, property, and freedom of movement, action, and opinion, as well as with professional training and academic education.

The changes in the status of Jewish women in Libya during the nineteenth and twentieth centuries were deeply intertwined with the wider processes of change that Libya experienced during that period, resulting from internal and external developments in the Middle East and North Africa, the Muslim and Jewish worlds, the Mediterranean basin, and the West. Consequently, the examination of the changes affecting Libyan Jewish women must take into account several partly overlapping circles of influence. Furthermore, each of the categories to be examined (i.e.,

---

8. On women in Judaism in general, see *Encyclopaedia Judaica*, s.v. "Woman."

status, family, work, education, and public life) was connected with the others. The achievements and experiences of women in each of these areas were influenced to a certain degree by their customary roles and modes of behavior inside and outside their homes, and the levels of achievement were not equal. Thus, the status of Libyan Jewish women at home and in public was shaped by tradition, economics, education, and external influences.

❖ ONE ❖

Status within the Family
and the Community

❖

The status of Jewish women in Libya was influenced by three main sets of factors: Jewish law and tradition; Muslim law and customs with their Arab, Berber, and Ottoman characteristics; and environmental conditions in the urban and rural areas. In addition, external influences, such as reforms in the Ottoman Empire and European penetration and rule, also had distinctive effects on the condition of Jewish women, just as they had on other segments of the population. Consequently, the status of Libyan Jewish women was not static. It also differed according to locale. Thus, one must examine status against a background of political, cultural, social, and economic conditions in Libya at each period.

There are few direct statements on the status of Jewish women in Libya during the late nineteenth century, and the existing reports were composed mostly by indigenous men or by Europeans. Since much of the information comes from external sources (i.e., not from Libyan Jewish women), it is often loaded with foreign concepts and lacking the personal point of view of these Jewish women. In addition, the information is uneven with regard to period, region, and source.

SUBORDINATION TO MALE RELATIVES

Descriptions of Libyan urban society during the late nineteenth century usually portrayed Jewish women as being mostly confined to the home. On the rare occasions that they left it, they were veiled, like their Muslim counterparts.[1] These women were generally under the authority of one of their close male relatives: father, brother, or husband. The male guardians were the ones who usually made the decisions regarding the present and future of the women, and their authority extended to economic matters. The most significant realm in which women were allowed some economic power was with regard to the dowry that they brought with them from their father's house (see chap. 2). The rules concerning the dowry represent, however, less the economic freedom of the woman and more the desire of her father's family not to let the property transfer into her husband's family. In other instances, the economic subjection of the woman to her male guardian was quite complete. Thus, for example, on the rare occasions that women went to work outside their homes during the Ottoman period, they usually had to give their earnings to their fathers (since most of those who worked were not yet married).[2] Some foreign observers remarked that the condition of Jewish women was "lamentable" among the lower classes,[3] and girls were even considered a burden by their fathers.[4] This was so apparently because in contrast to boys, it was less customary to send girls out to work, and as a result, they hardly ever brought home any income but had to be supported.

These observations were provided by French Jews of both sexes who stayed in Tripoli for a number of years and were involved in the Tripolitan Jewish community. These observers often felt themselves to be superior to the indigenous population, which they wanted to reshape according to the European, and preferably the French, model. Nevertheless, there are numerous grains of truth in these and other foreign descriptions. These observations refer to the general custom in Libya as well as in other North African, Middle Eastern, and Muslim

1. D. Arie, Tripoli, to the Alliance Israélite Universelle (henceforth, AIU), Paris, 1 June 1898, the AIU Archives, Libyan series (henceforth, AAIU), file IC-12.
2. A. Benchimol, Tripoli, to AIU, Paris, 11 March 1907, AAIU, IIIE-10.
3. D. Arie, Tripoli, to AIU, Paris, 10 July 1896, AAIU, IIIE-6b.
4. A. Benchimol, Tripoli, to AIU, Paris, 11 March 1907, AAIU, IIIE-10.

regions, especially in the urban areas, according to which women were protected by their close male relatives.[5] It was considered that this protection, from strangers and especially from themselves (women were assumed to be at the mercy of their irrational impulses and desires), could best be achieved when the women stayed at home: if they had to leave the house for some important reason, they had to be chaperoned as well as be completely covered and veiled. Furthermore, being under the authority and protection of male relatives also gave the latter a say with regard to the women's earnings. Jewish women, however, had a right to certain categories of private property and quite often were highly respected at home. Nevertheless, being honored did not mean having equal rights, and only very rarely could they attain an influential position outside the private domain.

Inside the home, much reverence was shown to wives and mothers, and they played a dominant role in the running of the household.[6] Yet, their position was not clear-cut. Although much honor was bestowed upon them, certain habits reflected their inferior status, and their decision making was limited by the boundaries set by men. Even as late as 1967, many Libyan Jewish women were still confined to their homes and were occupied only by their regular household tasks. Within the family circle, however, their opinions about family matters prevailed, and it was often they who made the decisions concerning the direction of family affairs. It was reported in 1967 that their strong character was often in contrast to their "feminine and humble appearance." In what were regarded by the observers as the "less progressive" families, women were more dependent on the man. There, he alone decided in all matters concerning the family, and he took care to answer its needs to the extent that he could and wanted. In the "more progressive" families, although women exercised greater intellectual independence, they still shared little in the material responsibilities.[7]

5. On this subject in general, see, e.g., R. T. Antoun, "On the Modesty of Women in Arab Muslim Villages: A Study in the Accommodation of Tradition," *American Anthropologist* 70 (1968): 671–97. On traditional concepts regarding Muslim women in Libya, see M. O. Attir, "Ideology, Value Changes, and Women's Social Position in Libyan Society," in E. W. Fernea, ed., *Women and the Family in the Middle East: New Voices of Change* (Austin: University of Texas Press, 1985), pp. 121–33.

6. I. J. Benjamin, *Eight Years in Asia and Africa from 1846–1855* (Hanover: The author, 1859), p. 286; A. Benchimol, Tripoli, to AIU, Paris, 9 January 1907, AAIU, IIIE-10.

7. De Felice, *Jews in an Arab Land*, p. 281.

SEGREGATION WITHIN THE HOME

During most of the period under discussion (even to the middle of the twentieth century), women usually ate separately from their male relatives. Since this practice concerned the private domain, which few strangers penetrated, reports concerning it are few. External influences were slower to cast their imprint here than in the public domain, but occasionally some changes were observed. Thus, for example, toward the end of the Ottoman period, changes were reported concerning the Sabbath breakfast. Whereas until then it was eaten separately by men and women immediately after the morning prayer (*shaḥarit*), among some rich Jews in Tripoli it became customary for both sexes to have it together at the table.[8] This observation by an indigenous Jew reflects two changes, albeit within a limited group and apparently only once a week. In this case, the physical environment of dining had changed together with the social behavior: breakfast was eaten at a table and by both sexes together. This resulted from the desire on the part of wealthy Jews who had close contacts with Europeans to copy some of their habits in order to appear as their equals. Consequently, the changing patterns of behavior in this case reflect a borrowing of a complete setting (i.e., using tables as well as eating together). This, however, was the exception that proved the rule, although similar behavior gradually spread.

Descriptions of eating habits in the countryside (in Yefren) state that after the males had finished their meal, the women ate theirs separately and consumed whatever was left over in the general plate. In Ottoman Libya it was usually considered "shameful and disgusting" to behave otherwise.[9] Nonetheless, some individual deviations from this custom were observed as early as 1906.[10] The traditional behavior in this respect continued during the Italian period. In the 1920s, in the west Tripolitan-

8. Ha-Cohen, *Higgid Mordecai*, p. 190. Among the Libyan Muslims it was also customary for females to eat separately, after the males had finished their meal, during which the women waited on them. See Miss Tully, *Letters Written during a Ten Years' Residence at the Court of Tripoli*, edited by S. Dearden (London: A. Barker, 1957), pp. 155n, 318; G. F. Lyon, *A Narrative of Travels in Northern Africa in the Years 1818, 19, and 20* (London: John Murray, 1966), pp. 46, 287.

9. Ha-Cohen, *Higgid Mordecai*, p. 289.

10. N. Slousch, *Travels in North Africa* (Philadelphia: Jewish Publication Society of America, 1927), p. 159. For a similar observation in Tigrina (Gharyan) in 1929, see D. Kleinlerer, "Cave Dwellers of North Africa: A Visit among the Picturesque Inhabitants of Djebel Garian," *Jewish Tribune* 94, no. 22 (1929): 1, 4.

ian coastal town of Zawiya the women used to grind the flour and bake the bread during the meal in order to serve it fresh to the diners: they waited on the men during the meal and ate separately afterward.[11] Even during the 1940s the men continued to eat by themselves at the table, while the women sat on the floor or on a mat in the corner of the room or in the kitchen. The only reported change was that some women "dared" to sit and eat at the table—but only after the men had finished their meal.[12] In addition to reflecting on women's status, this issue also had health implications. The reports make it clear that men had priority in the selection and consumption of food, and only what was left was the women's lot. Among the poor (i.e., a growing majority of the community) this could amount to very little food. There are no direct references regarding the quality of health care for both sexes. It was stated, however, that more Jewish females died than males in the cholera epidemic of 1910.[13] This might indicate that to start with women were in poorer health than men and that the medical treatment they received was worse than the men's.

ATTITUDE TOWARD CHILDREN

The status of Libyan Jewish women can also be deduced from the attitude toward children in the family. Thus, for example, there were several festivities connected with the birth of boys, and especially the first-born ones, but there were no similar celebrations regarding the birth of girls. Although it is true that many of these customs were not characteristic of the Jewish community of Libya in particular but reflect the Jewish tradition in general, there were certain local habits that went beyond the general Jewish practice. Thus, for example, when Libyan Jewish parents did not want to have more daughters, they used to call their newborn girl Yizza (meaning "that's enough").[14] This practice was

11. *Hed ha-Mizraḥ* 4, no. 32 (1945): 8.
12. Zamir and Yariv, Tripoli, to Yosifon and Ben-Yehudah, 7 November 1943, the Central Zionist Archives (henceforth, CZA), S25/5217. In the 1980s, in describing the situation in the 1940s, Ya'ir Duer (Yariv) gave a somewhat different description and said that his host family in Tripoli, which included the parents and three daughters, ate together. Another emissary, Naftali Bar-Giyora, wrote in the 1980s that while men sat at the table, the women sat on a rag on the floor. See B.-Z. Rubin, ed., *Luv: Hedim min ha-Yoman* (Jerusalem: Ha-Agudah le-Moreshet Yehudey Luv, 1988), pp. 36, 113.
13. Ha-Cohen, *Higgid Mordecai*, p. 185.
14. T. Sutton, "Les Israélites tripolitains," *Revue des Ecoles de l'Alliance Israélite Universelle* 8 (1903): 63. For an example, see *Ḥayenu*, Ḥeshvan 5705 (October 1944).

common not only during the Ottoman period but also well into the twentieth century. Needless to say, there was no similar custom with regard to boys, whose birth was cherished. Bearing a name that reflected rejection was a constant reminder of women's lower status.

Not only was the birth of girls often not wanted, it could also be interpreted as not having children at all; that is, "children" meant only male offspring. In Libya, as in many regions under Muslim rule, Jewish men could marry a second wife without divorcing the first one (or by divorcing her under easier terms) not only when the first wife did not have any children but also when she bore only daughters (see chap. 2). Although it seems that polygamy was not very widespread, it did, however, reflect the general attitude in this issue, which was not particular to Libya: women were the ones blamed for the lack of male descendants, and any wife who did not fulfill her duties in this respect could be replaced.

In comparing the position of sons and daughters in the family, it was noted by outsiders as late as the 1940s that boys had more rights than girls. Thus, girls were "protected"; that is, they were usually kept at home, where they had numerous household tasks to perform. Although it is known that a growing number of Jewish girls went out to study and work, many still had to stay at home during the day or following their authorized absence. According to some sources, this seclusion was one of the reasons why upon reaching the age of majority these girls tried to liberate themselves by marrying Christians.[15]

EDUCATION

Another aspect reflecting the status of Libyan Jewish women, and also influencing it, was education. Girls were very rarely educated, academically speaking, until the last quarter of the nineteenth century, and this prevented their full participation in public life (see chap. 4). During most of the period the spiritual leadership of the community viewed education as a means of preparing a person for worship in the synagogue and for work outside the household; consequently, it regarded as sufficient that girls learn from their female relatives and friends what-

---

15. Zamir and Yariv, Tripoli, to Yosifon and Ben-Yehudah, 7 November 1943, CZA, S25/5217; Zuarez et al., *Yahadut Luv*, p. 414. See also chap. 2, this volume, on mixed marriages.

ever was necessary in order to run the house properly. The communal leadership did not alter its attitude toward female education and did not provide women with any cultural services until the 1940s.

PARTICIPATION IN CEREMONIES

Women had special roles in ceremonies connected with family life, but many of these events had men as their focus.[16] There was a special custom related to pregnant widows. During the funeral procession, the coffin carriers would stop with the coffin of the late husband at the entrance of the room from which the corpse was taken, and the pregnant widow would walk under the coffin in full view of all those who had gathered to participate in the funeral. This was a sign that she was pregnant, and the custom was meant to prevent calumny concerning her later on.[17] Thus, although special care was taken to protect the honor of the widow and of her late husband, this habit also reflects mistrust in the woman's integrity and testimony. Another custom was connected with the circumcision ceremony of newborn sons. On the preceding day, female relatives would gather at the family's home and prepare incense that was to be distributed among the audience during the ceremony. Expert elderly female singers would accompany the preparation of the incense with special hymns in Judeo-Arabic based on popular tunes. These singers also participated in other family festivities.[18] On another occasion, during the preparation of the thirteen-year-old boy for his Bar Mitzvah ceremony, his mother would pour water on his hands while he asked for her forgiveness for all his follies up to that moment. This was considered one of the happiest moments for Jewish mothers in Libya.[19] All these customs were connected with some special memorable events related to a male member of the family. There were no similar customs related to female family members or performed by males in honor of females.

The position of women can also be determined from the way in which they were mentioned by the official bodies of the community.

16. It seems that several of the customs that were reported during the Ottoman period continued to exist during the twentieth century, though they are mentioned only sporadically.

17. Zuarez et al., *Yahadut Luv*, p. 396. If a son was later born, he was named after his dead father.

18. Ibid., pp. 386–87.

19. Ibid., p. 392.

Thus, in an announcement in Tripoli in 1949 calling for a commemorative prayer for those Jews who had been murdered during the riots of November 1945, male scholars and other men were mentioned first, followed by the women.[20] Since the list was not in alphabetic order, one can conclude that it was arranged according to the relative importance accorded by the community to those mentioned in it, and the least significance was assigned to those cited last, namely, to the murdered women.

Most of the customs connected with the dead mentioned only men. In one case, however, women were clearly included. It was stated that during the seven days of mourning (*shiv'ah*), Libyan Jews used to gather in the deceased person's home for three daily prayers, and that between the afternoon and evening prayers (*beyn Minḥah le-Ma'ariv*) a rabbinical scholar would praise the deceased—be it a man or a woman.[21] Since, however, in most cases, women were not mentioned, it seems that many customs for honoring the deceased were for men exclusively. On some occasions' it was even emphasized that only men were meant. Thus, when the dead was a male over thirteen years of age who had undergone his Bar Mitzvah ceremony, a candle was lit in his honor in the synagogue in which he used to pray.[22] No similar honor was bestowed upon women.

MODESTY AND PUBLIC APPEARANCE

Another aspect that reflected the status of Libyan Jewish women was related to the code of modesty. Much attention was paid to keeping proper morals, but punishment for their breach was much harsher for women than for men (see below). Libyan society, similar to other North African and Middle Eastern ones, regarded women as more prone to illogical, emotional, and irrational animalistic behavior, unable to restrain their desires. As a result, it was deemed necessary to protect them against themselves through severe punishment and by putting them under the complete authority of men.[23] This was felt more strongly in the towns than in the villages and resulted to a large extent

20. An announcement of "Ḥevrat Mora Shamayim," Tripoli, November 1949, Central Archives for the History of the Jewish People (henceforth, CAHJP), L-640.
21. Zuarez et al., *Yahadut Luv*, p. 397.
22. Ibid., p. 398.
23. On this issue, see n. 5.

from the greater economic responsibility of women in the rural society. This responsibility, in turn, carried with it greater personal freedom, which was, however, neither absolute nor equal to that of men. Since women were usually kept at home, mainly in the earlier period and in urban areas, men did all the shopping in the marketplace, based on the regular needs of the family and special requirements specified by their wives.[24] This was done in order to prevent any chance intergender meeting between nonrelatives.

Environmental conditions in the rural areas had significant implications for the status of women, including Jewish ones. Because the "household" and women's obligations within it were defined differently in the rural and urban areas, the status of women was also different. Women's role in the rural household was much more widely defined than in the urban areas and included work in gardens adjoining the house as well as in fields, wells, and woods further away. According to some European sources, in the countryside, and especially in the Tripolitanian mountain (in Yefren and Gharyan), Jewish women were almost equal to men and, in any case, were superior to their counterparts in other oriental communities: they mingled freely with men, sat side by side with them, ate with their husbands, and young girls were unveiled.[25] Similar observations, however, are not repeated by most local and foreign sources. Moreover, it should be noted that although some of the basic daily tasks that rural women were obliged to fulfill necessitated fewer restrictions on their freedom of movement, including their clothing, this did not drastically change their status and their position vis-à-vis men.

Clothing customs of Jewish women in Libya reflected Jewish traditions, neighboring Muslim habits, European influences, and regional characteristics.[26] Although there were some fundamental conventions

24. Zuarez et al., *Yahadut Luv,* p. 414; *Hed ha-Mizraḥ* 2, no. 12 (1943): 8–9. There were, however, a few women who worked as traders; see chap. 3, this volume. According to Attir, "Ideology," p. 124, Libyan Muslim women did not go shopping even in the 1960s.

25. N. Slousch, "Les Juifs en Tripolitaine," *Revue du Monde Musulman* 2 (1907): 32; idem, *Travels,* pp. 126, 159; Kleinlerer, "Cave Dwellers."

26. For general descriptions of the clothing of Jewish women in town, see Ha-Cohen, *Higgid Mordecai,* pp. 47–48; Benjamin, *Eight Years,* pp. 287–88; Ludvig Salvator, Archduke of Austria, *Yacht-reise in den Syrten* (Prague: H. Mercy, 1874), pp. 105–6; Lyon, *A Narrative,* pp. 17–18; T. Sutton, "Usages, moeurs et superstitions des Israélites tripolitains," *Revue des Ecoles de l'Alliance Israélite Universelle* 2 (1901): 154; A. Navon, Tripoli, to AIU, Paris, 14 May 1899, AAIU, IIE-5. On clothing in the village, see Ha-Cohen, *Higgid Mordecai,* pp. 47–48, 291; Benjamin, *Eight Years,* pp. 290–91; Slousch, *Travels,* p. 126.

within the Jewish community, there also existed numerous differences based on the divisions between urban and rural society and socioeconomic status. It seems that these differences resulted to a large extent from the particular life-styles necessitated by economic and environmental conditions, coupled with external influences, both Muslim and European.

During most of the Ottoman period, urban and rural adult and married Jewish women used to cover their hair in public with a hat (a fez during the late Ottoman period), which was wrapped with a kerchief. However, veiling exposing one eye was customary only in town for every woman over the age of thirteen years.[27] Covering the hair (and veiling for urban women) was common for all indigenous women, Muslim and Jewish alike. The covering of a woman's hair was regarded as one of the most important signs of modesty, and no respectable woman dared to be seen in public with her hair exposed.

All women wore a long square sheet, which was usually made of wool and covered the whole body. There were some differences in other items of apparel. Whereas urban women wore tunics, their rural counterparts did not, leaving their hands bare (except on their wedding day, when the bride had to cover her hands).[28] This difference in clothing apparently reflected working habits. Rural women, who had many tasks to perform both indoors and in the fields, could not limit the movement of their hands. There were also differences with regard to footwear. Urban women used to wear slippers (but no stockings), whereas in the village both men and women were often barefoot, because of the scarcity of footwear in the countryside.[29]

Another difference concerning the attitude toward women's apparel was with regard to pants. In Tripoli, the custom of wearing pants by women began to be accepted among the Tripolitan Jews in 1732, when the Jewish notable Shelomoh Khalfon gave a pair of pants to his daughter ʿAzizah as part of her dowry. Nonetheless, this practice was despised in the countryside even as late as the early twentieth century, where it was regarded as disgraceful due to its sexual connotations.[30] This differ-

27. Ha-Cohen, *Higgid Mordecai*, p. 47; Sutton, "Usages," p. 154; Slousch, *Travels*, pp. 126, 204.
28. Ha-Cohen, *Higgid Mordecai*, p. 291.
29. Benjamin, *Eight Years*, pp. 288, 291; Ha-Cohen, *Higgid Mordecai*, pp. 47–48, 287, 291.
30. Ha-Cohen, *Higgid Mordecai*, pp. 48, 291.

ence in attitude reveals that external influences introduced into the main urban centers were at times rejected in the hinterland.

Great importance was given to women's intimate apparel (i.e., kerchief and pants), because they had connotations of sexual intimacy. Married women were expected to keep their hair covered with a kerchief (*mḥarma*, "sacred, forbidden," in the Arab Tripolitanian dialect) in front of nonrelative males. This attitude toward the kerchief and its role in married women's lives came to the fore in the case of a Jewish gambler in Ottoman Tripoli who lost a lot of money. In order to recover his losses, he secretly took his wife's kerchief during her sleep, but unfortunately he lost it as well. As a result, his wife had to stay in her bedroom, because she lacked another kerchief and could not be seen in public without one.[31]

The attitude toward pants was even more strict. In addition to the fact that pants were worn only in town, those women who wore them took special care in handling them after washing. These women did not let their pants dry exposed in the sun for everyone to see but made sure to dry them only indoors. With the changing times, however, this custom, too, was not universally kept, and pants were observed drying openly already during the early twentieth century.[32]

The new times also brought with them changes in the materials from which clothing was made. These innovations, too, were adopted more quickly in the urban coastal centers than in the countryside. This difference was due to the stronger economic and social connections of the bigger cities with the outside world and to the larger number of rich people who could afford to acquire additional and fancy garments. Thus, silk and cotton started to replace wool toward the end of the Ottoman period.[33]

All women wore jewelry, but only urban women used cosmetics regularly, mainly blackening their eyelashes and brows and coloring their nails red. This difference resulted apparently from the fact that the rural women had to work more hours inside and outside their homes and consequently did not have the time required for elaborate beautification.

31. Goldberg, *The Book of Mordechai*, p. 172; Ha-Cohen, *Higgid Mordecai*, pp. 336, 380. For the practice of selling or mortgaging the wife's clothes and jewelry, see "Ha-Yehudim bi-Ṭripoli shel Afriqah," *Ha-Mevasser* 13 (18 2d Adar 5670 [29 March 1910]): 204.

32. Ha-Cohen, *Higgid Mordecai*, pp. 48, 291.

33. Ha-Cohen, *Higgid Mordecai*, pp. 291–92. According to Attir ("Ideology," p. 124), urban Muslim women in Libya started to take off the veil only in the 1960s.

Rural women could afford these luxuries only once in a lifetime, and they adorned themselves lavishly only for their wedding celebration. For instance, coloring the hands and feet of a bride red with henna (which does not wash off) was customary in both the urban and the rural areas.[34]

With the growing foreign influence following the Italian occupation of Libya, changes in the clothing of Jewish women started to take place at a more rapid pace. This was connected with other changes in Jewish women's social and cultural behavior, especially in the coastal urban region. As early as 1914, many young Jewish women in Tripoli stopped going out veiled, and the more traditional members of the community deplored what they regarded as a moral deterioration.[35] This was apparently influenced by the growing number of Jewish girls who went to Italian state schools and studied there in a European environment.

In the countryside, however, changes in the clothing and veiling of Jewish women were much less apparent. In 1923, for example, all Jewish women in Zawiya, those in Khoms who originated from Zliten and Mislata, and those in Zu'ara who came from Yefren and Zawiya (in contrast to the Tripolitan component in these places) were dressed like bedouin women, and at least in Zawiya and Gharyan they were always veiled when they left their houses.[36] Furthermore, rural Jewish women refrained as much as possible from appearing on the street and used to hide from strange men in order not to violate the local customs.[37] This was observed in 1949 when the rural Jews moved to Tripoli prior to their emigration to Israel. This stands in some contradiction to several reports from the late Ottoman period describing rural Jewish women mixing freely with men. It is possible that it was acceptable for these women to meet men of their extended family, and in the small villages the communities were composed of a limited number of extended families. Furthermore, the reports might also reflect habits in different parts of the country or the strengthening of some of the traditional customs in the face of the challenge of foreign influences.

34. Benjamin, *Eight Years,* pp. 288, 291; Ha-Cohen, *Higgid Mordecai,* pp. 47–48, 276–77, 292, 306; A. Navon, Tripoli, to AIU, Paris, 3 November 1890, AAIU, VIE-28. Color produced from the henna shrub (*Lawsonia inermis*) has been used since antiquity for coloring the skin and tinting the hair red. On the existence of the shrub in Libya, see Ha-Cohen, *Higgid Mordecai,* p. 53.

35. A. Levy, "Tripoli," *Bulletin des Ecoles de l'Alliance Israélite Universelle* 44 (April 1914): 207.

36. *Hed ha-Mizraḥ* 2, no. 12 (1943): 8; ibid. 4, no. 30 (1945): 6; ibid., no. 32 (1945): 8.

37. See *Ha-Tzofeh,* 22 November 1949.

University of Washington Press

P.O. Box 50096
Seattle, Washington 98145-5096, USA
Phone (206) 543-4050   Fax (206) 543-3932

Title: Change within Tradition among Jewish Women
in Libya

Author: Rachel Simon

Publication date: December 1992

Price: $30.00

Description: 230 pp., illus., bibliog., index

ISBN: 0-295-97167-3

LC: 91-35765

CIP: yes

Rights: world

Series: A Samuel and Althea Stroum Book

We take pleasure in sending you this book for review.
Please send us two copies of your published review.

Some of the differences in the public appearance of women stemmed from different life-styles. Customs similar to those of the rural Tripolitanian Jews were often in existence in Muslim rural and nomad societies, which seem to have influenced the Jews in many ways. In town, external Muslim pressure was strong enough during the Ottoman period to keep all respected and well-to-do women indoors and to ensure that their bodies were completely covered when they went out. This, however, was hardly possible in the village, because of the tasks women were obliged to fulfill. Rural women were more likely to have to work outdoors in the gardens close to the house or in fields and woods further away, often in harsh weather conditions. Consequently, it was necessary for them to have their eyes and even their whole face exposed, so that they could work properly. The same goes for their clothing: they had to have their arms free. These conditions also often prevented rural women from using makeup because they became dirty and sweaty during their labor, which started before dawn and continued until the late hours of the night. Only on rare occasions, such as during their own wedding celebration, could these women rest, rejoice, and adorn themselves with henna. Furthermore, town dwellers were more susceptible to external influences, and at least some of them were better off economically, enabling them to imitate foreign habits, including foreign dress. The society in the hinterland was much slower and more reluctant to adopt new customs, even though new practices, garments, and ideas did penetrate the countryside through peddlers, administrators, or occasional visits to religious centers to worship saints. The villagers were also quite poor, and could hardly obey every fashion whim. Thus, in the village, economic and environmental factors influenced the status and the public appearance of women, and external social and cultural trends were slow to penetrate the region and change the prevailing customs. In town, on the other hand, the influence of the majority of the population, especially of those who were considered models for inspiration and imitation, left its mark on women's status and apparel to a larger extent than did economic factors.

CONCLUDING REMARKS

During the Ottoman period, the surrounding Muslim society and authorities had a paramount influence on Jewish daily behavior, including the status of women, especially in the public domain. This situation gradually changed with the growing European cultural and economic penetration of Libya during the late nineteenth century and especially following the Italian occupation of Libya in late 1911. Under Italian rule, there was a growing relaxation of the observance of the strict customs regulating the status and the public appearance of urban Jewish women. Although many still kept the old customs, numerous others did not and, for example, went out to work and study unveiled. It seems that the main cause of this change was the growing number of Italians in Libya, who were accustomed to different modes of behavior. Furthermore, until 1943 the Italians were the government and, as such, the authority one had to obey. Although there were no laws regarding women's dress and appearance, the authorities wanted the indigenous population to resemble them, and they served as a model for proper behavior and imitation. Consequently, it became fashionable (mainly in the coastal urban areas) to imitate the Italians and not the Muslim Arabs or Berbers. During this phase, the Italians exemplified modernity and enlightenment, with which an increasing number of Jews wanted to be identified.

External changes, however, were not always followed by changes in the position of Jewish women at home or in public life, either within the Jewish community or in gentile society. Only gradually and very rarely did Jewish women in Libya reach positions of political or economic power, and when they did, it was mostly within the Jewish community and not within the larger society. More often than not, a Jewish women was honored by her relatives and coreligionists, and her rights within the family were observed, as were her rights concerning the property she brought with her from her father's house. The male guardians, however, had more rights both on a day-to-day basis and with regard to issues of principle or more far-reaching decisions. The fact that until a relatively late period most Jewish women were illiterate and uneducated hindered their active participation not only in religious but also in all other aspects of communal life (e.g., political, social, cultural, and economic). Women were quite active in the popular, emotional, and behavioral aspects of religious life, but hardly in any scholastic field. Thus, women did frequent the synagogue, mainly on the Sabbath and on holidays, helped maintain it, and at times even contributed to its establishment, but in accordance with orthodox Judaism they did not have any role in the service (see chap. 5).

Thus, despite the fact that a growing number of Jewish women adopted European clothing and looked Westernized, their position at home and in the community changed only slightly and very gradually. Furthermore, changes were experienced more by the richer and better-educated families than by the poor and, essentially, illiterate masses. However, the traditional low status of Jewish women continued to be very common even among the rich and educated classes until the final evacuation of the community to Italy in 1967. This can be concluded from the reports of the last remnants of the community, most of whom belonged to the higher socioeconomic strata.

The Jewish Quarter in Tripoli, 1943
(Photo by Dr. Nachum T. Gidal; Beth Hatefutsoth—Photo Archive)
❖

Jewish Family with Arab Neighbors at the Entrance of Their Home in a Village, 1936
(Janet and Dino Naim Collection, London; Beth Hatefutsoth—Photo Archive)

❖

The Rakah Family of Tripoli
(Cultural Center of Jews of Libya, Tel-Aviv; Beth Hatefutsoth—Photo Archive)
❖

Jewish Bride Leaving Her Parents' House on Her Wedding Day
(Janet and Dino Naim Collection, London; Beth Hatefutsoth—Photo Archive)

❖

Tripolitan Jewish Women in Traditional and Modern Dress
(Cultural Center of Jews of Libya, Tel-Aviv; Beth Hatefutsoth—Photo Archive)
❖

Jewish Mother and Daughter in Traditional Dress, Tripoli, 1914
(Janet and Dino Naim Collection, London; Beth Hatefutsoth—Photo Archive)

❖

Jewish Women Spinning in a Cave House, 1943
(Photo by Dr. Nachum T. Gidal; Beth Hatefutsoth—Photo Archive)
❖

Tripolitan Jewish Women Welcoming Eighth Army Soldiers at the Entrance to the
Jewish Quarter, April 1943
(Photo by Dr. Nachum T. Gidal; Beth Hatefutsoth—Photo Archive)

❖

❖ TWO ❖

Family Life

❖

Jewish communities in the diaspora were very careful to keep Jewish law and traditions regarding religious and daily life. This observance was the main guarantee for Jewish survival when small groups of Jews were spread across the world, often isolated from one another. It was deemed most important for the community members to know the basics of Judaism, to keep its laws and regulations, and to participate in the religious services. Jewish survival was dependent not only on knowledge and observance of religious laws but also on keeping the Jewish family a vital and strong entity. To guarantee Jewish survival it was essential that there be no mixed marriages and that the family itself—both the nuclear and the extended family—experience Jewish life in the full meaning of the term, making sure that no members went astray.

The Jews of Libya generally observed the traditional rabbinic laws and regulations with regard to marriage and family life. To these they added their own practices that developed during their lengthy existence in the region. The various marriage regulations and customs were meant to protect the sanctity of Jewish family life as a means of safeguarding the continued integrity and existence of the Jewish community. Marriage customs were slow to change among Libyan Jewry and many practices and habits reported for the Ottoman period continued well into the twentieth century. Under Italian rule, however, a growing number of departures from the old customs occurred. In the major coastal urban centers, and especially in Tripoli, these changes reflect significant independence of some Jewish women. In other cases, however, the changes show a decrease in religious observance but no increase in the social status of women. Marriages were usually arranged by the parents of the couple and were meant to last a lifetime. Polygamy was accepted in special cases, and divorce was practiced. Despite the fact that mixed marriages with gentiles were strongly rejected, they took place in ever-increasing numbers.[1]

MARRIAGE AGE

Jews in Ottoman Libya usually married young, especially the women.[2] The rationale was that according to the community, the main purpose of women was to be wives and mothers, and thus there was no reason to postpone marriage once a girl reached puberty. Brides were often between twelve and thirteen years old when they married (up to twenty years at the most). Men often got married at the age of sixteen, though some were younger. Many others waited until they were between twenty and thirty years old and were economically independent.[3] Early marriage continued to be the rule in most Libyan communities throughout the twentieth century. The improvement in female education and the growing numbers of working women were not significant enough to bring about a drastic change in this behavior. Thus, under Italian rule, in most places women married when they reached their fifteenth or sixteenth birthday,[4] but at times the brides were much younger.[5] Only

1. For an examination of marriage customs and practices among the Libyan Jews, see also H. E. Goldberg, "The Jewish Wedding in Tripolitania: A Study in Cultural Sources," *Maghreb Review* 3, no. 9 (1978): 1–6.

2. On marriage age according to Jewish law, see *Encyclopaedia Judaica*, s.v. "Marriage: Legal Capacity of the Parties."

3. Ha-Cohen, *Higgid Mordecai*, pp. 274, 305; Slousch, *Travels*, p. 37; T. Sutton, "Coutumes, croyances et légendes," *Revue des Ecoles de l'Alliance Israélite Universelle* 6 (1906): 425; H. Abravanel, "Les Juifs del'hinterland tripolitain," *Cahiers de l'Alliance Israélite Universelle* 90 (April–May 1955): 23.

4. *Hed ha-Mizrah* 4, no. 32 (1945): 8; "Ha-Yehudim be-Luv," *Yalqut ha-Mizrah ha-Tikhon* 1, nos. 7–8 (1949): 11; De Felice, *Jews in an Arab Land*, p. 281.

5. For example, in 'Amrus in 1923, girls were married as early as their eleventh year, or the twelfth at the latest, whereas their husbands were usually between the ages of fifteen and sixteen. Some fathers hurried to marry their sons when they reached thirteen and had

with regard to the rural community of Gharyan was it specifically emphasized that women there did not get married early but waited until they were twenty to twenty-five years old.[6] This is in contrast to reports from the Ottoman period and might indicate changes caused by the military and political upheavals in the region and the numerous tasks that rural women had to perform. It might also reflect only some individual exceptional cases.

COURTSHIP AND MATCHMAKING

During the Ottoman period, marriage was arranged by the parents and was often an economic-financial affair.[7] Nevertheless, in both town and village there were ample opportunities for marriageable youth to see each other and make their intentions known (especially for the men). Several of these customs continued in the twentieth century. Courting differed in the urban and rural areas due to the different life-styles and women's level of independence. In the villages, the instances in which Jewish men and women could meet were relatively frequent, because much of the women's work was outside the house, and women were unveiled prior to their marriage. In town, however, during the Ottoman period and in numerous cases also during the twentieth century, girls over thirteen years of age were obliged to be veiled. Furthermore, many urban families did not allow their daughters to step out of the house until they got married.[8] Thus, in Ottoman Tripoli there were no public occasions, save one, on which marriageable youth could see each other, and consequently, the preparations for this event were abundant. Even though during the twentieth century there were ample opportunities for Jewish youth of both sexes to meet, this traditional event was kept.

It was customary in Tripoli that once a year, on the afternoon of the

---

their Bar Mitzvah ceremony because the boys were then considered to be responsible for their deeds. In these cases, the boy was married on the evening following his Bar Mitzvah ceremony (*Hed ha-Mizrah* 4, no. 28 [1945]:7). In Benghazi, too, Jewish girls were sometimes married at the age of thirteen, but the bridegrooms were usually twenty-five to thirty-five years old and were at an age when they were well settled in life and had steady work and sufficient income (Yehoshafaṭ [Harkabi], Benghazi, to Professor S. H. Bergman, Jerusalem, 18 November 1943, CZA, S25/5217).

6. *Hed ha-Mizrah* 2, no. 12 (1943): 8.
7. Abravanel, "Les Juifs," p. 23.
8. Sutton, "Usages," p. 154; Slousch, *Travels,* p. 204.

last day of Passover, marriageable Jewish youth could see each other in public. The girls were allowed to expose their faces while they stood at the window, on the balcony, on the roof, or even outside the gate of the house. In order to appear at their best, the girls would put on their prettiest garments and jewelry. Meanwhile, young men walked to and fro in the street to view the girls and throw flowers in front of those they met. If a man found someone to his liking, all the other men and women would throw flowers in front of the couple. Thus, this day was referred to as the Festival of the Roses (*ḥag ha-shoshanim*). The young man would then communicate his intentions to the parents of the girl by bringing to the parents' house a basket full of lettuce and flowers on the same evening: the acceptance of this present meant the consent of the parents to the marriage proposal. This event was called Lettuce and Flowers (*khass wa-nuwwār*).[9] This custom refers only to the approval of the groom and was based solely upon the outward appearance of the bride: there is no mention in the sources of the bride being consulted for her opinion or of any intellectual exchange between the couple.

Engagements that resulted from this event were always celebrated on the last evening of Passover. A dinner party was organized in the house of the bride's parents, where singers and musicians playing drums and occasionally violins entertained the guests. The bridegroom arrived escorted by his parents, relatives, and friends. He brought baskets decorated with flowers and filled with lettuce, oranges, sweets, and flowers. These baskets were usually carried on the heads of young male relatives of the groom. When the groom and his entourage reached the home of the bride, they were welcomed by her family, and especially by the women, who voiced their joy by cheers and singing. The groom then distributed lettuce and flowers to those present. Afterward, the veiled bride sat at the back of the room, and everyone, following the groom, had to strike her head with the lettuce and the flowers. This done, a meal was provided for everyone, and the evening was spent in eating, drinking, and singing.[10]

9. Sutton, "Usages," pp. 154–55; Abravanel, "Les Juifs," p. 23; "Yoman Ṭripolitani," *Milḥamtenu* 8 (July 1943): 27; Zuarez et al., *Yahadut Luv,* p. 378. It is possible that this "beauty contest" was simply a means for the young men to see their future brides after marriage had already been discussed by the parents but before any formal agreement was signed.

10. According to Ha-Cohen (*Higgid Mordecai,* p. 196), the groom alone struck the bride with the lettuce. For other customs, see also Sutton, "Usages," pp. 154–55; Abravanel, "Les Juifs," p. 23; Zuarez et al., *Yahadut Luv,* p. 378.

During the Ottoman period and later, the betrothed often did not meet face to face until the recital of the Seven Benedictions (*sheva' berakhot*) during the wedding ceremony.[11] The marriageable Jewish girls were always veiled in the presence of nonrelated males, hardly ever spoke with a man who was not a close relative, and, when they heard that their fiancé was approaching, used to hide. A young man who did not see his fiancée during the Festival of the Roses sometimes became apprehensive lest he would not like the girl after the wedding and consequently demanded that her parents let him see her face clearly. For this purpose, a special ceremony named *tajliyah* (i.e., "exposure, discovery") was arranged. The *tajliyah* took place in the bride's parents' house, during a meal to which the groom had sent meat and whatever else was necessary. The groom came to this ceremony accompanied by his relatives, and the bride was handsomely dressed in order to present her to the groom at her best. If the groom approved, the conditions for the betrothal (*shidukhin*) were then agreed upon. This custom, however, was regarded by many as a disgrace, because if the groom rejected the bride, she was henceforth despised. As a result, some men tried to see their proposed brides through trickery (e.g., by posing as a peddler).[12]

Toward the end of the Ottoman period, many customs had changed: the separation between the sexes (at least in Tripoli) was less strict, the veil was often abandoned, and the betrothed could speak with one another face to face and even meet in solitude.[13] During the Italian period, and even more under British rule, the chances for young men and women to meet socially grew, mainly due to the existence of Jewish cultural activities and youth movements. During the 1940s, special parties were organized by the youth movements on Saturday nights for the entertainment of the youth, and quite a few marriages resulted from these events. Although some members of the older and more traditional generation disapproved of these activities, they nevertheless preferred the Jewish youth to meet among themselves, because otherwise some used to look for amusement among the gentiles, and occasionally this led to mixed marriages (see chap. 5). The troubled times of the early 1940s witnessed yet another kind of "courtship." Because of the dangers confronted by the Jews during World War II and the growing desire to

---

11. On the two phases of the Jewish wedding, see n. 42.
12. Ha-Cohen, *Higgid Mordecai*, pp. 274–75.
13. Ibid., p. 275.

immigrate to Palestine, some Jewish women and Jewish Palestinian soldiers entered into fictitious marriages to enable the women to immigrate to Palestine (see chap. 5).

In the villages, the Jewish youth had more opportunities to meet freely, and the most popular meeting place was by the well. In Yefren, the girls went each evening to draw water for all the family's daily needs. Since one well belonged exclusively to the Jews, the youth could meet in a relatively secluded Jewish environment. Due to the large size of the families, the water drawing could be a lengthy process, sometimes lasting from dawn until night during the dry season. This gave the Jewish youth ample opportunity to meet in public, although it was apparently more difficult to meet in solitude. After the young man had found a girl to his liking, she was not allowed to be seen with him face to face until their wedding. From the moment she was spoken for, she had to keep her distance from him, covering her face from him with the "veil of shame" (*mimzūza*).[14]

During the Ottoman period, a further element was sometimes involved in courtship in the rural regions. In Gharyan, for example, every Jew had a Muslim Berber patron who protected him from enemies and rivals, including fellow Jews. This arrangement could sometimes be utilized to secure a betrothal. When a father refused to give his daughter to a suitor, the latter would ask his Muslim protector to intervene and "convince" the girl's father to change his mind. As a result, the young Jew got the girl he desired even against her father's previous opposition.[15] As can be seen, in towns and villages alike the parents' approval for the marriage was necessary, and in both regions the groom could have a say in the process. Reference to the bride's opinion was never made.

BRIDE-PRICE AND DOWRY

During the early Ottoman period, there were more Jewish men than women in Tripoli. Consequently, not only were the bridegrooms required to give bride-price (*mohar*), but they also could not argue with the bride's father regarding the amount and composition of the dowry

14. Ibid., pp. 274–75; Slousch, *Travels*, p. 159.
15. Ha-Cohen, *Higgid Mordecai*, pp. 314–15. On Jewish "slaves" of Berber masters in the Tripolitanian mountain, see ibid., p. 284.

(*nedunyah*). In the late Ottoman period, however, the situation had reversed, and as a result, bridegrooms in Tripoli did not pay any bride-price and could even decide the size and composition of the dowry and how much of it should be in money.[16] In the early twentieth century, the dowry in Tripoli was usually between 400 and 800 francs, and among the rich it could reach 2,000 francs.[17] The dowry served for the basic needs of the family and often included sheets, furniture, kitchen utensils, and so on. This was the property that a divorced or widowed woman was allowed to take with her, and her husband had no authority over it.[18]

In the villages, the grooms had to contribute financially and in kind for the wedding. The amount depended on the personal status of the bride. During the late Ottoman period, the price for a virgin in Yefren was often 600 francs or at least 100 francs, but those whose fathers did not receive the higher price suffered a great disgrace. In addition to the gifts that were usually given during the betrothal, the bridegroom there also contributed wheat, olive oil, and other edibles to help the bride's father toward the expenses of the wedding feast. Unlike in Tripoli, Yefren grooms did not have a say over the amount of the dowry. If the bride's father was generous and good-hearted, he would provide a dowry that was equivalent to the bride-price that the groom had given him earlier. Sometimes, the bride's father gave a dowry that was worth more than the sum paid by the groom, but he was in no way obliged to do so. Since bride-price was obligatory in the hinterland but the dowry was not, whoever had only daughters could profit from these transactions. It was, however, reported that the main concern of the fathers of girls was not to make a profit but to find an appropriate match, so that their daughters would not fall into the hands of evil men.[19]

There are only a few references to the exchange of money in relation to weddings during the twentieth century, though this does not imply that the custom ceased to exist. For example, the dowry brought by the

16. Ibid., pp. 223, 275. For a report from 1877 on a Tripolitan Jewish man who paid fifteen maḥbūbs for his wife without seeing her, knowing only that she was referred to as "Bouba," see E. Rae, *The Country of the Moors: A Journey from Tripoli in Barbary to the City of Kairawan* (London: John Murray, 1877), p. 107.

17. Sutton, "Coutumes," p. 425.

18. Ha-Cohen, *Higgid Mordecai,* p. 275. On the dowry in Judaism in general, see *Encyclopaedia Judaica,* s.v. "Dowry."

19. Ha-Cohen, *Higgid Mordecai,* p. 306. On the various practices connected with the recording of the dowry in the wedding contract, see the next section.

bride in Zawiya during the 1920s could be as high as 300 napoleons.[20] At the same time, bride-price paid by grooms in Gharyan could amount to fifty to sixty napoleons when the bride was a virgin.[21] This might have reflected the continuation of the trend during the Ottoman period in the Tripolitanian mountain region for Jewish men to pay bride-price due to the relative scarcity of young women.

PRE-WEDDING CUSTOMS

The pre-wedding customs included the preparation of the new household and a festive transfer period immediately prior to the wedding. A few weeks before the wedding took place, the Tripolitan bridegroom bought the wool needed to make one or two mattresses. The families of the future couple departed from the groom's house in a cheerful and singing procession, quite a common sight in Tripoli, heading to the beach to wash the wool. Once this task was accomplished, they sat down in a circle on the sand and had a snack of fruit and biscuits as well as generous amounts of liquor. Later on, they returned to Tripoli in an even more cheerful manner, and on the same evening the bride offered a dinner to all the participants.[22]

As soon as the preparations for the wedding began among the rural Jews, the bride had to demonstrate her bashfulness. This was achieved through a number of traditional customs. The bride had to run away from her parents' house to one of her relatives and be wrapped in the "veil of shame." Her face had to remain covered, and she was not to be seen with any men until the wedding ceremonies began. This was an ancient custom in the Tripolitanian hinterland and was already documented in the sixteenth century. The groom, too, had to depart from his parents' home before the wedding. In the late Ottoman period, however, sometimes those young men who had been exposed to the habits of the big city—Tripoli—did not abide by the old usages and refused to flee from the parental home. Ignoring the pressure of the more traditional people, they stated that they had no reason to escape, not being thieves.[23]

The wedding was preceded by a week of celebrations in the urban

20. *Hed ha-Mizraḥ* 4, no. 32 (1945): 8.
21. Ibid. 2, no. 12 (1943): 8.
22. Sutton, "Coutumes," pp. 425–26.
23. Ha-Cohen, *Higgid Mordecai*, pp. 306, 375.

and rural areas alike. Although there were several similarities between the customs in the urban and rural areas, each region also displayed some distinctive characteristics, many of which continued well into the twentieth century. In the smaller places, where most of the Jews were related, weddings were almost a communal festivity, and wherever all weddings were conducted during the same period, for that time the whole village was in a constant state of rejoicing.

In the rural Jewish communities, a group of male friends (*shoshvinin* [Hebrew] or *shawwāsh* [Judeo-Arabic]) accompanied the groom during the seven days of festivities preceding the wedding. One of these friends had to be with the groom at all times. Similarly, the bride was surrounded by females. Relatives and friends used to invite the groom or the bride and their companions to dine with them, and the two groups would move from house to house accordingly. Before the wedding festivities began, the groom would send the bride some henna so that she and her female relatives could paint her hands and feet red.[24]

It was customary in the Yefren region that all weddings be performed on the eve of the Sukkot (Tabernacles) festival, and all those who decided to get married waited for this season. The reasons for this custom were economic, social, and religious. Many Jews in this region were itinerant peddlers, and some of them returned home only twice a year: for the High Holidays (i.e., Rosh ha-Shanah [New Year] and Sukkot) and Passover. The whole family could participate in the festivities only during these periods. Another possible reason for this custom was that local Jewish artisans who had previously lent money to Muslim farmers were usually paid back following the harvest of the autumn months or were supplied with gifts in kind by their Muslim clients at this time. Thus, during this period, most of the Jews were at home and could afford to finance the celebrations. It is also possible that they did not want to waste too many working days, since all the members of the extended family wanted to participate in the ceremonies. There were also some religious reasons for the custom. According to a Talmudic saying, one recites the benediction over the rain (customarily on the last day of Sukkot) after the groom goes forth to meet his bride. This saying was interpreted as indicating that one should fix the wedding shortly before the benediction over the rain. Another religiously motivated

24. Ibid., p. 306; Zuarez et al., *Yahadut Luv,* p. 393. Most of these customs were mentioned in relation to Yefren and Mislata.

reason was that the phrase "the time of our joy" is customarily recited during Sukkot, and the villagers thought it appropriate for weddings.[25]

On the eve of the eighth of the month of Tishri (i.e., one week before Sukkot), the bride in the Yefren region was brought back from her house of "exile" to that of her parents. On the following evening, the bridegroom brought to the bride's father's house a basket (*elqoffa*) with women's cosmetics wrapped in a silk sheet, as well as a dish of *bsisa* (cooked barley and wheat). After the Day of Atonement (the tenth of the month), kerchiefs were spread over a hand mill and a plow, and the bride was seated on top, demonstrating her mastery of milling and plowing. These were two of the Jewish women's normal tasks in the village, but this custom may also have had sexual connotations. Following this ritual, the female companions of the bride painted her hands and feet red with the henna that the groom had previously sent. It was also customary to expose the bride's unbound hair before a selected crowd in order to demonstrate that, indeed, she was a modest woman, as manifested by her long hair. On that occasion, the bride's hair was sprinkled with ground myrtle and powder as well as other cosmetics previously sent by the groom. During all this time, the bride's face was covered with a kerchief.[26]

In Ottoman Tripoli the festivities connected with the wedding, which was always set for a Wednesday, started eight days earlier. Each evening had its characteristic activities. The pre-wedding festivities began with an evening gathering during which the guests spread raisins (provided by the groom) and wheat (provided by the bride) around the groom's house in a ceremony called *tajlīl* ("spreading"). Both ingredients were put in a sifter, and the small children in the crowd collected whatever fell down. This ritual symbolized abundance and happiness.[27] After this ceremony, the bride was taken to the Jewish ritual bath (*miqveh*) by the female relatives of the groom. This was done not only because a bride is required to immerse herself in a ritual bath before her wedding but also in order to determine whether she had any physical defects.[28]

---

25. Zuarez et al., *Yahadut Luv*, p. 395; Goldberg, *The Book of Mordechai*, p. 180. On the festival of Sukkot, see *Encyclopaedia Judaica*, s.v. "Sukkot."

26. Ha-Cohen, *Higgid Mordecai*, pp. 306–7; Abravanel, "Les Juifs," p. 23.

27. Ha-Cohen, *Higgid Mordecai*, p. 275; Sutton, "Coutumes," p. 426.

28. Ha-Cohen, *Higgid Mordecai*, p. 275. There is no reference to a similar check with regard to the bridegroom. On rules and customs relating to purification, see the section "Purity" in this chapter.

The Saturday preceding the wedding was referred to in Tripoli as the Saturday of the Girls (*Sabbāt al-banāt*). On Friday night, the female relatives and friends of the bride and the groom put on their best clothes and went to the bride's father's house, in order to bless the bride farewell. The rejoicing and singing continued for the whole night. The females brought the bride from her room with her face veiled and her arms outstretched. Two women held her while everyone clapped their hands and sang special love songs. This performance was repeated Saturday afternoon and every night until Wednesday.[29]

On Sunday, the bride's father sent a messenger to invite his friends for supper. As a special treat for this occasion, the groom sent a beef heart, liver, and lungs for the bride and her relatives. The bride ate the "head of the heart," which was roasted and sweetened with sugar, symbolizing that the groom's heart was "sweet with her." The other part of the heart was sent back to the groom for him to eat. It was believed that this guaranteed understanding and love between the couple.[30]

On Monday night, the groom and his friends, accompanied by songs and music, went to the bride's father's house. The groom brought the bride a covered basket containing perfumes and jewelry, one white sheet, and four chicken eggs, two of which she was later to throw at the groom's house.[31] The groom also handed white sugar or honey sweets to his veiled bride. These were the first presents delivered directly by him to her, and symbolized a good omen and sweetness. Afterward, the guests circled the bride, while wax candles burned in front of her. Later on, the bride's father invited all the guests to dinner. When the meal ended, the long hair of the bride was exposed, but her face was kept veiled with a silk kerchief. Following this, female friends and relatives colored the bride's hands and feet red with henna, while she sat by the wall with her legs stretched in front of her. The groom, followed by the other guests (men and women alternating), threw money between the stretched legs of the bride. All this time, a group of musicians played and sang love songs. During the seven evenings preceding the wedding,

---

29. Ha-Cohen, *Higgid Mordecai,* p. 275; Sutton, "Coutumes," p. 426.
30. Ha-Cohen, *Higgid Mordecai,* p. 276; Abravanel, "Les Juifs," p. 23.
31. Ha-Cohen, *Higgid Mordecai,* p. 276; Sutton, "Coutumes," p. 426. According to Sutton, the basket (*elqoffa* in Judeo-Arabic, from the Arabic *al-quffah*) was sent on Sunday and also included cosmetics and shoes for all the bride's family, a coat (*barrakān*), soap, a mirror, a comb, candles, and sugar, but only two eggs, which the bride placed in a small stone mill. The bride distributed the sugar to her female companions, each of whom gave her a present.

the women would beautify the bride by coloring her hands and feet (and sometimes also her hair) red with henna and applying different cosmetics to her face.[32]

On the night before the wedding, the bride was brought from her father's house to that of her groom. In Yefren, this night was called the Night of the Journey (*laylat al-raḥlah*). Prior to her departure, the bride had to swallow seven twisted cotton wicks that were previously dipped in olive oil, symbolizing long life and the perpetuity of family ties.[33] Afterward, she slowly walked to the groom's house with her face veiled and two women supporting her. Meanwhile, all her other female companions clapped their hands and sang love songs composed in her honor. Simultaneously, the men chanted hymns loudly. The whole village of Yefren would be in a state of merriment, because several such processions usually took place at the same time. When the bride reached the groom's house, she took a chicken's egg out of her bosom and threw it against the wall of the house and thus soiled it. This was considered a reminder of the destruction of the Temple.[34]

In Tripoli, a similar procession took place on Tuesday. Before leaving her father's house, the bride was adorned, and all that she had to know as a woman was explained to her. In the evening, she went again to the ritual bath accompanied by the female relatives of the groom, to check on her once more. The groom, meanwhile, ordered a meal for his guests. At night, the groom went to the bride's father's house to bring the bride to his house. She was covered by the white sheet that he had earlier sent her. She wore a long veil on her head and walked slowly, her body stiff and expressionless. She appeared sad because of her departure from her parents' house and wept for her father and mother, and all her family also wept for her departure. As she proceeded, two female relatives or friends supported her. Sometimes, when the groom's house was very far, the bride would rest on a chair if she became weak or faint. The whole procession was accompanied by much turmoil. It included a group of male musicians and singers who played and sang love songs along the way. The women also sang and clapped their hands. The procession was surrounded by much light. One source of light were the

32. Sutton, "Coutumes," p. 426.
33. Goldberg, *The Book of Mordechai*, p. 126.
34. Ha-Cohen, *Higgid Mordecai*, p. 307.

wax candles that the girls held in front of the bride. In addition, lanterns were used, as well as an iron container holding live fire (called *raḥlah*, "journey"), which threw much light in front of the bride. When the procession reached the groom's house, everybody refrained from entering and waited for the groom to ascend to the roof. From there, he hurled a jug of water to the ground and called: "If I forget thee, O Jerusalem, let my right [hand] forget itself," in memory of the destruction of the Temple. This act was accompanied by cries and wailings from the women and was followed by yet another ceremonial act. Before the bride entered the room reserved for her and her groom, she stepped through the broken pieces of the jug. She then took from her bosom a chicken egg, which had been sent to her earlier by the groom, and threw it vigorously at the external wall of the room, just above the door. After she entered the room, she threw another egg inside the house, and thus soiled the outside and the inside of the house alike, as a sign for mourning over the destruction of the Temple. Later, in the absence of the groom, she took hold of one of his garments, put it on the sofa, and sat on it. This act was regarded as symbolizing her authority during her marriage.[35]

In Tripoli, following the bride's arrival in the groom's house, he offered a meal to all the guests, who were entertained by musicians playing love songs. Meanwhile, the bride sat on a chair, and although her face remained veiled, her long hair was exposed in front of everyone, in order to demonstrate that she was a proper and modest woman. After the meal, her hands and feet were once again colored red with henna. Simultaneously, the groom, followed by the guests, threw money between her legs. All the money thrown at the bride inside the groom's house belonged to him, and he used it to cover the wedding expenditures, though often a large amount remained in his hands. All these donations, as well as the meals prepared by various friends and relatives during the pre-wedding festivities, were recorded in the family's register, and the groom was obliged to repay an equivalent sum on

---

35. Ibid., p. 277; Sutton, "Coutumes," p. 427; Zuarez et al., *Yahadut Luv,* p. 393. These processions were usually conducted in a cheerful but orderly manner. In 1847, however, an internal conflict in the Tripolitan community resulted in some Jewish men trying to unveil the bride by force. See reports on this event by the British consul in Tripoli to his Tuscan colleague, starting on 22 September 1847, Public Record Office, London (henceforth, PRO), Foreign Office Archives (henceforth, FO), file 169/11.

the occasion of a family feast in the donor's house (e.g., circumcision, Bar Mitzvah, or wedding ceremonies).[36]

THE WEDDING CEREMONY

After the bride had been brought to the groom's house, her dowry was written into the marriage contract (*ketubbah*).[37] In Yefren, the items of the dowry were appraised by assessors who were chosen from among the notables of the community. The sum written into the marriage contract was, however, twice or three times the appraised value of the dowry, in order to protect the woman in case of divorce or widowhood. It also reflected the bargaining power of the couple's families with regard to the economic aspects of the marriage. Quite often they had disagreements concerning the evaluation of the dowry and the sum that should be recorded in the marriage contract. Consequently, lengthy discussions occasionally took place before an agreement was reached. In any event, the decision concerning the sum to write in the *ketubbah* was not made by the groom, although he was present during the negotiations. When this issue was resolved, the local rabbi read aloud the *ketubbah* in front of all those assembled, in order to make public the sums written in the *ketubbah*. The reason for this custom was that sometimes the obligatory witnesses to the wedding did not sign the marriage contract, and the public reading by the rabbi was considered a sufficient alternative. The avoidance of signing the contract might have resulted from the fact that most of these rural Jews in Yefren were related and as such were not legally valid witnesses and might have even nullified the marriage contract had they signed it.[38]

In Tripoli, after the assessors appraised the value of the dowry, it was customary for the groom to record at least 50 percent more in the *ketubbah,* although he was free to decide on a higher sum.[39] The sums

36. If the groom tried to evade this duty, the donor could refer the issue to a religious court (Din Torah) to force the groom to repay whatever he had received, which was considered an interest-free loan. See Ha-Cohen, *Higgid Mordecai,* p. 277; Zuarez et al., *Yahadut Luv,* pp. 393–94; M. L. Todd, *Tripoli the Mysterious* (Boston: Small, Maynard, and Co., 1912), pp. 113–18.

37. On the *ketubbah* in general, see *Encyclopaedia Judaica,* s.v. "Ketubbah."

38. The signing took place on the day of the wedding or on the day preceding it (Ha-Cohen, *Higgid Mordecai,* pp. 306–7; Goldberg, *The Book of Mordechai,* p. 126).

39. In the early nineteenth century it was customary in Tripoli to write down in the appendix to the marriage contract (*tosefet ketubbah,* "increment" *ketubbah*) at least the sum

written down in the Tripolitan marriage contract served as a basis not only for payments to a widow or a divorced woman. According to a regulation (*taqanah*) in force since 1717 and referred to as *hishavon* (namely, the return of an item to its owner), if a wife died without having a son, all her dowry returned to her father's house.[40]

In comparing the two practices for fixing the sum written in the marriage contract, one can see that in the village it was at least twice or three times higher than the appraised value of the dowry, depending on the results of the negotiations between the couple's families. In Tripoli, it was at least 50 percent higher, depending on the good will of the groom. In both cases, this sum was intended to ensure the economic future of a widow or a divorcée and the integrity of the property of her father's family.

Dressing the bride for her wedding was considered a good deed, and female relatives and friends were invited to join in this undertaking.[41] Later in the evening, the wedding took place in the groom's house. It was customary in Tripoli that the *qiddushin* ("betrothal"; literally, "sanctification") and holding the *ḥuppah* (traditional bridal canopy covering the couple with a *ṭalit* [prayer shawl] during the marriage ceremony) took place at the same time, and whoever violated this regulation had to pay a penalty.[42]

In Tripoli, weddings were conducted on Wednesday. Following the betrothal blessing, the groom sanctified the bride, whose face was unveiled on this occasion in full view of the wedding witnesses and the whole crowd. The *ḥuppah* was usually in the form of a *ṭalit*, with which

---

of 66 golden maḥbūbs (equal to 264 francs or 1,320 Turkish ghurush) when the bride was a virgin and half that sum for a widow. When half the value of the dowry was appraised at more than 66 maḥbūbs, the groom had to add half the value of the dowry to the 66 maḥbūbs. At times, they used to specifically indicate the exact monetary value of the dowry. See Ha-Cohen, *Higgid Mordecai,* pp. 207–10, 220–21, 277; on *tosefet ketubbah,* see *Encyclopaedia Judaica,* s.v. "Ketubbah."

40. For the text of this regulation see Ha-Cohen, *Higgid Mordecai,* pp. 209–10; Zuarez et al., *Yahadut Luv,* p. 394.

41. Sutton, "Coutumes," p. 427.

42. In the early nineteenth century, this penalty was 50 doro (250 francs) for the rich, 25 doro for the middle class, and 12.5 doro for the poor (Ha-Cohen, *Higgid Mordecai,* p. 220). A Jewish wedding consists of two phases: betrothal (*qiddushin* or *erusin*) and marriage (*nisu'in*). After the first ceremony, each member of the couple is forbidden to marry anyone else, but only following the second ceremony is the couple allowed to live a marital life. For details, see *Encyclopaedia Judaica,* s.v. "Marriage."

the father of the groom[43] covered the groom; the latter then took a corner of the *talit* and put it over his bride's head. They remained standing like this, covered with one *talit* until the end of the reading of the Seven Benedictions. Afterward, the groom broke a glass in memory of the destruction of the Temple. This glass was the one from which the groom and the bride drank during the ceremony. It was broken while still almost full of wine, and when the wine spilled all around, the female guests would wail, commemorating the destruction of the Temple, but say at the same time *mazal ṭov* ("good luck").[44] In Yefren, the Seven Benedictions were recited on the night preceding the eve of Sukkot. Due to the lengthy discussions concerning the value of the dowry, it sometimes happened that the benedictions were not read until midnight.[45]

It was customary in Tripoli for the bride's mother to remain in the groom's house the night of the wedding. She did this to ensure that intercourse took place, so that the groom would not falsely complain that he had not found the hymen. As a further precaution, the bride's mother took her daughter's dress spotted with the hymen's blood as proof of her daughter's virginity.[46]

Jewish marriage in Libya was in fact a three-phase process. During the first part, the economic security of the bride and the integrity of her father's property were guaranteed. In the village, the bride's family had the upper hand in this issue. This is the only phase in which the bride herself was not present. During the second phase, the betrothal and marriage ceremonies were performed, and during the third phase, the marriage was consummated. The modesty of the bride was closely watched in Tripoli. Whereas prior to the wedding the female relatives of the groom doublechecked the bride to make sure she had no physical defects, the bride's mother made sure to get proof of her daughter's virginity once the marriage was consummated.

43. If the father was no longer living or was not available, another male relative of the groom performed this function.

44. Ha-Cohen, *Higgid Mordecai*, pp. 277–78; Zuarez et al., *Yahadut Luv*, p. 393; Todd, *Tripoli the Mysterious*, pp. 113–18.

45. Ha-Cohen, *Higgid Mordecai*, p. 307. In another small place, Mislata, after the groom and bride drank wine from the cup, the groom took this cup and poured the remaining wine into an empty cup held by the rabbi, who then poured it back into the groom's cup, and vice versa. This exchange continued until all the wine was spilled, to the loud encouragement and hand clapping of the rejoicing guests, and the merriment was great. See Zuarez et al., *Yahadut Luv*, p. 393.

46. Ha-Cohen, *Higgid Mordecai*, pp. 277–78.

POST-WEDDING FESTIVITIES

The wedding was followed by another week of festivities, though not as elaborate as during the preceding week. During these seven days, the couple stayed together as much as possible. They also entertained relatives and friends together or separately, at home or outside. The groom was especially honored in the synagogue when he was called to read from the Torah scroll. During this week, great amounts of food, sweets, and liquor were consumed.

It was customary in Tripoli that on the Thursday following the wedding, the bride's father sent to the groom's house honey, sweets, and wafers fried in olive oil for distribution among the guests. On Friday, the groom arranged a meal for his male friends. At this meal, his married friends, to whom he had given money on their weddings, "returned" the money to him. Unmarried friends were also invited, and they gave the groom money, which he would repay when they got married.[47] Later that evening, it was customary to go to the groom's house following the evening prayer (*'arvit*) or to pray it in his house. Afterward, all who were present recited the Seven Benedictions with the bride and the groom standing as they did during the wedding. This was repeated the following day (Saturday) after the morning prayer (*shaharit*), during which the guests received sweets and drinks.[48]

In Ottoman Tripoli, shortly after the wedding, a female relative of the bride called upon the groom and made a knot over his hand with a string she had brought with her. This precaution was made to ensure that the husband would never forget to be faithful to his wife. During the whole week following the wedding the couple stayed at home (with the exception of the groom going to the synagogue). The groom did not work during this period of feasting. During the first three days he was considered a "king"; in the following two, "deputy"; and for the rest of his life, a "slave," providing food for his family. At the conclusion of this week, the bride's father sent a special meal to his daughter and son-in-law. On Tuesday following the wedding, the first thing that the groom did was to go and buy a basket full of green vegetables and a big fish. When he returned from the market, he threw the vegetables at his

47. Ibid., p. 278.
48. Ibid., pp. 210, 278; Zuarez et al., *Yahadut Luv,* pp. 394–95, including details on the groom's participation at the Sabbath prayer.

wife's feet and sprinkled water over them. Afterward, they held opposite ends of the fish and took turns cutting it. It was believed that the first act ensured abundance and fertility and that the second served to fight the evil eye.[49]

The week of wedding celebrations in Ottoman Yefren corresponded to Sukkot. During the eve of Sukkot, the groom was forbidden to leave his house, because this was his wedding day, in which "his heart rejoiced." He was dressed in festive garments, and for one whole day he was to devote himself entirely to the woman he married and make her happy. Afterward, the husband was free to meet anyone he wanted, with the exception that during the first month after the wedding he and his wife were not supposed to be together in a room with his parents, because he was embarrassed to face them.[50]

THE CONFLICTING AUTHORITY OF THE COMMUNITY AND STATE REGARDING JEWISH WEDDINGS

Family life was highly respected, and the Jewish community had various regulations and institutions to ensure proper marriage procedures and opportunities. During the late Ottoman period and even more in the twentieth century, the intervention of the communal bodies in marriage procedures increased in Tripoli and Benghazi. In these towns communal organization became more institutionalized during this time and was later governed by special Italian laws. In the smaller towns and rural communities, communal organization was less formal, and the community intervened to a lesser degree in personal affairs. Thus, for example, in Tripoli the groom was required to get a permit from the chief rabbi in order to hold the wedding.[51] This was done to ensure that the bride and the groom were single and marriageable and that the groom was able to support a family.

In order to provide for poor couples, and especially poor brides, there was a special time-honored institution named Mohar ha-Betulot

49. Ha-Cohen, *Higgid Mordecai,* p. 278; Sutton, "Coutumes," p. 428.
50. Ha-Cohen, *Higgid Mordecai,* p. 307, including details on the special role of the groom in the synagogue. There are a few descriptions of wedding ceremonies during the twentieth century. It was mentioned that weddings in the Gharyan region lasted for eight days, during which the bride was forbidden to leave her house. See *Hed ha-Mizrah* 2, no. 12 (1943): 8.
51. Ha-Cohen, *Higgid Mordecai,* p. 277.

(Bride-Price for the Virgins). This society helped poor women who could not afford to pay the expenses required for a wedding. These operations were financed at first by donations and later also by a special communal tax. Many synagogues had a collection box named after a saintly Moroccan Jewish woman, Solika del Maroc. For many years, the revenues from this collection were the main financial source for Mohar ha-Betulot.[52]

During the twentieth century this society became a department bearing the same name within the Jewish communal council of Tripoli. Community members had to apply to this department for a betrothal permit, and the decision of the department was based on the personal status of the couple as well as on the groom's ability to provide for a family. This department used to levy a "betrothal tax" from every couple whose registration for marriage was approved[53] (see table 2).

In Tripoli, it was also customary for the bridegroom to give a certain percentage of the dowry (1 percent at the beginning of the twentieth century) to the community. In Benghazi, too, couples had to pay a fee to the rabbinical court in order to get engaged. These sums, together with special donations by rich people, served to assist poor women when they got married. It seems that the income from these sources was higher than the expenditures.[54] It is possible that the gap between these

52. The collection box commemorated the pious Sol, the most important female saint of Moroccan Jewry, whose tomb in Fez is venerated by Jews and Muslims alike. She was a member of the Hajwal family of Tangier and became a martyr in 1834 when she refused to convert to Islam as her Muslim judges had ruled. Similar collection boxes existed in many synagogues outside Morocco (I. Ben-'Ami, *Ha'aratzat he-Qedoshim be-Qerev Yehudey Maroqo* [Jerusalem: Magnes Press, 1984], pp. 577–81; Zuarez et al., *Yahadut Luv*, pp. 104, 111–12).

53. Ha-Cohen, *Higgid Mordecai*, p. 275; Zuarez et al., *Yahadut Luv*, p. 21. For an example of the help provided to a poor couple and how the husband understood it to be a package deal, see the story related in Rubin, *Luv*, p. 41, about how a man agreed to marry a blind orphan after the community promised him a horse and carriage.

54. Thus, for example, during January–September 1931, the tax on dowries brought the community of Tripoli 17,220.50 Italian lire (henceforth, IL) (out of a total income of IL 502,085.95), whereas the expenses were only IL 500 for regular dowries and IL 1,500 for dowries accorded by lot ("doti sorteggiate") (out of an expenditure of IL 502,085.95) (see De Felice, *Jews in an Arab Land*, pp. 334–36; idem, *Ebrei in un paese arabo* [Bologna: Mulino, 1978], pp. 178–79). Furthermore, in August 1949, the community of Tripoli received 46,768 Military Administration Lire (henceforth, MAL) as dowry taxes and MAL 14,250 as donations from rich people to help poor women on the occasion of their marriage (out of a total income of MAL 885,076), but only MAL 2,250 was spent to assist poor women to get married (out of a total expenditure of MAL 960,532) (see Report by the Jewish Community of Libya, Tripoli, to the Joint Distribution Committee [henceforth, AJDC], 6 September 1949, CZA, S20/555; Zuarez et al., *Yahadut Luv*, pp. 21, 23; *Ha-Tzofeh*, 8 December 1946).

Table 2. Engagements, Weddings, and Divorces

		ENGAGEMENTS		WEDDINGS		DIVORCES	
YEAR	PLACE	*No.*	*Fees*	*No.*	*Fees*	*No.*	*Fees*
1949	Tripoli	316		336		17	
1949	Benghazi	22	2,220	42	21,940	1	250
1950	Tripoli	91		102		10	

SOURCES: The annual reports on Tripolitania and Cyrenaica, PRO, FO 371/80864 (for 1949) and 371/90314 (for 1950). The fees in Benghazi were paid in Egyptian liras; the sums paid in Tripoli were not reported. By 1950, most of the Jews of Benghazi had moved to Tripoli on their way to Israel.

sums resulted from the fact that this tax was obligatory by law, but the manner in which welfare money was distributed was not.

In spite of the high respect accorded family life by the Libyan Jews, there were occasional instances of irreverence toward marriage, usually due to ignorance. One case took place in Khoms during the last quarter of the nineteenth century. A Jewish physician jokingly put a ring on the finger of an eleven-year-old girl and recited the required marriage formula in the presence of two witnesses, but without the knowledge of her father. When this man was told that as a result of this act he had to marry the girl or divorce her, he ran after her in order to take the ring from her finger. In an inquiry conducted by the chief rabbi of Tripoli, Eliyahu Ḥazzan, it turned out that the man and the girl were not acquainted with marriage regulations and proceedings and that the girl's father opposed the marriage once he heard about it. Rabbi Ḥazzan ruled that the affair was conducted jokingly and out of ignorance. He preferred to decide leniently, so that the girl would not have to be divorced and thus be forbidden to marry a Cohen.[55] Another reason for this decision was "in order to break the teeth of the rascals of our generation who do their evil deeds in the dark."[56]

Even during the last years of Ottoman rule in Libya, the Ottoman state did not intervene in issues connected with the personal status of the Jews, including those who were Ottoman citizens, and left these issues to the Jewish community and its religious bodies. Under Italian

55. Despite the rarity of Cohanim in Libya at the time.
56. E. Ḥazzan, *Ta'alumot Lev* (Livorno and Alexandria, 1879–1907), 2:31b, no. 2.

rule, however, the situation changed. Although the Italian authorities acknowledged the rights of the Jewish community and its institutions, they believed it to be their duty to intervene in personal matters for the well-being of the state, and they intervened when they were asked to do so, especially if the request came from Italians from Italy living in Libya (in contrast to Libyan Italians). Some of these interventions brought about real conflicts between the community and the Italian authorities.

One of these cases involved a private wedding.[57] Although private weddings were not common in Libya, the local rabbinical court, following Jewish law, accepted their validity. In Tripoli in 1935, a private wedding caused an internal conflict in the community and a rift between the spiritual leadership of the Jews and the Italian authorities. This dispute reached such a level that the chief rabbi of Tripoli was dismissed by the Italian authorities, who sent him back to Italy. In that year, a Tripolitan Jew, Gino Hassan, aged thirty-five, and Linda Nemni, the fifteen-year-old daughter of Raffaelo Nemni, one of the leaders of the community, decided to get married. Since their decision was against the will of their parents, they arranged a private wedding.[58] The validity of the wedding ceremony was confirmed by the rabbinical court of Tripoli, after the father of the bride challenged the procedure. Following his rebuttal, the father appealed against the rabbinical ruling to the governor of Tripolitania, Italo Balbo. The governor informed the chief rabbi of Tripoli, Gustavo Castelbolognesi, that the marriage had to be nullified, because according to Italian law the girl was a minor, and her father, under whose guardianship she still was, objected to the marriage. The governor also stated that private marriages were a remnant of "primitive customs" that prevented the modernization and Italianization of Libyan Jewry. Because the chief rabbi sided with the rabbinical court, he was dismissed by the Italian authorities and sent back to Italy.

The approval of the Hassan-Nemni marriage by the Jewish rabbinical court encouraged other Jews to follow suit. Thus, a Jewish shoemaker, Ghebri Fitusi, decided to leave his sick and paralyzed wife of many years and privately marry the young Meri Gerbi. With regard to this case, the

57. Private weddings are not conducted in front of a rabbi and lack the permission of the communal institutions. They are performed by the couple and some Jewish witnesses according to legal Halakhic procedures.

58. This wedding was referred to in the Italian correspondence relating to the affair as a *qiddushin* ("sanctification"). On the terminology relating to Jewish marriage, see n. 42.

governor decided not only to nullify the marriage but also to have the shoemaker publicly flogged.[59]

These cases, and especially the Hassan-Nemni one, reveal the attitude of the community leadership and the Italian authorities toward the right of Jewish women to independently make decisions about marriage and the tactics each party used to buttress its position. The Hassan-Nemni case also shows that some fifteen-year-old girls could meet freely with nonrelated adult Jewish males, even against the approval of their fathers, and that Italianized Jewish women in Tripoli were ready at times to refer to older habits and practices when it better suited their needs. Furthermore, despite the fact that the Hassan-Nemni wedding was against the will of the bride's father, some Jews were ready to serve as witnesses in the ceremony. By doing so, they demonstrated their approval of the free mixing of the sexes as well as of conducting a wedding against the will of the father. The rabbinical court, too, showed that it put the validity of the marriage process before what was traditionally considered proper behavior of unmarried people as well as the rights of the father concerning his children, and especially girls. When the situation was explained to Linda Nemni, apparently by her father or in the presence of members of her family, she changed her mind. She claimed that she did not understand that the ceremony had changed her personal status to that of a married woman, and she stated that she did not want to get married. One can conclude from this exchange that once under the influence of her family, she did not dare to oppose their will. The authority of the close male relatives concerning the women under their guardianship came to the fore in several instances in this case. Mr. Nemni demanded a passport for his daughter in order to send her away for a while, whereas Mr. Hassan claimed that since he was her husband, his permission for this act was required. From these two statements it can be concluded that no weight was given to the opinion of the woman. According to Italian law the woman was a minor, and consequently, the state regarded the authority of her father over her as final, and no consideration was given to her opinion or well-being.

59. De Felice, *Jews in an Arab Land,* pp. 155–60; H. Abravanel, Tripoli, to AIU, Paris, 10 June 1935, AAIU, IC-29.

POLYGYNY

As was generally the case in Muslim countries, the Jewish community of Libya did not follow the edicts relating to marriage and divorce promulgated by Rabbi Gershom Me'or ha-Golah of Mainz ("Light of the Diaspora," c. 965–1028).[60] These edicts forbade polygyny and required the husband to obtain his wife's consent to a divorce. These rulings were accepted by European Jewry but were not binding in the realm of Islam. This difference, as well as others, reflects the influence of the surrounding non-Jewish society on the customs and communal legislation of the Jews living under non-Jewish rule.[61]

Although polygyny was not prohibited in Libya, most Jews remained monogamous. Some Jews married a second wife, but this was usually done only when the first wife did not bear a son. If after ten years of marriage the couple had no children (or no son, according to some sources), the husband could divorce his wife or marry a second one, if both women agreed.[62] In Gharyan, however, even those who had a son sometimes married a second wife.[63] According to a field study conducted in the 1960s in Israel among Jewish immigrants from Gharyan, only a few, prominent members of the community had entered into a polygamous marriage in Libya; most were restrained by tradition and costs.[64] The acceptance of polygamous marriages in the Libyan Jewish community was known in Europe and prompted some European Jewish men who did not have a son by their first wife to come to Libya to marry a second wife.[65]

DIVORCE

Although Jewish law permits divorce, the religious authorities usually do not view it with favor. Furthermore, it is often easier for a man to

60. On these edicts see *Encyclopaedia Judaica,* s.v. "Gershom Ben Judah Me'or ha-Golah."

61. Goldberg, *The Book of Mordechai,* p. 32; B. Lewis, *The Jews of Islam* (Princeton: Princeton University Press, 1984), p. 82.

62. Ha-Cohen, *Higgid Mordecai,* pp. 42, 203. For some examples, see ibid., pp. 260–63; Benjamin, *Eight Years,* p. 286 (Rabbi Haim Serrusi); Zuarez et al., *Yahadut Luv,* p. 112 (Yosef Fargion). The distribution between divorce and polygyny is not clear.

63. Ha-Cohen, *Higgid Mordecai,* p. 313.

64. Goldberg, *The Book of Mordechai,* p. 143.

65. Ha-Cohen, *Higgid Mordecai,* pp. 117, 231. This was one of the reasons for European Jews to settle in Libya, though how many came for this reason is not clear.

seek a divorce than for a woman.[66] As a general rule, the Jewish religious courts in Libya used to work slowly whenever they had to deal with a divorce case, hoping that the couple would make peace and agree to continue to live together. If, however, it was rumored that the wife had committed adultery, the judges hurried to get a divorce.[67] In this case, as well as in others connected with adultery, women were punished much more severely than men. If a husband divorced his wife against her will, he had to add a sixth to the sum written in the marriage contract. If, however, she had not borne him children, he could divorce her without increasing the sum written in the contract.[68] In most places in Libya, although weddings were conducted by the local rabbis, divorce cases were not, due to their complexity or specific problems. Thus, for example, during most of the period under study, the Jewish court in Benghazi referred divorce cases to Tripoli. Consequently, a warning by a husband in Benghazi, "We shall go to Tripoli," was a threat of divorce.[69] Cases of *halitzah* were also referred to the rabbinical court of Tripoli.[70]

PURITY

The Jews of Libya, and especially those in the Tripolitanian mountain, were very strict concerning purity, mainly with regard to menstruant women and women after giving birth, and even went beyond the Jewish

66. On Jewish law regarding divorce in general, see *Encyclopaedia Judaica*, s.v. "Divorce."

67. No reference is made to instances in which the husbands were involved in adultery.

68. Ha-Cohen, *Higgid Mordecai*, pp. 202–3. In Libya, as in other Jewish communities, great emphasis was placed on the accuracy of personal names and place-names in the divorce document (*get keritut*). Furthermore, the Hebrew names of the husband and his father were always used in the divorce document, even when these men had nicknames by which they were known locally. When the name of the father of the husband was not known, it was omitted from the divorce document.

69. The reason for this was uncertainty about the spelling of the town name (i.e., in one word, Benghazi, or in two, Ben Ghazi). See Zuarez et al., *Yahadut Luv*, p. 26. During the twentieth century this question was resolved, and the name of the town was written as one word composed of two parts: BenGhazi. From Gharyan, too, divorce cases were referred to Tripoli, due to their complexity. See Ha-Cohen, *Higgid Mordecai*, p. 313.

70. The *halitzah* ceremony enables a widow whose husband died without a son to marry a man who is not her late husband's brother (or other close relative) (*Encyclopaedia Judaica*, s.v. "Levirate Marriage and Ḥaliẓah"). *Hed ha-Mizrah* 4, no. 33 (1945): 8, mentions a case from Misrata being referred to Tripoli.

law in this matter. Women were very careful regarding menstruation, and even if there were only a few drops of blood, they had to count seven clean days afterward.[71] The Libyan Jewish husband was not allowed to touch his wife when she was in a state of impurity and was not even supposed to throw things to her. In Yefren, the husband was forbidden to step on the same straw rug that his menstruant wife had walked on, to look at her, or even to speak to her, with the exception of the most necessary issues, and then their conversation had to be as brief as possible. Libyan Jewish women were considered sexually impure for forty days following the birth of a son and eighty days following the birth of a daughter.[72] Beginning in the late Ottoman period, however, people decreased the number of impure days.[73] In accordance with Jewish law, at the end of seven clean days after menstruation or after the specified number of days of impurity after childbirth, women had to go to a ritual bath (*miqveh*).[74] In Libya, they had to wash in cold water even during the winter months, and only in 1913 was a warm-water *miqveh* constructed in Tripoli. In some places, like Zanzur, there was no *miqveh*, and the women used the sea for their ritual immersion.[75]

Jews around the world obeyed similar regulations, but the regulations were more strictly interpreted in Libya in comparison with many other places. Elsewhere, it was usually only forbidden for the husband to touch his menstruant wife. In addition, the increased period of impurity following the birth of a daughter was a Libyan interpretation, which reflected the attitude toward women and newborn girls. The postponement of establishing a warm-water ritual bath might also reflect the attitude of the male leadership of the community toward women, who according to Jewish law have to take this bath regularly each month.

71. On Jewish law regarding purity, see *Encyclopaedia Judaica*, s.v. "Niddah."
72. According to Jewish law, a wife is forbidden to her husband for seven days after the birth of a son and fourteen days after the birth of a daughter. In addition, she is not allowed to touch any consecrated objects for another thirty-three and sixty-six days respectively (*Encyclopaedia Judaica*, s.v. "Niddah; Woman after Childbirth").
73. Ha-Cohen, *Higgid Mordecai*, p. 272.
74. On regulations relating to the *miqveh* and its uses, see *Encyclopaedia Judaica*, s.v. "Mikveh."
75. Ha-Cohen, *Higgid Mordecai*, pp. 252, 272, 304, 319.

SANCTITY OF JEWISH FAMILY LIFE

Much emphasis was laid on preserving the Jewish family intact: inter-marriage was forbidden and women who engaged in adultery or prostitution were severely punished. From a number of remarks and regulations it is apparent that occasionally breaches did occur in the urban and rural regions alike, and in most cases women suffered a heavier punishment than men.

The Jewish community of Ottoman Tripoli had its "secret spies" to supervise the behavior of its members and prevent adultery. Whenever a case of improper behavior was discovered, the woman was severely punished, both physically and mentally. She was beaten with a big stick and her hair was cut short and tied to a long pole, to be publicly exposed by Talmud Torah (Jewish religious school) students. This was done with much fanfare, in order to make the woman's misbehavior widely known.[76] Since long hair was a sign of a woman's modesty, its cutting and public display were considered a great shame. Furthermore, adulterous wives could even be stoned, and there was a special field outside the city walls of Tripoli where the stoning was said to have taken place.[77] Although there is mention of the method of punishment, no actual instances of stoning were reported during the period under review. Usually, here as elsewhere, only the punishment of women was referred to. In only one reported case, at the beginning of the nineteenth century, was a Jewish man suspected of adultery beaten, while the woman and the Arab notable, who was the real culprit, were spared (see the next section).[78]

From the existence of regulations regarding illegitimate children, one can conclude that despite all the precautions and punishments, extramarital sex did occur. Thus, it was customary in Tripoli that when the name of the father of a boy was unknown, the boy was named "Israel" during his circumcision and was afterward considered a full-fledged Jew.[79] Also, the omission of the name of the father of the husband in divorce documents indicates that at times there was ambiguity as to the identity of the father.

76. Ibid., p. 255.
77. Rae, *The Country of the Moors,* p. 98 (he visited Tripoli in the 1870s); N. Slousch, *Sefer ha-Masa'ot* (Tel-Aviv: Devir, 1938–43), 2:75.
78. Ha-Cohen, *Higgid Mordecai,* pp. 120–21.
79. Ibid., pp. 216–17. According to Lyon, *A Narrative,* p. 91, it was customary among the Libyan Muslims at the beginning of the nineteenth century to kill illegitimate babies.

MALE-FEMALE RELATIONS BETWEEN JEWS AND NON-JEWS

Jewish laws and institutions as well as the members of the community did their utmost to prevent mixed marriages between Jews and gentiles, in order to guarantee Jewish survival. Nevertheless, the lengthy coexistence with gentiles and certain connections between the groups, based not only on politics and economics but also on cultural and social links, prevented total seclusion. As long as women were kept at home, the possibilities for contact with undesirable males were small. However, once women started to go to school, work, and various social and cultural functions, it was very difficult to prevent them from meeting nonrelated men, Jews and gentiles alike.

Jewish-Muslim

During the Ottoman period, contacts between Libyan Jews and Muslims were very common. Nonetheless, Jewish families tried to keep their women away from Muslim men as much as possible, even more than they tried to prevent any contact between nonrelated Jewish women and men. Due to the behavior patterns in the Muslim state, relations between Muslim females and non-Muslim males were hardly possible (unless the latter were of a lower social class, such as slaves or peddlers) and endangered both parties.

Before the return of direct Ottoman rule (1835) and the growing intervention of European powers in Libya, the Jews were at times quite hesitant to demand the protection of the authorities against the molestation of Jewish women by Muslim officials. At times it was even impossible, because the abuse originated from the highest authorities. A rare case of a forced giving of a Jewish woman to a Muslim man occurred in 1793. The ruler of Tripoli at the time, ʿAlī Burghul al-Jazāʾirī, gave to one of his officers the widow of the Jewish agent of the British consul, who had been put to death for betrayal. It took her father several weeks to collect a thousand dollars in order to buy her back.[80] This was apparently a rare case in which the authorities distributed the "property" of a convict, including his widow, among their supporters. ʿAlī Burghul was infamous for his cruelty and for his attempts to extract money from the population, and this incident was in line with his general conduct but was not typical for the Ottomans as a whole.

---

80. Tully, *Letters,* p. 376 (a letter from 20 November 1793).

This, however, was not the only case in which senior officials tried to take advantage of their position. In the early nineteenth century, during the rule of Yūsuf Qaramānlī, a Jewish Tripolitan married woman was repeatedly raped by a senior Muslim administrator, who was referred to in the Jewish source only as "Al-Kakhya."[81] Her husband was afraid to complain, because of the political status of the rapist, and consequently the woman went secretly to seek the support of the Jewish religious court. The members of the court were also afraid to intervene in the case for similar reasons. They stated that since the Muslim notable was so important, nothing could be done against him. When the issue came to the knowledge of the leader of the Jewish Strongmen (*biryonim*),[82] he decided to take the matter into his own hands. He hid himself in the woman's house in order to take revenge on the rapist when he arrived. The Jewish court, however, was informed of this scheme and suspected the Jewish Strongman of indecent behavior with a married woman. As a result, this plan was canceled, and the Strongman was sentenced by the Jewish court to a beating. Later on, the temporal leader of the Jews of Tripoli, Raḥamim Barda (died 1807), consulted with the leader of the Strongmen and his deputy. They decided to invite the unsuspecting rapist to Barda's house for a meal, during which the Strongmen would attack him and force him to agree to change his behavior. Because of Barda's position in the community, it was not uncommon for him to entertain Muslim dignitaries, and the invitation aroused no suspicions. During his visit, the Strongmen severely beat the Muslim official and threatened to bring his evil deeds to the knowledge of Yūsuf Qaramānlī, who was renowned for his favorable attitude toward the Jews. The beaten and frightened Muslim promised not to repeat his crimes and begged to be pardoned and to have his former actions kept secret.[83]

The situation revealed by this case is interesting. It seems that the Muslim notable was so important that no judicial or disciplinary action against him was considered feasible by the Jews. This was apparently due to the deputy's influence over lower officials, who would be afraid to enforce the law. Even when this notable was caught by the Jews, they

81. A title usually referring to the deputy of the ruler. In Tripoli during that period there were a senior deputy and a junior deputy.

82. On this group, see Ha-Cohen, *Higgid Mordecai*, pp. 118–23. The Jewish Strongmen protected the Jews in Tripoli and the countryside. Until 1845, they would wrestle every Saturday afternoon on the city wall next to the Jewish quarter. The Ottomans forbade their wrestling in 1850, and the group apparently ceased to exist as security improved.

83. Ibid., pp. 120–21.

were satisfied with his promise to end his relations with the woman and did not press the matter further to bring him to court, punish him, or get some compensation. Also of interest is the fact that the Jewish woman had access to the Jewish court of law, even against the will of her husband. The temporal leadership of the community and especially the unofficial association of Jewish Strongmen were more willing to protect the honor of a Jewish woman than the Jewish spiritual leadership was, and the former two decided to use unconventional methods to achieve this end. It also appears that the Jewish court was very strict with the Jewish Strongman, on whom it could lay its hands, but was quite reluctant to protect a woman against a personal attack by a senior official who was regarded as unattainable. It was, however, a rare case in which the man, and not the woman, was punished for what was suspected to be a sexual offence.

During the mid-1870s, the protection of the honor of a Jewish woman was the cause of a diplomatic conflict between the United States of America and the Ottoman authorities in Tripoli and almost resulted in the outbreak of war. In the summer of 1875, Ottoman naval ships carrying marine cadets came to Tripoli during their training. While walking around town, a group of cadets headed by an officer started to make immodest remarks to a Jewish female servant who was at the gate of the orchard of the American consul in Tripoli. The consul came to her rescue, and together with a male servant cursed and shouted at the cadets. As a result, the latter filed a complaint against the consul in the penal court of law. This case, in which the diplomatic immunity of the American consul was not honored, caused an American naval force to be sent to Tripoli, and offensive demands were placed before the Ottoman authorities. After some negotiations, the Ottomans and the Americans reached a compromise, and the issue was resolved.[84] This case shows the liberties that some Muslims took toward unaccompanied Jewish women. Furthermore, it appears that employers assumed a position of guardianship over their female employees, as long as the latter were in their service, when their natural guardians were unavailable.

84. According to the Jewish source (Ha-Cohen, *Higgid Mordecai*, pp. 157–58), this incident happened in 1876. American sources reveal 1875 to be the correct year, but they give a different reason for the conflict, which does not involve the insulting of a Jewish maid. See House of Representatives, 44th Cong., 1st sess., *Papers Relating to the Foreign Relations of the United States*, 1875 (Washington, D.C.: Government Printing Office, 1875), 2:1311–15; *New York Times*, 11, 13, 19, 23, 25, 27, and 28 August, 26 September 1875. See also *The Daily Levant Herald*, 20 September 1875.

Despite the efforts of the Jewish community, contacts between Jewish women and Muslim men took place, more frequently in the countryside than in the cities. At times, these contacts ended in staged or forced kidnapping of the women. Some Muslim men even took advantage of their administrative positions to force their will upon Jewish women. Some cases ended with the return of the woman to her family following the intervention of the authorities. This happened only after the latter were alarmed by the Jews and the woman was confronted by her Jewish relatives. During the 1940s, the return of kidnapped women at times provoked outbreaks of violence by the Arabs against the Jewish community, in which Jewish public and private property was destroyed. The region and period of the kidnappings had some bearing on their outcomes, and in those areas where Arab political power was supreme, it was less likely that the kidnapped women would be released.

During the late Ottoman period, there were a number of reported cases of kidnapping of Jewish females by Muslim men in both the larger and the smaller population centers. In all of the cases in which the females were Ottoman citizens, the higher Ottoman authorities hastened to intervene in order to return them to their families and to prevent their forced Islamization. Between 1868 and 1908, three Jewish girls ranging in age from six to twelve were kidnapped from Benghazi, Tripoli, and Khoms. No details are provided on how the first kidnapping took place. In the second the girl was kidnapped from the streets of Tripoli in 1907 by a Moroccan Muslim dressed like a *murābiṭ* (Muslim mystic). In the third case, occurring in 1908, the twelve-year-old girl ran away with a Muslim from Khoms to Tarhuna, where they got married. The reaction in the case involving the *murābiṭ* was the fastest: a Christian passerby caught him, and the authorities sent the kidnapper in chains to the Libyan region of exile: Fezzan. In the two other cases, Jewish institutions in Libya, Istanbul, and Paris called upon the Ottoman authorities to intervene in favor of the Jews, and the girls were eventually returned to their families.[85]

Whereas two of these cases seem to be genuine kidnappings, it is quite probable that in the third incident there was collaboration between the somewhat older girl and the Muslim man. That case also

85. For details on the 1868 case, see M. Franco, *Essai sur l'histoire des Israélites de l'Empire Ottoman* (Paris: A. Durlacher, 1897), p. 219. On the 1907 case, *Ha-Yehudi*, 29 August 1907. On the 1908 case, *Ha-Yehudi*, 24 September 1908.

reflects the greater freedom of movement enjoyed by Jewish women in the smaller communities in the rural areas and the newly developed towns alike. Also of interest is the involvement of the Jewish administrative bodies in these events. Although one of the cases occurred in Khoms, the services of the Tripolitan and the Istanbuli Jewish leaderships were called upon to secure the intervention of the local and the imperial authorities in favor of the Jews. This apparently reflected the fact that although the officials of the big communities did not have the power to interfere in the affairs of the smaller, hinterland communities, the latter regarded the Jewish Tripolitan and Istanbuli leaderships as their representatives before the provincial and imperial authorities. The difference of opinion between Jews and Muslims with regard to the age of majority, and specifically with reference to women, was also stressed. One might conclude that when the issue involved an Ottoman citizen, the Jewish point of view prevailed. This was the case apparently because of the responsibility that the Ottoman authorities felt toward the Protected People as the Muslim ruler[86] and the repentance of the girl, and less due to foreign pressure on the Westernized governors to protect the rights of all citizens. Furthermore, even Muslim dervishes could not reap the fruits of their evil deeds, and they were not immune from punishment for kidnapping.

Even when the kidnapper was an Ottoman official and the victim could be claimed to be an adult, the Ottoman authorities sided with the Jews and demanded the return of the woman to her family. This was evident in 1903, when the local governor (*kaymakam*) of Misrata kidnapped a fourteen-year-old Jewess. The case was brought to the attention of the leadership of the community of Tripoli, which asked for the intervention of the governor (*vali*) of Tripolitania as well as of its military commander. When the kidnapper and the girl were interrogated, the man stated that the girl had cooperated in what was really a voluntary escape and not a kidnapping. Nevertheless, the authorities demanded that she return to her family. As a result, the girl was brought to Tripoli with her father and brother, in whose presence she denied that she had wanted to convert to Islam. Simultaneously, the governor of Misrata brought forth a statement signed by seventy Muslim *shaykh*s (religious leaders or civilian chiefs) that confirmed that the girl converted to Islam voluntarily. She was, however, returned to the Jewish

86. For details, see n. 2 in the Introduction.

community at the demand of the provincial authorities.[87] Of interest is the fact that the administrative position of the kidnapper did not ensure success in his undertaking. Although he had managed to get a statement signed by seventy *shaykh*s, something that an ordinary citizen might have found extremely difficult to achieve, especially in such a short period of time, the provincial authorities in Tripoli sided with the Jewish community. This position of the provincial authorities reflected a known tendency of the Muslim state to restrain government officials, especially when confronting a weaker segment of the population, lest they take undue advantage of their office.

The Ottoman authorities reacted differently when the kidnapping involved a foreign citizen. In 1910, an eighteen-year-old Jewish girl of an Algerian family (i.e., having French citizenship) in Benghazi left her home and wanted to become a Muslim. The Jewish vice-consul of France in Benghazi stated that according to the French law the girl was a minor and until the age of twenty-one she could not convert without the permission of her parents. In answer to an appeal, the Ottoman minister of the interior replied that since she was over fifteen years of age, she could decide for herself issues of principle and religion and did not need her parents' permission. The Ottoman minister ordered the Muslim religious judge (*qāḍī*) to convert the girl, and the ceremony took place in the presence of the Administrative Council of Benghazi.[88] In this case, Ottoman law was applied to a French citizen. It seems that the authorities were less inclined to show favor to demands of non-Ottoman Jews, and especially in a remote place like Benghazi, where events were regarded as less likely to arouse foreign pressure and intervention than in Tripoli.

During the Italian period there is only one report of a Muslim man kidnapping a Jewish woman (although more kidnappings might have occurred). This could be the result of the inferior position of Muslims during that period and the strong presence of Italian-led military and police forces in the country. In 1941, a Jewish girl from Mislata was kidnapped by an Arab municipal official. She was returned to the Jewish community the same night by the police and stayed in the house of the

87. M. Levy, Tripoli, to AIU, Paris, 23 November 1903, AAIU, IC-16.

88. Bernabi, Benghazi, to the Ministry of Foreign Affairs, Rome, 28 June 1910, Archivio Storico e Diplomatico (henceforth, ASD), Serie Politico (henceforth, SP), 7.

head of the community. Later that night, indigenous Arabs attacked Mislatan Jews and their homes, beating every Jew they encountered. The Arabs also assembled and shouted in front of the homes of the head of the community and the director of the local Jewish school, who were instrumental in securing the return of the kidnapped girl. The violence culminated toward morning, when the Arabs set fire to the only synagogue in Mislata, which also served as the Jewish school and library.[89] This is the first reported case in which the return of the kidnapped Jewish woman was followed by an outbreak of violence by the Arabs. In this instance, although the authorities took immediate steps to return the kidnapped girl, they did not manage—or did not try hard enough—to prevent the violent reaction of the Arabs to the failed kidnapping attempt. It is possible that due to the war situation, the Italians had sufficient power in Mislata to enforce the return of a kidnapped girl but were not in a position to bring large peacekeeping forces to Mislata. This incident may have served as a warning to both sides: although kidnapping would not be officially tolerated, the price might be too high for those seeking justice in this delicate issue.

A resurgence of kidnapping occurred in the late 1940s and may have been the result of the growing self-assurance of the indigenous Arab population in expectation of the declaration of Libyan independence. In addition, during this period the Israeli War of Independence took place and enflamed nationalistic feelings among Jews and Arabs in Libya. Furthermore, because of the Jewish mass emigration from Libya to Israel following the establishment of the state of Israel and in expectation of Libyan independence, an ever-decreasing number of Arabs in the towns and the countryside felt themselves to be responsible for the safety of their Jewish neighbors or dependent on their services, as had been the case in the past.

During the mass emigration from Libya to Israel (1949–51), quite a few cases of kidnapping of Jewish women by Arab men occurred in Libya, although only a few were reported officially. In Tripolitania, the British-supervised police managed in most cases to force the return of the women to their families, but the police usually failed to prevent the violent Arab reactions that followed. In Cyrenaica, where the political power of the Muslim Sanusi order was on the rise, it became

89. Zuarez et al., *Yahadut Luv,* p. 179.

impossible to return kidnapped Jewish women, who were immediately Islamized.[90]

In 1949, three cases of kidnapping of Jewish women by Arab men were reported in Tripolitania (in Misrata, Tarhuna, and Khoms).[91] They were but the tip of the iceberg, and other attempted and successful kidnappings occurred. Although the British police intervened in all three cases, the women were returned only in two. This success was, however, very costly. Both times there were outbreaks of violence by local Arabs against Jewish individuals as well as toward private and public property, including the synagogue of Tarhuna, which was set on fire. During these and similar incidents, the traditional Arab leadership usually tried to explain to the Jews that this was the work of irresponsible "kids" and did not reflect the age-long friendly attitude of the local Arab population toward their Jewish neighbors. It seems, however, that the village elders did not do much to prevent these incidents. If, on the other hand, they did try but failed, it would be evidence of their deteriorating authority vis-à-vis the younger generation, a state of affairs that was also developing in many other areas.

During the same period, the Sanusi leader Idris acquired great power and authority in Cyrenaica, although the region was still under the BMA. This division of power had an impact on some kidnapping cases. Thus, for example, following a complaint by the parents of two kidnapped Jewish girls from Barce in late 1949, Idris stated that the girls remained with the Muslims voluntarily and should not be returned to the Jewish community against their will.[92] Because of the particular situation in Cyrenaica, where the British did not want to infringe on the rising power of Idris, the Jews failed in all their attempts to get the British authorities to intervene in this case. This incident, as well as several others, convinced the Cyrenaican Jews that their safety under an Islamic Arab government was not guaranteed, and they lived in constant fear with regard to their

90. The Sanusiya was an Islamic order founded in 1837 by Muḥammad b. ʿAlī al-Sanūsī. Combining orthodoxy and Sufism, it aimed to unite all Muslim religious orders by returning to the sources. It established itself in Cyrenaica and its main support was tribal, based on a network of religious compounds. It played a central role in the resistance to Italian rule in Libya (1911–33), and many Sanusi leaders and followers were killed or went into exile. With the British occupation of Libya in 1942–43, many Sanusis returned, and the British appointed Idris al-Sanūsī, the last Sanusi leader, to the leadership of the indigenous administration in Cyrenaica. When Libya attained independence in late 1951, Idris became its king.

91. *Ha-Tzofeh*, 18, 21, and 22 November 1949.

92. Ibid., 9 December 1949.

future. As a result, most Jews did not trust the promises and reassurances of local Arab dignitaries regarding their well-being, and they tried to emigrate from Libya—legally or illegally—before the country became an independent Arab state.

The involvement of people from different religions in the kidnappings highlighted the differences in the legal systems in Libya. In one case in 1948, a Tripolitan Jewess, Giulia Surfir, aged seventeen years and nine months, cooperated with her Arab kidnapper and was converted to Islam in a Muslim religious (*shar'i*) court of law. Her parents appealed to the civil (*ahli*) court of law, claiming that she was a minor and could not decide by herself on such issues as conversion and marriage. The civil court, composed of two Muslim Arabs and one Jew, ruled that the girl should be returned to her family and that the Arab kidnapper should be imprisoned for three months. Following this ruling, the chief Muslim judge of Tripoli complained that because the woman had converted, she was under the jurisdiction of the Muslim religious court, and consequently the case should be decided according to Muslim law and not civil law. The opinion of the chief rabbi of Tripoli, based on Jewish Halakhic law, was that the age of majority of women is thirteen (or in some cases twelve and a half) years for marrying a Jewish man and twenty years for economic transactions; in no instance, however, and regardless of age and gender, is apostasy accepted. The British chief civil affairs officer commented that it was impossible to effect a compromise between the two religious systems. He therefore suggested that the administration should try and convince the father and the Muslim judge to wait until the girl became eighteen years old, the age of majority according to civil law, when she would be considered by a "neutral" system to be the sole responsible party for her acts. He further stated that in the meantime it should be emphasized that both religions have great respect for family life and the right of the father to bring up his children according to his religion until the children reach majority and are considered capable of deciding these matters for themselves.[93] It is of interest to note that even in the words of the British official, the emphasis was on the authority of the father—and not both parents—with regard to the children.

93. M. C. Hay, Tripoli, to the Legal Department, Cairo, 5 April 1948, and enclosed documents, PRO, War Office (henceforth, WO) 230/160. On Jewish law regarding apostasy, see *Encyclopaedia Judaica*, s.v. "Apostasy."

Jewish-Christian

During the Ottoman period, contacts between Jews and Christians occurred mainly in the big coastal towns. Most of these connections involved upper-class Jews who had commercial, social, and cultural contacts with Europe and Christians. The major difference between the Ottoman and the Italian periods was that during the Ottoman period it seems that Jewish men married Christian women, but during the later period there are also records of Jewish women marrying Christian men. The increasing numbers of Italians in Libya during the twentieth century and the growing involvement of Jewish women in non-Jewish education and employment made contact between Jewish females and Christian males much more easy and common than before. This led to a significant rise in mixed marriages.

There are two reports on marriages between Tripolitan Jewish men and Catholic women during the Ottoman period. In both cases the men were European (British and Italian). The first wedding was conducted in the British consulate, and the second in a church. There was strong pressure from the community in both cases to break up the marriages. The first couple was excommunicated and emigrated to Tunis. In the second case, the husband repented, and although he died young, he raised his son as a Jew as long as he lived.[94]

Whereas mixed marriages of Jewish women and Italian Christian men were quite rare in the 1920s, they became more frequent in the 1930s.[95] Apart from general reference, however, there are few details on such marriages. One incident, which aroused much uproar, took place in Tripoli in 1920–21. It triggered a conflict involving the families, the Jewish community, and the authorities. This case focused on the fifteen-year-old daughter of Mario Nunes Vais, a metropolitan[96] Italian citizen who served a number of times as a member of the Jewish community's council. The girl became engaged to an Italian Christian officer who was close to the governor of Tripolitania, Luigi Mercatelli. At first, the

94. Ha-Cohen (*Higgid Mordecai*, pp. 188–89) discusses the case of Raphael Abu ʿAziz, a British citizen from Gibraltar, who was married in the British consulate of Tripoli and later emigrated to Tunis. Slousch (*Sefer ha-Masaʾot*, 2:75–77) reports this case as well as that of Gustavo Arbib, a journalist and publisher, who was married in church but later repented. The community regarded his death soon after as punishment for his marriage to a Christian.

95. De Felice, *Jews in an Arab Land*, pp. 85, 135.

96. There was a difference between Italian citizenships held by people originating in Italy (metropolitan citizenships) and those held by local Jews.

father gave his consent to the engagement, but he later retreated when he became aware of the strong and vocal opposition of the community. As a result, the girl appealed to the Italian civil court, which accepted her application and approved her right to get married to the officer. The community's leadership, headed by Chief Rabbi Elia Samuele Artom, sent memoranda to several state and Jewish bodies (e.g., the governor of Tripolitania, the president of the Libyan court of appeal, the Italian ministers of justice and the colonies, the Italian Rabbinical Federation, and the Board of Italian Jewish Communities). In these memoranda, the Tripolitan Jewish leadership invoked the principle of freedom of conscience and the right of the father to educate and bring up his children according to his principles. The governor angrily rejected these statements, stressing the unacceptability of a petition criticizing the highest judicial court in Libya. He also objected to the attempt to deprive a young metropolitan Italian citizen in Tripoli of her acknowledged prerogatives.[97]

This case shows the growing freedom of Italianized upper-class Jewesses to become acquainted with nonrelated males, including non-Jews, to the point of getting married. When the father tried to prevent the marriage, the girl was independent enough to appeal to the Italian civil court against her father and her community. The attitude of the Italian authorities must have encouraged mixed marriages. In contrast to the Hassan-Nemni case, in which a fifteen-year-old girl was regarded by the authorities to be under the authority of her father, the Nunes Vais girl, who was the same age, was regarded as a full-fledged adult citizen who was qualified to enjoy the prerogatives of an Italian citizen. It seems quite possible that the husband's ties to the governor also influenced the attitude of the authorities toward the status of the girl.

Marriages between Tripolitan Jewish women and Italian Christians continued in the 1940s.[98] One source speculated that this was due to the

97. Ibid., pp. 119–20. According to Zuarez et al. (*Yahadut Luv*, p. 139), in 1918, the Zionist leader Elia Nhaisi (died 1918) and a group of young Jewish strongmen disrupted the wedding ceremony of the daughter of the head of the community and an Italian Christian officer. The police arrested the attackers, but the girl's father intervened in his capacity as head of the community and arranged their release, because he understood the motive for their action. Since no names were provided, it is not clear if this report refers to another case or to an earlier incident in the Nunes Vais affair.

98. In 1949, some Italian Christians asked the rabbinical court of Tripoli to convert them to Judaism. In answer to an inquiry of the court, the Sephardic chief rabbi of Israel, Benzion Ḥay 'Uzi'el, stated that he was inclined to convert them, so that Jewish girls would not marry Christians. See *Ha-Tzofeh*, 2 November 1949. This incident shows once

relatively greater degree of freedom enjoyed by women in Italian Christian families. According to this view, some Jewish women married Christians as a protest against their seclusion, which was in accordance with local customs, Jewish and Muslim alike, until the Italian occupation.[99] Once Jewish women had more freedom to leave their homes and even began studying in Italian state schools, and once the customs of Italy became the models to be imitated, habits that had prevailed in the Jewish community for generations started to erode and change. This included the behavior of women; they attempted to change their position by various means, including departure from the Jewish community and joining the Italian Christian world.

CONCLUDING REMARKS

Family life among Libyan Jews was strongly shaped by Jewish laws and tradition as well as by the influence of the neighboring society, which was almost exclusively Muslim for most of the period under discussion. Jewish regulations and customs relating to women were at times more strictly applied in Libya than in other parts of the Jewish world. There were a number of reasons for this. The main purpose of these laws was to guarantee Jewish existence, but they were also influenced by customs in the surrounding society. Thus, some regulations regarding women were implemented more strictly in Libya due in part to the attitude toward women in the neighboring Muslim society. This strictness, however, also served to keep the two communities separated. The impact of these external influences and customs was felt in many aspects of daily life, resulting in the overall inferior status of women.

Italian rule and the growing numbers of Italians entering Libya greatly influenced Libyan Jewish life. These changes were felt mainly in the public domain (e.g., work and education) and much less in family life. Thus, a Libyan Jewish woman still had almost no say regarding the selection of her mate. Very little changed in this respect until the 1940s, and then, too, only in certain groups who were under strong Italian or Zionist influence.

---

again that the issue of mixed marriages was an acute one in Tripoli. The request for conversion possibly arose because the women wanted to emigrate to Israel but hesitated to arrive in Israel as members of mixed marriages.

99. Zamir and Yariv, Tripoli, to Yosifon and Ben-Yehudah, 7 December 1943, CZA, S25/5217.

In many respects, Jewish women continued to be viewed as belonging to their male guardians. This was reflected, for example, in the economic arrangements related to marriage, when much attention was paid both by the bride's family and by her husband to the property listed in the marriage contract. The community regarded family life as the basis and a guarantee for Jewish survival. Although there were individual attempts by Muslims to take Jewish women, the autonomous status of the Jews under Ottoman rule precluded the intervention of the state or external legal systems in Jewish family life. Under Italian rule, however, the organization of the community was dictated by Italian laws. Furthermore, Fascist Italy regarded intervention in personal issues, including marriage, to be the right and even the obligation of the state for the benefit of the society as a whole. Consequently, one can find during the Italian period several examples of state intervention in purely Jewish marital issues, whereas Muslim courts intervened only when one party was Muslim.

❖ THREE ❖

Work

❖

There was a clear division of economic activity in Ottoman Libya between Muslims and non-Muslims and between men and women, with relatively few exceptions to the rules. Economic conditions to a large extent determined the occupations of the various segments of the population and their social and political status, and changes in economic conditions had significant effects on the socioeconomic behavior of the population. There was also a high correlation between increased economic involvement and freedom of action. Yet, social and cultural concepts were slower to change in response to changing economic needs than occupational behavior. Consequently, an increase in economic leverage did not necessarily carry with it improved social status and political power.

The major change between the Ottoman and the Italian periods with regard to Jewish women's work in Libya was the growing number of women who worked outside their households. Until the end of the nineteenth century, the standard was that women stayed at home. Thus, they were honored by the family and had much influence on its management, but most women were not income producers and lacked the authority that a breadwinner has. Due to the then-existing social order in Libya, extreme economic necessity and uniquely feminine needs were for a long time the only legitimate justifications for women to work outside their households. Furthermore, those professions that were solely services for other women (such as midwifery and cosmetics) were only part-time jobs and were performed in addition to regular household tasks. Some women had a sporadic income from various home industries (e.g., woven rugs), which were undertaken in addition to the women's regular chores at home. Thus, most of the women who worked full-time outside their households during the Ottoman period were poor, performed unskilled labor, and were regarded with disrespect, and their morals were at times suspected. The penetration of European ideas contributed to a change in attitude toward women's work among the Jews. Although the growth in numbers of working women was triggered by economic needs, work gradually also became a sign of increased independence and of having the power acquired by providing income. Although many women continued to stay at home and numerous others were employed in unskilled jobs, the number of professional women gradually increased and respect for women and women's self-respect grew.

HOUSEHOLD TASKS

Jewish women in Ottoman Libya did all the household work, but the definition of housework was much wider in the village than in town. Thus, although many of the tasks inside the house were similar in the urban and rural areas, rural women had to perform several chores outside the house, in the family's domain as well as in public areas. These tasks were, nevertheless, regarded as part of household work and earned no external income for the woman. In town, most women worked only at home.

There was also a difference in the attitude toward female work in the urban and rural areas. In the village, there was public pressure on the women to be industrious. It was considered shameful to be regarded as lazy, not to be busy all day long, and not to perform all work independently. In town, on the other hand, women did not hesitate to employ servants or buy manufactured products if they could afford them, thus freeing themselves from many of their chores. Furthermore, it was relatively easier in town than in the village to get this kind of help because there was a growing number of urban women who were obliged to work outside their homes due to economic pressures, and most of them became servants and laborers. Moreover, those urban women who opted to employ servants were not despised. In addition, some of the products that were previously manufactured by women at home (e.g., wool, cloth, clothing, flour) were more available in town than in the village. Thus, the main differences concerning women's work in the rural and urban areas were the general attitude, needs, opportunities, and scope.[1]

During the Ottoman period and in many places well into the twentieth century, rural Jewish women of the Tripolitanian mountain performed most of those tasks that according to Jewish tradition a wife was obliged to do for her husband. These traditional tasks included grinding, baking, laundering, cooking, nursing, making the bed, and weaving.[2] The one task Jewish women of the Tripolitanian mountain did not need to perform was making the bed, because in many rural places, such as Yefren, they did not use beds during that period. People slept on the ground on mats of straw, sacks, carpets, or skins, laying their heads on a stone or in a small hole dug in the ground.[3]

The workday of rural Jewish women lasted from well before dawn until late at night. They started each day by grinding enough grain for the needs of the entire household for that day. In Yefren, they got up before dawn and ground for about two hours. Whoever did not get up early to do the grinding was considered lazy and could not erase the shame. There was only one exception to this rule: newly married wives were exempt from this task for one month. They brought the required amount of flour with them as part of their dowry, so that they could be free to enjoy themselves with their husbands until dawn.

The women accompanied the grinding by singing special songs composed for this occasion. This singing can be viewed as a way of passing the time and entertaining oneself, but it might also have served as a vocal sign to the neighborhood that the singer was indeed an industrious woman who was diligently performing her duties. The grinding was done in a stone hand mill, made up of two wide, flat, circular stones

---

1. For an examination of the working conditions of Libyan Muslim women, see Attir, "Ideology," p. 121.

2. Ha-Cohen, *Higgid Mordecai,* p. 308. These tasks are enumerated in the Babylonian Talmud, Tractate Ketubbot.

3. Ha-Cohen, *Higgid Mordecai,* p. 309.

bored through the middle. Although camel-driven mills existed in Yefren and Mislata in the early twentieth century, most of the rural women continued to grind by themselves at home every day, either because of tradition and the social pressure upon them or because they did not have the economic means to pay for this work with money or with a portion of the flour.[4] In town, there were some camel-driven mills and later also steam mills. Urban people had no scruples about using these facilities, and in the early twentieth century they often bought flour imported from Europe.[5]

Before the beginning of the month of Nisan (March–April), as part of the preparations for Passover, the Jewish women of Yefren also ground an amount of unleavened flour sufficient for fifteen days (the days of the feast and the week preceding it) to be used for the baking of the special Passover bread. In order to ensure that the flour would not be fermented by saliva, they would cover their mouths with a kerchief and would not talk or sing during this special grinding.[6] The grinding of the unleavened flour was, of course, in addition to their regular daily grinding.

In the villages, every Jewish home had an earthen oven, in which the women baked bread every day. The ovens opened from the top and were heated with straw, rakings, peat, and wood. The dough was placed on the sides of the oven for baking. During the meal, the women would prepare the dough, knead it, and bake the bread, which was then served fresh to the dining men.[7] During Passover unleavened bread was baked daily.[8] In Tripoli it was quite usual to bring prepared dough to be baked in ovens operated by men from Fezzan (and later also by others).[9] This is another instance of the town offering facilities that released the women from part of their work, and they did not hesitate to take advantage of it. Rural Jewish women cooked using earthenware and copper pots and kettles. They cooked directly over flames while

4. Ibid., p. 308; Slousch, *Sefer ha-Masaʿot*, 1:82; idem, *Travels*, pp. 63–64, 159; Benjamin, *Eight Years*, p. 291.

5. Ha-Cohen, *Higgid Mordecai*, p. 50.

6. Ibid., pp. 194, 302–3. On the special regulations and customs relating to Passover, see *Encyclopaedia Judaica*, s.v. "Passover."

7. Ha-Cohen, *Higgid Mordecai*, p. 308; *Hed ha-Mizrah* 4, no. 32 (1945): 8. The females ate after the males finished their meal; see chap. 1 on women's status.

8. Ha-Cohen, *Higgid Mordecai*, p. 303.

9. Ibid., pp. 49–50, 149; Sutton, "Usages," pp. 155–56 (on Tripoli); Slousch, *Travels*, p. 63 (on Mislata).

columns of smoke rose straight up from the burning leaves and broom roots.[10]

Another task that the rural women performed individually was the laundry. In contrast to grinding and baking, which were performed daily, laundry was rarely done, because most people were poor and had only one set of clothing. Relatively few people had special garments for holidays and feasts. One's regular working clothes were hardly ever washed. Holiday attire was worn much less frequently but was sometimes washed. In Yefren, the women used a substance made from natron instead of soap for the laundry. Groups of women hewed the natron out of a nearby cave.[11] This was apparently cheaper than buying or producing soap from oil, but the searching, walking, and hewing added to the women's workload. In this case as in others, the rural women procured the raw materials and produced the necessary substances themselves even when the latter could be bought; this was in keeping with tradition and to keep costs low. The fact that the extra work had its price apparently did not count.

Everything connected with clothing was prepared by the rural Jewish women themselves. They spun sheep's wool, wove the cloth, sewed the clothing, and embroidered carpets. They did this work in the traditional manner, both with regard to equipment and with regard to styles. Cotton garments, however, were bought, because cotton did not grow there. Silk products were introduced to the hinterland in the late Ottoman period. The clothing and carpets that the Jewish women produced were mainly for private use. Sometimes, as a result of hard work well into the night, the women managed to produce surpluses of clothing and rugs, which were sold to the neighbors or exchanged for foodstuffs.[12] Usually, however, these women did not have much spare time to produce surplus items for sale.

Rural Jewish women drew water and chopped wood. In Yefren, Jewish girls went each evening to draw water for all the daily household needs from the one well (out of three) that belonged to the Jews. On Passover eve, they also drew enough water to last throughout the holi-

10. Ha-Cohen, *Higgid Mordecai*, p. 308. On their diet, see ibid., pp. 288–91.
11. Ibid., p. 308.
12. Ibid., pp. 290, 308; Slousch, "Les Juifs," p. 29 ('Amrus); idem, *Sefer ha-Masa'ot*, 1:82 (Misrata); idem, *Travels*, pp. 63–64 (Mislata), 129 (Beni 'Abbas), 159 (Yefren); *Hed ha-Mizraḥ* 2, no. 12 (1943): 8 (Gharyan).

day. Getting the water could take a long time, depending on the size of the family and the flow of the water. In a dry year, when the springs were weak and thin, the water drawers had to stay by the well from dawn until night, taking their turns, because the crevices of the rock would merely drip water. This tedious work not only provided for the daily needs of the family but also contributed to the continuity of Jewish existence: as a result of this chore, the young men of the community could see the girls and choose their future wives.[13]

Just as the rural women supplied the natron for the laundry and the water for cooking, cleaning, and drinking, they also obtained the wood for cooking and baking. Each Friday morning the women went out in family groups and scattered in the forest and fields to find a week's supply of wood and straw. At times they had to make a two-hour journey from their villages, walking barefoot over thorns and briers. When they returned by noon, each carried on her head a bundle of wood weighing more than a hundred pounds. This chore was viewed with disfavor by urban Jews, because the women were on their own for a long period of time in the wilderness, far from the residential areas and away from the control of their male guardians. Consequently, the rabbinical authorities in Tripoli issued a decree that threatened to excommunicate all those women who went out to chop wood. The women of Yefren, however, paid no attention to this decree, because had they not fulfilled this task, they would have been regarded as lazy, and none of them dared to bear that shame, which must have been considered worse than excommunication, which, in any case, was never implemented. Furthermore, because gathering wood was considered women's work, it was highly unlikely that men would have performed it.[14]

In the countryside, Jewish women also participated in the agricultural work. They worked in plots of land adjacent to the house as well as in fields and orchards farther away. They plowed and reaped the fields, beat olive trees to make them release their fruit, worked in the olive

---

13. Ha-Cohen, *Higgid Mordecai,* pp. 303, 305–6, 309. On the water drawers in Gharyan during the early 1920s, see *Hed ha-Mizrah* 2, no. 12 (1943): 8.

14. Ha-Cohen, *Higgid Mordecai,* pp. 302, 309. This event also reflects the failed attempt of the rabbinic court of Tripoli to extend its authority to the hinterland. Although the small communities in the countryside occasionally referred their difficult cases to the court of Tripoli, they rejected its attempt to spread its authority over the whole region. For the situation during the twentieth century, see *Hed ha-Mizrah* 2, no. 12 (1943): 8.

press, and raised egg-laying chickens. Their young children helped them tend the animals.[15]

In addition to these household and agricultural tasks, the women cared for their children. To avoid interrupting their work, Yefreni mothers used to carry their infants on their shoulders or put them in cagelike cradles suspended by ropes so they could swing the cradles back and forth and rock the babies to sleep.[16]

Besides their regular work, rural women had special tasks related to the holidays, and mainly to Passover. From the feast of Purim onward (i.e., during March–April), the women cleaned every part of the house, checking everywhere for leavened bread. The house itself was whitewashed, dishes for eating leavened bread were stored away, and new utensils were bought or special ones used only during Passover were taken from storage. The requirement to get rid of all leavened substances was also the reason for laundering all the clothing. As mentioned above, the women also drew extra amounts of water and ground special flour for the feast's needs. Furthermore, all the holidays called for numerous special delicacies, which were prepared by the women in addition to their regular work.[17]

Although it is true that Libyan Jewish women (especially in the countryside) had very little time to rest, Jewish law and local customs took care of some of their basic needs. In addition to the Sabbath and other holidays in which, with few exceptions, work is forbidden by Jewish law, Jewish women in Libya also did not work on several other dates. Thus, on the first day of each Jewish month (when many women used to fast) and also during the whole eight days of Hanukkah, married women did not work. Furthermore, on the first of the month of Teveth, unmarried women, too, were exempt from work (and as a result, this day was referred to as the "New Month of the Girls").[18]

Being a Jewish homemaker in Libya was indeed a full-time job, especially in the villages and during the Ottoman period. However,

---

15. Ha-Cohen, *Higgid Mordecai,* p. 309; Slousch, "Les Juifs," p. 32 (Tigrina); idem, *Sefer ha-Masa'ot,* 1:82 (Mislata); idem, *Travels,* pp. 63–64 (Mislata), 129 (Beni 'Abbas), 159 (Yefren).

16. Ha-Cohen, *Higgid Mordecai,* p. 308.

17. Ibid., pp. 193, 303; Sutton, "Coutumes," pp. 421–22.

18. Ha-Cohen, *Higgid Mordecai,* p. 197. During the twentieth century, many Jewish women continued the custom of not working on the first day of the month of Teveth (Zuarez et al., *Yahadut Luv,* p. 373). There is no mention of their habits on the first days of the other months. It is probable that this custom was practiced only at home and not by women who went out to work.

even these women found the time and energy for projects that were not directly connected to their regular tasks, in order to provide an extra income or to attend some special religious or social functions. It is also apparent that even in this limited area of household tasks, the wider the variety of work, the greater the responsibility, authority, and independence of the women.

PAID LABOR

Most Libyan Jewish women did not work outside their households. There were, however, some exceptions to the rule, and their number increased from the late nineteenth century onward. During the whole period under discussion, some Jewish women specialized in services that were required by other women. Fewer Jewesses chose the field of entertainment and became dancers and singers. Although some members of the latter group gained influence among the rich and the mighty, they had a bad reputation within the community because of the way in which they acquired their power, namely, by mixing with nonrelated males and showing off, even if no immoral acts were performed. Some women produced merchandise for sale, but only very few were actually involved in any level of commerce. Due to economic crises, growing numbers of urban women became servants and laborers. As a result of European cultural penetration, some chose to be trained in more specialized professions, such as sewing. Economic changes and the increased presence and authority of Western powers during the twentieth century influenced the participation of Jewish women in the work force in a growing variety of professions. Although the number of working Jewish women, the diversity of jobs they held, and their working conditions were all lower in comparison to men, there was a significant change in each. Furthermore, Jewish female involvement in the work force was much greater than that of Muslim women.[19]

During the Ottoman period, the most respectable female work geared toward the public was either an extension of the household tasks or the supplying of specialized female services. The first category included mainly the production of textiles and agricultural produce. Surpluses were sold or exchanged. Sometimes women worked late into the

19. For the low participation of Libyan Muslim women in the work force as late as the 1960s, see Attir, "Ideology," pp. 123–26.

night in order to meet the demand for textiles. All this work was done privately at home, and there was no cooperation among several women to increase production and efficiency.[20]

Specialized Female Services

Some of the traditional female occupations were not conducted at home but were nevertheless performed in completely female surroundings, Jewish and non-Jewish alike. Such was the case with midwives and cosmeticians. The work of midwives was not regulated by the authorities during the Ottoman period, and women learned the skill from other females.[21] During most of the period it was not customary to have male physicians attend women at childbirth or otherwise. Consequently, midwives performed an important and responsible service that was in high demand. The work of cosmeticians was more popular in the urban than in the rural areas due to the different working and living conditions in the regions. During the Qaramānlī period (1711–1835), this profession was apparently in Jewish hands in Triopoli.[22]

Commerce

The participation of Jewish women in commerce was more problematic throughout the whole period under review. This was because it required public contact with nonrelated males (including non-Jews). Consequently, it was regarded as men's work and generally considered to be an improper occupation for women. Nevertheless, throughout the Ottoman period and the twentieth century, some Jewish women did participate in trade in the urban and rural areas, but their numbers were limited, and their reputation was often low. Either they were considered immodest and suspected of lewdness, or they were elderly, past childbearing age, and as a result had more freedom of movement than younger females. Thus, for example, it was reported in the late Ottoman period that in Mislata Jewish women were engaged in trade, but this had led some of them into licentiousness.[23] In Tripoli, local tradition as reflected in the folklore knew of an elderly Jewish female peddler who

20. Ha-Cohen, *Higgid Mordecai,* pp. 308–9.

21. Ibid., pp. 272, 370.

22. According to local Jewish tradition as reflected in folktales, at one point there were in Tripoli three Jewish women who specialized in applying makeup for brides, Jewish and gentile alike (D. Noy, *Shiv'im Sippurim ve-Sippur mi-Pi Yehudey Luv* [Jerusalem: Bi-Tefutzot ha-Golah, 1967], p. 109).

23. Ha-Cohen, *Higgid Mordecai,* p. 322.

through her trade had close contacts with the ruling elite, reaching as high as the governor's mother, who had great influence over her son.[24] Female merchants were not only legendary figures: one whose business was in expensive garments and precious stones was killed in Tripoli in 1911 by a Muslim female patron and a servant.[25] Even itinerant female peddlers were mentioned during the Ottoman period (in Yefren),[26] but it seems that this was a very unusual phenomenon. On a different level was Esther Arbib ("Queen Esther") who had a hand in the foreign trade of Tripoli during the late eighteenth century.[27]

Even during the twentieth century, it continued to be very unusual for Jewish women to be involved in commerce. Nevertheless, some went to the market to sell their products. Thus, for example, Jewish women from 'Amrus went to sell their merchandise (e.g., cloth, felt hats, woolen socks) in Sūq al-Jum'ah, where thousands of villagers from all over the region as well as people from Tripoli used to gather on Tuesdays.[28] Usually, however, rural women who produced surpluses exchanged them on an individual basis with neighboring women—Jewish or Muslim—mainly for foodstuffs and did not themselves go to the market.[29]

Entertainment

Of a quite different nature were the entertainers. In the eighteenth century, many female dancers and singers in Tripoli were Jewish, and they were usually invited to entertain the rulers and the rich at special events, which could at times be quite gruesome. For example, Jewish entertainers, including female singers and dancers, were invited to perform by Yūsuf Qaramānlī in 1790 in the presence of the body of his brother Ḥasan, whom he had just murdered.[30]

Although some entertainers may have gained influence over the authorities and the rich through this channel, this occupation was not considered a respectable one for women, and the participation of Jewish women in it was ignored by indigenous Jewish sources. Performances

24. Noy, *Shiv'im Sippurim,* p. 58.
25. *Ha-Yehudi,* 20 November 1911.
26. Slousch, *Travels,* p. 159.
27. On Esther Arbib, see chap. 5 on leadership.
28. *Hed ha-Mizrah* 4, no. 28 (1945): 6–7. It is not clear when the weekly market moved from Fridays to Tuesdays. On not allowing Muslim women to shop in the market, see Attir, "Ideology," pp. 122, 124.
29. *Hed ha-Mizrah* 2, no. 12 (1943): 8.
30. L. C. Feraud, *Annales tripolitaines* (Paris: Librairie Vuibert, 1927), p. 284; Slousch, *Sefer ha-Masa'ot,* 2:44.

within Jewish family circles were, however, viewed differently. Thus, throughout the whole period, Jewish singers used to entertain the community during special family events, primarily marriage festivities.[31] Because these performances took place in a Jewish environment and because the participants were often segregated according to gender, these entertainers did not carry the same stigma as those who appeared before the gentiles.

Effects of External Changes on Women's Participation in the Work Force
During the nineteenth and twentieth centuries, Libya witnessed an economic transformation that resulted from shifts in international trade, European economic penetration, wars, and changes in the regime and legislation. These developments had a marked impact on the society as a whole and, in particular, on urban women because there was an increased demand for female work outside the household to help balance family budgets. This demand, in turn, enabled some women to receive vocational training, which exposed them to academic studies. The improved educational level of women, coupled with the gradual increase in cultural and social openness in the Jewish community and the society at large, made it more acceptable for women to work even when economic necessity was not a cardinal factor.

Throughout the Ottoman period, the Muslims were mainly farmers, shepherds, caravan owners and personnel, military and police personnel, and administrators. Most Jewish men during that period were involved in various trades and crafts, and decreasing numbers of them were farmers. The main source of revenue for the Jewish community during the nineteenth century was the trans-Saharan trade between sub-Saharan Africa and Europe. Several Jewish trading houses in Tripoli had a prominent role in this operation. In addition to financing caravans, these Jewish traders employed numerous workers, including many Jews, in their establishments. These wealthy Jews were accustomed to donating generously to the communal funds. In this way, as long as the economy was strong, international trade served as an important employer as well as a source for public welfare.

The 1860s witnessed a recession in the trans-Saharan trade, but the

---

31. See chap. 2 on marriage festivities. In 1943, the Tripolitan communal leadership agreed to send young Jewesses to dance with British officers, following the latter's request and the refusal of the Muslims (an unsigned letter from Tripoli to the Jewish Agency, Jerusalem, 12 July 1943, CZA, S25/5219).

trend was dramatically reversed between 1870 and 1883, mainly due to an exceptionally high demand by the European female fashion industry for ostrich feathers. In 1883, however, there was a sudden drop in the European demand for this product, which caused a significant drop in the volume, composition, and value of the goods in this trade and resulted in a substantial fall in revenue.

This, in turn, brought about bankruptcies and dismissal of workers from establishments that were directly or indirectly connected with the trans-Saharan trade, and the number of the poor and unemployed increased. Simultaneously, there was a decrease in private donations for public services, at a period when reliance on welfare grew. Even though there was some improvement in the trans-Saharan trade later on, periods of economic crisis and standstill recurred and forced the population to search for new economic ventures. Furthermore, this situation necessitated the contribution of all family members for economic survival and paved the way for a less negative attitude toward women working outside the home. The economic crises coincided with new opportunities resulting from the European cultural and economic penetration of Libya. Thus, when many Jewish women felt the need to go out to work, they could for the first time be institutionally trained in modern professions, while simultaneously acquiring some academic education.

The late nineteenth century also witnessed a growing population movement in Libya, which was caused in part by economic changes. The constant shifts in the trans-Saharan trade negatively affected many population centers along the caravan routes, which supplied the caravans with needed services. Many inhabitants in these centers became underemployed and were forced to migrate from the Tripolitanian hinterland to bigger population centers, mainly on the Mediterranean coast. Consequently, the number of the poor and the underemployed in the cities grew and forced the authorities to search for ways to support the growing number of those who relied on welfare.[32]

Maids

The economic condition of large parts of the urban Jewish community in Libya began to deteriorate in the last quarter of the nineteenth

---

32. For a further discussion of these issues, see R. Simon, "The Trans-Saharan Trade and Its Impact on the Jewish Community of Libya in the Late Ottoman Period," in *Proceedings of the American Historical Association, 1987* (Ann Arbor: University Microfilm International, 1988).

century as a result of the aforementioned factors as well as events connected with the Turkish-Italian war and World War I. One result was that an increasing number of Jewish girls from poor families had to work as servants in the homes of the rich.[33] At times, rural families also sent their daughters to serve urban Jews. Thus, for example, in 1923 Abramo Forti (a member of the chamber of commerce of Tripoli) had a fourteen-year-old maid from Gharyan (a distance of some eighty-five miles) who was sent to him in 1916 following the death of her mother and the remarriage of her father. She received food and board in exchange for her services around the clock but apparently earned no wages. Apart from occasional greetings from Gharyan, there was hardly any contact between the girl and her family.[34] It is not clear, however, how common the practice was of sending poor or orphaned rural girls to work in town.

The working conditions of Jewish maids in Tripoli (mostly aged seven to twenty years) were generally rough. They worked for long hours, had toilsome work to do, ate little, froze from the cold, and collected poor wages, if any at all, which they usually had to give to their male guardians. Because these maids were generally unmarried, the recipients of their meager and hard-earned salaries were often their fathers.[35] These servants did not need any special qualifications for this work, which did not differ from what they used to do in their own homes. On the other hand, this experience did not provide them with any new skills that might have been of use in a more sophisticated and better-paying job. Many of these women worked in Jewish households, but as the number of well-to-do Italian families in Libya grew, increasing numbers were employed by gentiles. The fact that Jewish women were working in gentile households (and not their arduous working conditions) became a growing concern of the male leadership of the community, especially because from the 1920s onward, Jewish women also had more opportunities to meet gentiles in school and work in general. As a result of this concern, the leadership tried to train destitute Jewish women in professions that would allow them to work in a

33. De Felice, *Jews in an Arab Land,* p. 85. For the 1940s, see S. U. Nahon, "Yehudey Luv," *Yalquṭ ha-Mizraḥ ha-Tikhon* 1 (January 1949): 23–24.

34. *Hed ha-Mizraḥ* 2, no. 11 (1943): 5.

35. Ha-Cohen, *Higgid Mordecai,* p. 157; A. Benchimol, Tripoli, to AIU, Paris, 11 November 1907, AAIU, IIIE-10. According to the Report on the Tripolitanian Jews, Tripoli, received by the AIU, Paris, on 23 July 1933 (AAIU, IC-27), maids earned between 40 and 150 Italian lire a month during the 1930s.

protected Jewish environment and to collect a decent income.[36] Their motives were, however, mainly to protect the Jewish entity and less to improve female working conditions.

The chances of Jewish females finding themselves in "delicate" situations grew as the number and variety of places seeking female help increased. During the Italian period and later, pubs and coffeehouses proliferated in Tripoli, becoming particularly widespread during and after World War II, due to the presence of a large number of Italian, German, and later British troops in and around town. Coffeehouses also existed in Ottoman Tripoli, but it was not customary for decent women to visit them, and certainly not to work there. Because of the Islamic prohibition on alcoholic beverages, pubs did not exist in Ottoman Libya and were first introduced there under Italian rule.[37] In the mid-1940s, but possibly also earlier, Jewish women were working in pubs and coffeehouses. The wages there might have been better than in domestic service, but this was not considered respectable work, and it was rumored that women who worked in such places were often corrupted. The communal leadership felt a growing urgency to provide these women with the means and qualifications to acquire an alternative and more respected employment.[38]

Crime

The deteriorating economic conditions and the wartime situation also brought about an increase in crime in the Jewish community, including that perpetrated by women. Although details are not provided, the general impression of several observers was that prostitution among Jewish women had increased, and whereas it was very rare in the 1920s, it became more widespread during the 1930s. Furthermore, the prison population of Tripoli in 1949 included one Jewish female inmate during three separate months. No details were provided regarding the cause of imprisonment and whether the same Jewish woman was held behind bars each time.[39] Although this information is quite vague, it points to

36. S. Yelloz, Tripoli, to AJDC, New York, 17 August 1946, CZA, S6/1984; Nahon, "Yehudey Luv," pp. 23–24. See also chap. 4 below on vocational education.

37. During the Ottoman period, however, Jews were allowed to produce and consume liquor, and it was not uncommon for the Muslims to get drinks from the Jews.

38. S. Yelloz, Tripoli, to AJDC, New York, 17 August 1946, CZA, S6/1984.

39. Annual Report on Tripolitania, 1949, PRO, FO 371/80864. The female prison population in Tripoli during that year was mostly Muslim, and numbered between thirty-seven and fifty-seven inmates. One Jewish woman was imprisoned during each of the months of March, April, and July.

some moral deterioration in the community to a degree that women, who were once completely secluded, had turned to improper and even criminal activities. Signs of moral deterioration were also felt in the family circle, and instances of adultery became more numerous as did incidents of wife and child abuse.[40]

Begging and Welfare

During World War I, when only a few coastal towns were under Italian rule and the rest of the country was under Arab and Berber domination, the Libyan Jewish community became increasingly impoverished. Many Jews fled from the Muslim-controlled hinterland to find refuge among the coastal communities, adding to the number of the poor who asked for communal support. Because the economic opportunities during this period were decreasing, the combined economic, social, and moral effect on the community, including its women, was very strong. Many of these indigent Jews could not find work and turned to begging, resulting in hundreds of poor Jews, including young women, roaming the streets of Tripoli, especially on Fridays and holiday eves, and begging for alms.[41] The further economic deterioration of the community, especially in the 1940s, drove an increasing number of Jews to rely on communal welfare. Because the welfare funds were dependent on the dwindling contributions and taxes of the community's members, the Libyan Jews were compelled to rely to a growing extent on the support of international Jewish organizations. This reliance, in turn, increased the influence of external factors on the Libyan community.[42]

Processing of Ostrich Feathers

Changes in economic conditions also served to change the economic behavior of Libyan Jews. In the late nineteenth century the trans-Saharan trade diversely affected Libyan society. The fluctuations in this trade caused several economic crises but also opened up new economic possibilities. When the trade in ostrich feathers was active, Jewish girls in Tripoli were engaged to clean and dye the feathers, which were shipped to Europe after undergoing this basic treatment. In 1907, as a

40. De Felice, *Jews in an Arab Land,* pp. 85, 135, 164.
41. Ibid., p. 314.
42. The most important organization in the early period was the AIU, and since the 1940s, the AJDC. On the AJDC, see n. 6 in the Introduction.

result of changes in this trade, about four hundred girls were laid off.[43] The large number of females who were engaged in this occupation reflected the economic deterioration necessitating that women work outside the household. The work with the ostrich feathers did not require much training and was regarded by the community as permissible for Jewish women to perform outside their homes (apparently because it was conducted in an all-female environment), as can be seen from the large number of girls who participated.

Needlework and Vocational Training
All these jobs were an extension of household work, work among other females, unskilled services, or, sometimes, reprehensible tasks. A major breakthrough concerning Jewish female work in Libya took place during the 1890s as a result of a severe economic crisis and the new educational opportunities connected with the European penetration of Libya. Following the repeated economic crises resulting from fluctuations in the trans-Saharan trade, the impoverishment of the Jewish community rapidly increased and women had to seek work outside their households. In 1896 the AIU opened a vocational school for girls in Tripoli to answer these needs and to deepen the organization's involvement in Libya. This school provided training in Western-style sewing, cutting, knitting, embroidery, and ironing, as well as in some academic subjects. Proficiency in these professions promised improved payment and working conditions as well as expertise in a European occupation, with a better chance for upward mobility. As a result, numerous girls from the lower classes enrolled in the AIU school. This was the beginning of systematic vocational training for women in Libya, which enabled them to acquire respectable and profitable jobs. Furthermore, it paved the way for comprehensive Westernized female education, which for some fifty years was the only education open to females in Libya (for more details, see chap. 4). The AIU continued to provide these courses until its institutions in Libya were closed during World War II. Meanwhile, other Jewish organizations provided similar opportunities in vocational training for Libyan Jewish females.

During the twentieth century there were several attempts by the community and special Jewish organizations to train local adult

43. Levy, "Tripoli," p. 207.

Jewesses in needlework. This was done to improve the economic condition of the community and also to prevent women from becoming underpaid domestic servants or maids in what were regarded by the communal leadership as unsuitable places (e.g., pubs and coffeehouses), not to mention beggars or even criminals. The first attempt in this direction was undertaken shortly after the Italian invasion. The initiative came from a special women's organization that was established for the purpose of raising the "moral level" of young Jewish women through work. Details on the number of women who took advantage of this program were not provided, and it is clear neither how long the experiment lasted nor how successful it was. There was, however, some progress in this field, albeit slow.[44]

In 1934 ha-Tiqvah evening school for Hebrew and Jewish studies added to its curriculum special vocational courses for women that included sewing, cutting, knitting, and embroidery. About a hundred students, most of them young girls, participated. This program came into being thanks to the contribution of sewing machines by Issaco Nahum Ididia, the Tripoli representative of the sewing machine company Necchi. Ididia's wife was among the women who volunteered to teach sewing in this program.[45]

Yet another attempt in this direction began in April 1947, at the initiative of the new chief rabbi of Tripoli, Shelomoh Yelloz. The teachers in this course were all Jewish women, who were either volunteers or were selected from poor and revered families who were in need of help. Some four hundred girls were enrolled in the new enterprise, and about the same number had to be turned down due to lack of space and equipment. They received vocational training (in sewing, cutting, knitting, and embroidery) complemented by some academic courses (Italian, Hebrew, and arithmetic). The works produced by the trainees were sold, and one quarter of the revenues was kept for the future needs of the girls, following the approval of the institution's board. It was emphasized that this endeavor was undertaken to stop Jewish girls from working as servants in unsuitable places.[46]

---

44. Slousch, *Sefer ha-Masa'ot*, 1:24; idem, *Travels*, p. 7.

45. Zuarez et al., *Yahadut Luv*, p. 149; De Felice, *Jews in an Arab Land*, p. 98. Details on the outcome of this enterprise were not provided. For more details on ha-Tiqvah school, which ran the project, see chap. 4.

46. *Nitzanim* 24 (Elul 5707 [Summer 1947]): 5; A. Guetta, Tripoli, to the Youth Department, Jerusalem, 23 July 1947, CZA, S32/123; F. Zuarez and F. Ṭayyar, *Ḥokhmat Nashim* (Tel-Aviv: Vaʿad Qehilot Luv be-Yisraʾel, 1982), p. 16. See also n. 36.

Work Resulting from Italian Enterprises

Although the Italian authorities were busy from 1911 until the early 1930s in crushing the local Muslim resistance to their rule (mainly in Cyrenaica), they also launched several development programs. These were geared mainly toward Italians, but they also had a significant influence on the Jews. The number of Italians grew substantially in the urban centers and in agricultural colonies in the countryside. This resulted from administrative and military needs as well as state initiatives to increase Italian rural settlement in Libya in order to solve domestic problems in Italy, mainly related to unemployment and emigration to America. The increase in Italian population in Libya necessitated urban and rural development in the areas of housing and public services to reach European standards. Furthermore, the Italian Fascist regime was famous for its interest in establishing impressive public monuments and installations. These activities improved the living conditions not only of the newcomers but also of some of the indigenous population, and boosted the economy. The construction industry was one business that benefited during the Italian period. There was a strong demand for builders, carpenters, technicians, mechanics, and contractors, as well as a growing need for building materials and equipment. Jews had an important role in this industry, especially as contractors. The increase in the European population also required a growing supply of goods and services that met European standards. Although many Italians entered the commercial and service sectors in Libya during this period, indigenous Jews continued to have a significant role in both, because the Jews usually had long-standing and better contacts with indigenous suppliers and laborers. Thus, the increased demand for European goods and financial services greatly improved the economic standing of those Jews who were connected with these services.

The development of state health and education services in Libya and the establishment there of several industries that were state monopolies opened up new employment opportunities for Jewish women. Among the professions opened to Jewish women during the 1930s was nursing in government hospitals. They were employed in the wards of Jewish and Muslim women alike, because no Muslim women were willing to work as nurses.[47] The importance of the role of the Jewish nurses in

---

47. On a similar problem as late as the 1970s, which necessitated the employment of foreign nurses in Libya, see Attir, "Ideology," p. 126.

Tripoli is evident from a letter by the governor of Tripolitania, Italo Balbo, to the Italian leader, Benito Mussolini, in 1939. In his letter Balbo stated that it would be almost impossible to implement in Libya the racial legislation calling for the dismissal from state hospitals of all Jewish nurses. He argued further that the same was true with regard to the role of Jewish women in government monopolies, where Jewish women made up a large part of the work force, especially in the tobacco industry. Balbo stated that in both cases it was impossible either to find an alternative work force in Libya or to import it from Italy.[48] Even though it is quite possible that Balbo exaggerated the dominance of Jewish women in these fields in order to convince Mussolini not to implement in Libya the economic regulations of the racial legislation, it is beyond doubt that Jewish women in Libya had an important role in these fields.

There are no details on the training of the nurses. It was apparently very rudimentary and conducted at the workplace, since nursing schools did not exist in Libya at the time. It is known that in 1942, when the Cyrenaican Jews lived in the Jado concentration camp in the Tripolitanian mountain, the Italian camp physicians gave some basic training in nursing to several Jewish female inmates following the outbreak of epidemics.[49] Somewhat later, during the mid-1940s, several female teachers, mothers of students, and members of women's organizations received basic training in nursing from a private Jewish physician.[50] The main purpose of this program, however, was not to train nurses but to instruct teachers and mothers how to improve children's hygiene. A secondary goal was to provide them with the principles of first aid to enable them to assist the medical staff in hospitals and clinics in taking care of wounded and sick Jews.

Teaching

Another important innovation in Jewish female work in Libya took place in the 1930s when indigenous women entered the field of teaching. The first step in this direction occurred in the mid-1870s, with the beginning of secular Western female education in Libya. Although there had been female teachers in Libya before the 1930s, they were

48. De Felice, *Jews in an Arab Land,* pp. 172–73.
49. Simon, "Yehudey Luv ʿal Saf Shoʾah," p. 68.
50. E. ʿAzarya, Tripoli, to the Youth Department, Jerusalem, 28 December 1945, CZA, S32/106; Report on the Hebrew School, Benghazi, 25 April 1944, CZA, J17/8064.

mostly Europeans and taught in European institutions (Italian and French). There were also some indigenous teaching assistants, but their main role was to keep order in class. The entry of local Jewish women into teaching was connected with the comprehensive cultural, political, and social changes that were part of the revival of the Hebrew language in Libya. The advocates of this revival called for equal educational opportunities for both sexes. Furthermore, they emphasized that for this project to succeed, girls should be taught by females. The female instructors were locally trained, usually by autodidact indigenous male teachers who often did not have much more experience than their students.

Female involvement in Jewish education increased during the 1940s, and women teachers became the majority within the modern Hebrew school system. Several local Jewish women were instructed by Jewish soldiers and emissaries from Palestine, some of whom were qualified and experienced educators. The teacher training courses were quite intensive but usually relatively short (between two and seven months long), and consequently the knowledge of the graduates was not extensive. These seminars were innovative not only in their curriculum but also in their structure: they were usually coeducational, and the training of the female teachers was the same as that of the males. The new teachers, most of whom were women, were very dedicated to their work and were responsible for much of the progress of the new Hebrew schools in Libya.[51]

Data on salaries suggest, however, that female teachers were in the lowest income bracket of the teaching staff (see table 3). In 1944, all the female teachers in the Hebrew school in Benghazi were paid less than the male teachers, and in 1945, one regular male teacher and four "rabbis" (male teachers for religious subjects) were paid the same as the four female teachers, whereas two other male teachers were paid 20 and 50 percent more. Only the school's janitors and medic (the latter also a female) earned less than the female teachers.

Due to the lack of further details, it is not clear how many male teachers were more veteran than the females who had just graduated from the teachers' seminar and were at the entry level. It is, however,

---

51. The more veteran male teachers were mostly rabbinical scholars. Their expertise was limited to Jewish religious studies, they lacked pedagogical training, and their teaching methods were less advanced. For more details on the training and activities of the teachers, see chap. 4.

Table 3. Monthly Wages at the Benghazi Hebrew School, 1944–45 (in Egyptian Liras)

		1944		1945	
POSITION	SEX	No.	Salary	No.	Salary
Director	M	I	20	I	20
Teacher	F	4	7	4	IO
Teacher	M	2	IO	I	I5
Teacher	M	—	—	I	I2
Teacher	M	—	—	I	IO
Rabbi	M	—	—	4	IO
Janitor	M	I	6	3	8
Medic	F	—	—	I	5

SOURCES: E. Khalfon, Benghazi, Report on the Community of Benghazi, January 1944, CZA, S6/4582; Report on the Budget of the Benghazi School in 1945, attached to a letter from A. Ze'iri, 7 June 1945, CZA, S25/5217. The Egyptian lira was used in Cyrenaica during the BMA.

known that at least some of the male teachers were also novices. Since the teachers for religious studies taught a reduced number of hours and the regular teachers taught two shifts (in the morning and in the afternoon), the gap between the men's and the women's salaries becomes even bigger. Details on wages in other professions and periods are not available, and as a result it is impossible to make further direct comparisons between the salaries of men and women. Because women were often employed in unskilled jobs, one can assume that their salaries were usually lower than the men's. From the example relating to teachers' salaries, however, one might conclude that even in the same profession, women's salaries were often lower.

The Impact of World War II and the BMA on the Work Force

World War II brought about economic hardship to the majority of the Jews in Libya due to restrictions in the work field imposed by the racial legislation. Furthermore, thousands of Jews were sent to concentration and labor camps, and hundreds were deported. Nevertheless, those whose professions were vital to the regime were frequently spared, and at times they even prospered. Due to the large presence of Italian and German civilian and military forces in Libya during the war, there was an increased demand for supplies and services, as well as a growing need for construction work. Despite the enrichment of part of the Jewish community during the war, large segments of it, especially "enemy citizens" (citizens of the Allied countries, mainly Britain and France) and inhabitants of Cyrenaica, suffered greatly—physically, economically, and emotionally. Before all enemy citizens were deported in 1942, numerous men from this category were incarcerated for various periods of time. Some other Jewish men were sent to labor camps. This situation forced many Jewish women to become more involved in economic and public life.

Under the BMA (1942–51), Libya witnessed economic stagnation and deterioration. This resulted from changes in policies and economic conditions. The Italian regime viewed Libya as part of Italy and strove to develop it in order to attract settlers and, through development and settlement, also to increase the prestige of the regime. The British, on the other hand, regarded their administration as temporary, lasting only until the United Nations decided on the political future of Libya. The scarcity of British investment in Libya was also a result of the postwar economic standstill in Britain, which decreased British investments at home and abroad. Consequently, although services were needed for the BMA officials and troops as well as for the indigenous bureaucracy and population, only the most essential construction works and services were undertaken, and there was hardly any state support for private enterprises. Furthermore, although the BMA operated various services, it did not rely solely on the local population to provide staff. It brought many of the required personnel with it; at times these were Arabs who were recruited in Palestine and Egypt. As a result, the indigenous population benefited only slightly from the presence of the military and administrative personnel in Libya.

Several droughts during the 1940s also contributed to the economic deterioration in the countryside. As a result, food prices rose and underemployed agricultural workers flocked to the cities. These immigrants competed with the townspeople for unskilled jobs and contributed to the lowering of wages in certain nonprofessional positions. This situation added to the worsening economic condition of numerous poor Jews. Large segments of the community were destitute even before the war, but developments during the war and in the postwar period greatly increased the number of indigent Jews and the severity of their poverty. Also contributing to the economic deterioration of the Jews in the 1940s were the November 1945 anti-Jewish riots on the Tripolitanian coast, which claimed the lives of some 130 Jews and destroyed much property.[52]

The growing economic difficulties in the 1940s, improved educational facilities, and the presence and encouragement of Palestinian Jewish soldiers and emissaries all played a part in increasing the number of urban Jewish women who worked outside their homes. During this period, women entered additional work fields. Many Jewish women became regular teachers in the new Hebrew schools, and others worked in military laundries. In both fields one could see a growing sense of trade unionism. This is significant not only for the growing self-confidence of Jewish women in Libya but also for the development of the labor movement and working conditions in Libya as a whole. Thus, a teachers' association was established and became quite active in supervising the curriculum and working conditions (for more details see chaps. 4 and 5). Under the BMA, Jewish women began to work as cooks and laundresses in British military camps in the Benghazi area. Due to the deportation of the Cyrenaican Jews to Jado by the Italians and the Germans in 1942 and their stay there until mid-1943, and as a result of the destruction of large parts of Benghazi during the war, it was deemed necessary to allow the women, including girls, to go out to work for the army. As it turned out, these Jewish women got accustomed to their new situation to such a degree that they were even ready to struggle for better salaries. Through the influence of some Jewish soldiers from Palestine—Communists, according to one report—they held a strike in one military laundry to demand a salary equal to what was customary for a similar job in Palestine.[53] The strike lasted for only a few days, and although it is not clear on what terms these women returned to work, the mere fact that they were ready to go on strike for improved salaries was a real innovation not only for the Jewish women of Libya but also for the indigenous work force as a whole.

CONCLUDING REMARKS

Over sixty years, one can observe several important changes in the occupation of Libyan Jewish women, although the majority continued to work only in their homes. Economic necessity, educational opportu-

52. Zuarez et al., *Yahadut Luv*, pp. 207–27.
53. Report by Gad, Benghazi, 20 September 1943, CZA, S25/4973; E. Khalfon, Benghazi, Report on the Community of Benghazi, January 1944, CZA, S6/4582.

nities, imitation of the Italians, and sociopolitical awakening all contributed to the widening of the variety of professions open to indigenous
Jewish women in Libya. Furthermore, whereas previously it had been
considered a sign of failure of the family's head (i.e., the father or the
husband) when women had to seek outside work because of poverty, it
gradually became an indication of female independence and involvement in public life. Although most of the working women were still
employed in unskilled jobs and often received lower wages than their
male colleagues, some women started to demand equal rights with
regard to working conditions and salary. The move into teaching was
also of great significance: it indicated the move from manual to
spiritual-scholarly work and a shift in the attitude of the traditional male
communal leadership that only males are to be educated and are qualified to be spiritual mentors.

❖ FOUR ❖

Educational Opportunities

❖

U ntil well into the nineteenth century, the Ottoman Empire did not concern itself with educating the masses. The state educated only its military and administration; religious bodies undertook the education of the rest of the population (i.e., the Muslim religious endowments for the Muslim majority, and the communal leadership of the non-Muslim communities for their members). Only during the nineteenth century, as a result of the Ottoman reforms, did the state begin to get involved in various cultural and social services, including public education, for the population at large. These reforms applied to Libya also, and Ottoman schools were opened there. Due, however, to the traditional character of the indigenous population, these schools were frequented mostly by children of people who were affiliated with the regime. Nonetheless, Ottoman state education did have some influence on Jewish education in Libya through its supervision of Jewish institutions and because a small number of Jews studied in Ottoman schools in Tripoli. Furthermore, each element in the regional education had its impact on the entire system, through its offerings and competition over student enrollment.

In Libya, as in the Ottoman Empire as a whole, Jews usually frequented their own educational institutions. Education was viewed by the community as a means of preparing the adult Jew for participation in communal life and the required religious activities. In order to do this, one must be able to read the holy scriptures, prayers, and commentaries in Hebrew. However, according to rabbinic law, women are not required to participate in the public religious service.[1] As a result of these two dispositions, parents as individuals and the community leadership as a body took special pains to ensure that boys would be able to read the Hebrew script. Consequently, the education offered by the community until the 1940s was only for boys, and women usually remained illiterate. They were trained by their female relatives in the proper way to run the house and occasionally learned some traditional crafts. A very few women received informal academic education from their male relatives who attended Jewish traditional religious schools or who had private tutors. As for the boys, the communal leadership in Libyan towns and villages set up religious schools (Talmud Torah), which were modernized in stages starting in the 1890s. Even in upper-class homes, where the boys had private tutors, the girls usually did not study. Thus, for example, whereas information was provided on the studies of the two sons of the head of the Tripolitan community in 1850, Shalom Tito, nothing was mentioned regarding the instruction of his two daughters.[2] Still, there was some female education in Libya in the nineteenth century. There was a girls school run by Catholic nuns in Tripoli, which was set up mainly for the foreign Christian community in town (composed mostly of Maltese and Italians). Because of its Christian religious character, only a few Jews sent their daughters to study there.[3] Since most Jews did not deem it necessary to educate their

1. See *Encyclopaedia Judaica,* s.v. "Woman," on the nonparticipation of women in the service in the synagogue.

2. Benjamin, *Eight Years,* p. 286. In Ottoman Libya, many Jewish men were functional illiterates: although they could often decipher the Hebrew script, many of them did not understand the Hebrew language and could not write their own Judeo-Arabic or Judeo-Berber dialect (which was written in the Hebrew alphabet). On Jewish education in Libya during the late Ottoman period in general, see Y. Kaḥalon, "Ha-Ma'avaq 'al Demuta ha-Ruḥanit shel ha-'Edah ha-Yehudit be-Luv ba-Me'ah ha-19 uva-'Asor ha-Ri'shon shel ha-Me'ah ha-20," in H. Z. Hirschberg, ed., *Zakhor le-Avraham* (Jerusalem: Va'ad 'Adat ha-Ma'araviyyim bi-Yerushalayim, 1972), pp. 79–122.

3. A. Steele-Grieg, *The History of Education in Tripoli from the Time of the Ottoman Occupation to the Fifth Year under British Military Occupation* (Tripoli: British Military Administration, 1948), p. 13; Hazzan, *Ta'alumot Lev,* 1:14b, no. 4.

daughters anyway, they were obviously reluctant to send them to a religious Christian institution.

The illiteracy of Libyan Jewish women during the Ottoman period was clearly pointed out, even by indigenous sources. They stated that during the service in the synagogue, the women were unable to read from the Torah scroll.[4] In one Tripolitan synagogue (Dar Barukh, established in 1830), however, European Jewish women used to read their prayers from the book. This ability was mocked by the indigenous women,[5] apparently because the European women were viewed as trying to exceed their traditional place in society by performing roles reserved for men.

Western and Westernized education did not have much impact on Libyan Jewry until the mid-1870s, because until then it had served either Christian religious or Ottoman military and adminstrative purposes. However, some Jews were unsatisfied with the kind and level of education offered by the Jewish community. This became evident once Western secular education that took into consideration special Jewish needs became available in Libya. Western secular education in Libya, as in other parts of the Ottoman Empire, came to serve political goals. This does not mean that Western education was totally indoctrinational but rather that European governments used education as a tool in order to penetrate into the empire. They focused their attention on target audiences among the local population, whom they tried to bring closer to them through education and other cultural activities. As time passed, societies, clubs, and journalism complemented the European school systems and engendered in the local population increasing levels of support and loyalty to a foreign political power.

Changes in Jewish female education in Libya were implemented only with the introduction of European secular and Jewish education in Tripoli in the last quarter of the nineteenth century. The main participants in the foreign educational endeavor in Ottoman Libya were Italy and France. Whereas the Italian enterprise was sponsored by the state of Italy, the French one was conducted by a Jewish organization (AIU) with varying levels of blessing and support from the French regime.

---

4. Ha-Cohen, *Higgid Mordecai,* pp. 192, 248, 337. On illiteracy among Libyan Muslim women, see Lyon, *A Narrative,* p. 59.
5. Ha-Cohen, *Higgid Mordecai,* pp. 248–49.

THE ITALIAN GIRLS SCHOOLS IN OTTOMAN LIBYA

Italian secular education in Libya started in 1876 when a boys school was established in Tripoli.[6] In the second year of its operation, the Italian educational system in Libya also addressed itself to the female population. This was already customary in Italy and was intended to further deepen Italian influence in the local society. Until 1896, when the AIU girls school opened in Tripoli, the Italians had hardly any competition regarding female education within the Jewish community. This was because Jewish parents were usually reluctant to send their daughters to the Catholic school, especially once secular female education became available. Still, female education was not too popular, due to the common perception that education is either a religious or a professional tool, preparing the young person for religious obligations and for a professional career outside the house; women did not belong to either category. Nevertheless, several dozen girls, mostly from well-to-do families with European backgrounds, enrolled each year in the Italian girls school. This was apparently done because their families, who had economic and social ties with Europe, wanted the girls to adopt European habits and life-styles. It appears that hardly any girls from the lower classes attended the Italian schools at that time, because their help was needed at home, and it was not thought that the kind of education offered by the Italian schools would in any way improve their condition in the accepted framework of living and social interaction.

The first Italian girls school in Libya was opened in Tripoli in 1877 and was directed by a Jewish woman from Livorno, Carolina Nunes Vais (1856–1932), who held that position until her death.[7] In 1911, there were 348 students in this school, and its total annual expenditure was 12,500 francs (out of 100,000 francs for the whole Italian educational system in Tripoli). In that year, out of twelve Italian schools in Libya, another two were for girls: one in Benghazi (160 students) and one in Khoms.[8]

---

6. Steele-Grieg, *History of Education*, p. 13; Ha-Cohen, *Higgid Mordecai*, pp. 53–54, 129; Zuarez et al., *Yahadut Luv*, pp. 166–67.

7. B. Nunes-Vais Arbib, *Gli Ebrei di Tripoli*, CAHJP, P-66, pp. 6–7; Zuarez et al., *Yahadut Luv*, p. 54; G. V. Raccah, *Lunario ebraico libico 5698* (Tripoli: Zerd, 1938), p. 12.

8. M. Levy, Tripoli, to AIU, Paris, 10 September 1911, AAIU, IVE-22c (based on articles in *Corriere d'Italia* and *Tribuna*, but offering no dates); Ha-Cohen, *Higgid Mordecai*, p. 324; Steele-Grieg, *History of Education*, pp. 13–14. According to official Ottoman

At first, all the teachers in the Italian girls school in Tripoli were from Italy. Gradually, the teaching staff was augmented with indigenous women, some of whom were graduates of the school. It seems, however, that the Italian directorship was not always satisfied with the professional level of the local staff. Thus, for example, it was decided in 1895 to dismiss the local instructor of sewing because her teaching was not up to standards, and she was consequently replaced by an instructor from Italy.[9]

The Italian girls schools emphasized the study of Italian culture, general studies, and some needlework. The main subjects taught were reading and writing Italian, arithmetic, sewing, and embroidery. Due to public demand caused by the competition of the AIU network from the mid-1890s onward, the Italians introduced new subjects to their curriculum, which were either an innovation at the AIU or were not taught there. Thus, in 1895 the instruction of French was added, and the number of hours of its instruction was soon doubled. Moreover, English, history, and geography were also introduced.[10]

Most of the pupils in the Italian schools were Jews with Italian citizenship. Although these were not Jewish schools, the directors and many of the teachers and pupils were Jewish. In order to attract Jews to the Italian schools, especially in the face of the competition of the AIU schools and the improvements in Jewish traditional religious education, Jewish subjects were introduced in the 1890s.

The curriculum and the general atmosphere in the Italian schools attracted numerous Jewish girls. These girls stemmed mostly from well-to-do families who were already influenced by European customs through their commercial and financial activities. There were several reasons why these families decided to send their sons and daughters to a European secular school—and the Italian school was the first in this category. These mercantile families, who had strong economic connections with Europe, wanted their sons to be well trained in the appropriate languages as well as in commercial and financial skills, so that they would be better qualified to participate in the family businesses. These

data, there were 241 girls in the Italian schools in Tripoli in 1903. See Turkey, Maarif-i Umumiye Nezareti, *Salname-yi Nezaret-i Maarif-i Umumiye* (Istanbul: Asr Matbaası, H1321 [1903]), p. 696.

9. D. Arie, Tripoli, to AIU, Paris, 1 December 1895, AAIU, IIE-6a.

10. Ha-Cohen, *Higgid Mordecai*, p. 167; D. Arie, Tripoli, to AIU, Paris, 18 December 1895, AAIU, IIE-6a.

subjects were not taught in the traditional Jewish schools, which strongly opposed any attempt to introduce new subjects into the curriculum. These business-oriented families were not interested in providing similar professional skills for their daughters, because they did not intend to incorporate females into their local and international operations. On the other hand, these businessmen wanted to be Westernized and knew about the improved educational level of women in Europe. Their wish to imitate European customs brought them to accept female education out of cultural and social motives, and not due to economic needs. As a result, Jewish girls were sent to the Italian schools, which in contrast to the Catholic school offered secular education and, in later years, Jewish subjects also.

In the mid-1890s, political pressure was added to the social and cultural attraction of the Italian schools, when the Italian consulate in Tripoli exerted pressure on Italian citizens to send their children only to the Italian schools and not to the AIU ones. Families were even warned that their citizenship would be abrogated, economic sanctions against them would be taken, and pupils in the Italian schools would be expelled if their siblings attended the AIU school. Occasionally, the Italians even threatened to close their schools altogether.[11] The last threat was against Italian interests in Libya and was apparently not taken seriously by the local population, who knew that Italy was dedicated to maintaining its interests in Libya even in the face of a heavy economic burden. Some of the former warnings, however, had their impact, and several children whose siblings attended the Italian schools left the AIU schools.

A great attraction of the Italian system was that all education there was free of charge, whereas the AIU continuously tried to impose tuition fees on its pupils. It is true that this might not have been a financial burden on the well-to-do families, whose children were the majority of the students in the Italian schools. It was, however, customary in Libya for school education (in contrast to private instruction) to be free of charge, and families refused to pay for this service when it came from either a communal or a public institution. For these reasons, the establishment of the AIU school for girls did not bring about a decrease in the number of Jewish girls attending the Italian school in Tripoli (those in Benghazi and Khoms did not have any competition), and families with

11. D. Arie, Tripoli, to AIU, Paris, 28 October 1895, AAIU, IIE-6a; ibid., 8 January 1899, AAIU, IIIE-6c; M. Levy, Tripoli, to AIU, Paris, 8 January 1902, AAIU, IVE-22a.

connections with Italy preferred stronger emphasis on Italian studies anyway, which they could get only at the Italian schools.

THE AIU GIRLS SCHOOL DURING THE OTTOMAN PERIOD

In the 1890s, when the AIU decided to launch its educational activities in Libya, it had to take into consideration the two existing networks that were already serving the Jews there: the veteran communal system and the newer Italian system. In accordance with its basic custom to cooperate with the local communities in order to protect and advance them, and not wishing to come into conflict with another European institution, the AIU tried to answer those communal needs that were not taken care of by the other educational networks. The innovation brought about by the AIU in Libya was the combination of Western vocational training and academic studies in a Jewish environment. Vocational training was of prime importance for the urban lower classes at that period. They suffered heavily from the economic crisis of the 1880s following the dramatic changes in the trans-Saharan trade. Whereas most of the big merchants were able to alternate their investments and redirect their trade, numerous small businesses connected with the trans-Saharan trade collapsed, and many poor artisans and laborers became unemployed. In the 1890s, many indigent urban families were in desperate need of any additional source of income. Consequently, despite the local custom, families were ready to let their daughters leave the house in order to go out to work. Furthermore, parents were even willing to send the girls to school, so that they could be trained in new professions that promised employment and higher wages. These parents, however, had to accept a package deal: at the AIU school, the vocational training was tied to regular academic studies. In the beginning, these Jewish, urban, lower-class families were not very interested in obtaining general education for their daughters, but they were ready to agree to it when it was secondary to vocational training. These families were usually more traditional and religious than the upper classes, and they avoided as much as possible cultural contacts with the non-Jewish world. Consequently, those destitute and traditional parents who decided to send their daughters to school so that the girls could learn a profession, usually preferred the AIU to the Italian schools, because the former emphasized vocational training in a Jewish environment.

In 1890 the AIU started its educational activities in Tripoli with vocational training for boys. This was followed six years later, in October 1896, by a similar institution for girls.[12] During the Ottoman period, mainly poor girls attended the AIU school in Tripoli, and most of the richer girls went to the Italian school. The number of better-off girls attending the AIU institution gradually increased, however. This difference was probably the result of the character of the schools and their educational offerings, coupled with political pressure. Those who sent their children to the Italian schools wanted first and foremost an Italian education, geared primarily toward commerce and banking (in the case of boys), complemented by Jewish education. In the case of girls, the practical preparation for adult life in the Italian school consisted of academic subjects and some sewing and embroidery, mainly for household needs rather than as a profession. The AIU schools emphasized vocational training complemented by some general and Jewish studies, in a comprehensive Jewish environment. Gentiles were not excluded from the AIU network, but it appears that non-Jewish girls did not attend the AIU school in Tripoli (in contrast to the boys school in town, which occasionally had Turkish and Arab pupils).

Whereas the competition between the various boys schools in Tripoli (i.e., the Italian, AIU, and Talmud Torah) was strong, it seems that the girls schools did not suffer as much from rivalry, because each one of them answered the needs of a different segment of the population. The growth of the AIU girls school was hampered only by the management's decision to limit the number of pupils due to lack of funds, facilities, and staff. The school became very popular, and the number of applicants always exceeded that of those who could actually be enrolled. The prestige of the AIU school can also be seen from the fact that in some cases girls who had graduated from the Italian school came to the AIU to study additional subjects that were not taught in their former school. Furthermore, they did so despite the demand for payment of tuition fees.

In 1895, a new AIU school director, David Arie, and his wife, Esther, arrived in Tripoli. He introduced changes in the AIU boys school and strengthened the focus on academic studies, due to difficulties in properly operating the vocational workshop. This move triggered a lengthy conflict between the AIU and the Tripolitan Jewish leadership, who

12. The following discussion is based mainly on the AIU correspondence, especially files IIE-5, IIE-6, IIIE-6, IIIE-10, and IVE-22.

approved of the AIU activities in vocational training but viewed its growing inclination toward academic studies to be in competition with the community's own educational operations. As a result, whereas the community's leadership was ready in 1890 to financially support the AIU vocational workshop, it stopped its payments in 1895 and tried to prevent the AIU from operating in Tripoli.

In this hostile atmosphere, the Aries started to discuss the issue of a girls school in Tripoli. It was clear to them from the beginning that the community's leadership would not support the new venture financially for a number of reasons. It was obvious that as long as the conflict over boys' education was not solved, the community would oppose any AIU initiative. Furthermore, the community was in a severe economic crisis and had little income for its growing regular needs. On top of it all was the traditional concept that girls' education was an unnecessary luxury. Although a growing number of individuals accepted the need for girls' vocational training because of economic difficulties, the communal leadership did not see any reason to change its basic view on the issue, which was based on religious and not on temporal grounds.

Following the AIU's decision in late 1895 to establish a girls school in Tripoli, it started to search for funding for this enterprise. It figured out that at least 600 francs would be needed annually for this purpose. Because they realized that the Tripolitan Jewish communal treasury would not support the venture, the local AIU committee suggested that Esther Arie should work toward the creation of an indigenous women's society that would support the establishment and general operation of the new school. Because many Tripolitan Jewish women supported the idea, the Italian consul in Tripoli, Motta, became alarmed. He warned the Italian Jewish men in town that if their wives joined the proposed society, he would advise his government to close its schools in Tripoli. In order to curb the Italian opposition, David Arie met with Motta to clarify the issue. He explained that the purpose of the AIU in Tripoli, as in any other place, was to uproot ignorance from among the youth of both sexes and definitely not to compete with any existing educational activity, Italian or otherwise. He argued that since there were still some four hundred Jewish girls who did not attend any educational institution, there was ample room for an additional facility. Following these explanations, the consul promised the AIU director reciprocity in the field of education: the Italians would not oppose the

Table 4. Pupils and Teachers at the AIU Girls School in Tripoli

	PUPILS								
YEAR	*Total*	*I*	*II*	*III*	*IV*	*V*	*VI*	*Vocational (atelier)*	TEACHERS
1896/97	40–44								
1897/98	70–102	28	29	45					4
1898/99	95–109	24	22	25	24				4
1899/1900	88–112	34	30	24					7
1900/1	100								
1909/10	150+								
1910/11	245	30	34	30	39	40	42	30	

SOURCE: Annual reports and letters of the AIU staff in Tripoli. The Total category reflects fluctuations during the year.

AIU schools nor would they try to lure pupils from the latter to their own.[13]

The AIU girls school was opened in Tripoli on 1 October 1896 under the directorship of Esther Arie. The AIU decided to start with a relatively small number of pupils (between forty and fifty) due to the novelty of the project and because of financial constraints (see table 4).[14] As a result of this decision, quite a few candidates were rejected, and Ms. Arie was able to choose the most promising ones. This situation continued even when the number of pupils in the AIU school increased, and during the Ottoman period there were always more candidates than could be accepted.[15]

The prestige of the school was manifested by the tuition fees issue. From the very beginning, the directors tried to collect tuition fees, albeit symbolic and low sums, from their pupils, at least from the wealthier among them. The management's lack of success stemmed from two sources: poverty and custom. Most of the families who sent their daughters to the AIU school were very poor and could not afford to pay. In addition, they knew that no other educational institution in Tripoli demanded payment. During the first ten years of the school's operation,

13. D. Arie, Tripoli, to AIU, Paris, 28 October 1895, AAIU, IIE-6a.
14. Ibid., 10 July 1896, AAIU, IIE-6b.
15. Ibid., 15 September 1898, AAIU, IIE-6b.

Table 5. Tuition Fees at the AIU Girls School in Tripoli

YEAR	PAYING PUPILS	AMOUNT (FRANCS)	TOTAL/YEAR
1896/97	2 (40)	2–2.5/month	
1897/98	6 (102)		
1898/99	2 (95)		
1899/1900	3 (102)–2 (88)[a]		
1905/6	All new and rich	0.1–0.15/week	29.85
1907/8	All new	0.4–0.9/month	100
1908/9			140
1910/11	55 (245)		

SOURCES: A. Benchimol, Tripoli, to AIU, Paris, 14 January, 15 June 1906, AAIU, IIIE-10; M. Levy, Tripoli, to AIU, Paris, 2 January 1908, AAIU, IVE-22b; 31 May 1911, AAIU, IVE-22c.
NOTE: Numbers in parentheses show the total number of pupils.
[a]By the end of the year, there were only 2 paying pupils out of a total of 88 pupils.

no more than six girls paid tuition fees per year, and these were inconsiderable sums (table 5). Sometimes, the parents promised to pay at the beginning of the year in order to guarantee their daughters' registration, but once the girls were enrolled, the parents refused to pay, claiming that no one else paid.

After many attempts to collect tuition fees at the AIU girls school in Tripoli had failed, the director tried another approach. In 1905 she demanded the weekly payment of a *sou du pauvre* ("a penny for the poor") in the amount of 0.10 to 0.15 francs from new and well-to-do pupils. Since the competition among candidates to enter the school continued to be strong, in part because there were fewer institutions to choose from for female education, many promised to pay in order to register. In contrast to the past, however, the parents realized that the director had no intention of retreating from her financial demands, and they had no alternative but to pay or take their daughters out of school. Consequently, the number of paying pupils gradually increased, though it never reached beyond a third of a class or 22.5 percent of the whole student body (in 1910/11) (tables 6 and 7). The lowest percentage of paying pupils was in the vocational class (the *atelier*), which was attended by the poorest pupils. The issue of fees shows the high esteem with which many Jews in Tripoli started to regard the advantages that were gained from sending their daughters to the AIU school, for which

Table 6. Paying and Nonpaying Pupils at the AIU Girls School in Tripoli

YEAR	CATEGORY	GRADE						Vocational (atelier)	TOTAL
		I	II	III	IV	V	VI		
1897/98	Paying	2	2	2	—	—	—	—	6
	Gratis	26	27	43	—	—	—	—	96
	Total	28	29	45	—	—	—	—	102
	% paying	7.2	6.9	4.4	—	—	—	—	5.9
1898/99	Paying	1	1	0	0	—	—	—	2
	Gratis	23	21	25	24	—	—	—	93
	Total	24	22	25	24	—	—	—	95
	% paying	4.2	4.6	0	0	—	—	—	2.1
1899/1900	Paying	0	2	0	—	—	—	—	2
	Gratis	34	28	24	—	—	—	—	86
	Total	34	30	24	—	—	—	—	88
	% paying	0	6.6	0	—	—	—	—	2.3
1910/11	Paying	5	10	7	5	12	14	2	55
	Gratis	25	24	23	34	28	28	28	190
	Total	30	34	30	39	40	42	30	245
	% paying	16.6	29.4	23.3	12.8	30	33	6.6	22.5

SOURCE: Same as in table 5. The data are for year's end.

they were now ready to pay. The fact that it was not presented as a tuition fee but as charity probably also contributed to the readiness of the parents to pay this sum.

The sums received by the AIU in this manner were very small and were only a small fraction of the total annual school budget. Thus, for example, the annual budget in 1896/97 was 12,700 francs, and the school collected only 140 francs from the parents in 1908/9.[16] Knowing the economic conditions in Tripoli, this was a matter of principle for the AIU rather than a real source of income to finance the activities of the AIU there, and they decided to continue charging fees regardless of its

16. Ibid., 19 June 1898, AAIU, IIE-6b; ibid., 16 July 1899, 1 June 1900, AAIU, IIIE-6c; M. Levy, Tripoli, to AIU, Paris, 2 January 1908, AAIU, IVE-22b; ibid., 31 May 1911, AAIU, IVE-22c.

Table 7. Payment of Tuition Fees at the AIU Girls School in Tripoli in 1923

| | GRADE | | | |
STATUS	*I*	*II*	*III*	TOTAL
Paying	30	38	57	125
Gratis	5	11	13	29
Total	35	49	70	154
% paying	85.7	77.6	81.4	81.2

SOURCE: L. Loubaton, Tripoli, to AIU, Paris, 7 June 1923, AAIU, IC-25. The level of the fees was not provided.

profitability. It was very important for the AIU that the parents be involved both morally and materially in the education of their children, and the amount of that participation was less relevant than accepting the principle.

Due to the lack of facilities and the limited number of pupils who could be enrolled, the AIU decided to limit the ages of its female students to eight to fourteen years. During the first ten years of the school's operation, the students were divided by age and not according to their academic accomplishments. From 1905 onward, classes were formed according to academic achievements.[17] Most new pupils entered the first grade, and some, the vocational class. However, no new students were admitted to higher grades, because of Italian political and economic pressure on Italian citizens not to transfer their children from the Italian to the AIU school. Altogether, there were six grades and a purely vocational class in the AIU girls school during the Ottoman period. In 1908, a kindergarten for both sexes was established adjacent to the girls school, under the supervision of a special teacher.[18] Through this enterprise, the cultural and social activities of the AIU spread further, and it enabled the AIU to attract future students at a tender age.

The curriculum at the AIU girls school included at first French, Hebrew, arithmetic, singing, and sewing. To this were later added history, geography, sciences, drawing, knitting, sewing lingerie, and ironing. After the program had stabilized, the regular school day started with

17. E. Arie, Tripoli, to AIU, Paris, 4 October 1896, AAIU, IIE-5; A. Benchimol, Tripoli, to AIU, Paris, 6 January 1905, March 1905, AAIU, IIIE-10.
18. A. Benchimol, Tripoli, to AIU, Paris, 21 June 1908, AAIU, IVE-22b.

three hours of academic studies followed by three hours of vocational training.[19]

Some pupils had a more concentrated vocational program than others, and they took academic courses for about one hour and vocational training during the rest of the day. Thus, for example, a sewing atelier was established, and during the years 1901–7, thirty-six girls were trained there. This program had two important advantages for the poor. While they were acquiring a profession, the girls also earned some money. During their training, the apprentices earned between two and sixteen francs a month, because they were still learning most of the time and could not sell all their products. The creation of a professional craftswoman was considered by the AIU to be an important contribution to the improvement of the status of Tripolitan women. Consequently, the AIU was proud of the achievements of this course. Twenty-one pupils finished the course by 1907, including fifteen who continued their training, with five of them serving as teaching assistants. Among the graduates, eight worked and earned money, one just started to work, and two worked at home. As to the rest: one went to Paris, six were married, and three died.[20] The AIU regarded it as an important achievement that more than half of the living graduates were working in their new profession. What these figures also reveal, however, is that it continued to be undesirable for married women to work professionally in addition to their regular household tasks.

The founder of the AIU girls school in Tripoli, Esther Arie, believed that it was important for her pupils to learn Hebrew because of the character of the community and its future. She assumed further that it would make a good impression on the religious Tripolitan community if the AIU advanced the knowledge of Hebrew and that this in turn would improve the relations between the community and the AIU. She also thought that it was important for the future Jewish mothers in Tripoli to know "our sacred language" and the basics of the Jewish religion.[21]

The AIU, however, found it difficult to hire suitable teachers for

19. D. Arie, Tripoli, to AIU, Paris, 15 September 1898, AAIU, IIE-6b; Ha-Cohen, *Higgid Mordecai,* p. 239.

20. A. Benchimol, Tripoli, to AIU, Paris, 11 March 1907, AAIU, IIIE-10; M. Levy, Tripoli, to AIU, Paris, 19 March 1907, AAIU, IVE-22b. In 1898, a group of fifteen indigent girls participated in a special vocational course that concentrated on sewing lingerie and ironing (E. Arie, Tripoli, to AIU, Paris, 1 November 1898, AAIU, IIE-5).

21. E. Arie, Tripoli, to AIU, Paris, 4 October 1896, AAIU, IIE-5.

Jewish subjects. This problem was not unique to the AIU girls school; the Italian and the AIU boys schools, which employed indigenous religious scholars, had the same problem. The regular teachers in the European schools were not trained in Hebrew and Jewish subjects but only in Italian or in French and in general studies. Most of the local teachers in Libya at the time lacked the professional pedagogic training that the European teachers had. Consequently, the academic standards in the courses on the Hebrew language and Jewish subjects were usually lower than those of the general studies courses. The problem was even more complicated in the AIU girls school, because in order to keep the girls in a female environment, the management was reluctant at first to employ local Jewish males.[22] During this period, two women were mentioned as teaching Hebrew, and the fact that one of them had only a little knowledge of Hebrew contributed to her low salary. It seems that this problem continued to hinder the study of Hebrew and Jewish subjects at this school, and the pupils did not make much progress.[23]

Throughout the Ottoman period, the AIU girls school combined vocational training with academic studies. Although the former was of great importance to the poor, it seems that at least some families were attracted by the scholastic potential of the school and were especially fond of the opportunity to learn French. Thus, some female graduates of the Italian school enrolled in the AIU school in order to learn French.[24] Some mothers believed that the chances of their daughters for a good match improved if they knew French. This preference was apparent even in a traditional family where the daughter was betrothed to a religious judge (*dayyan*).[25] This attitude reflected the view that knowledge of foreign languages was needed for upward mobility. It was believed that in order to mix with the wealthier Jews who were more Westernized and whose wealth often came from commercial contacts with Europe, knowledge of European languages was essential.

During the first years of the school's operation, most of the teaching was done by the director, who taught between twelve and twenty-five hours a week. The director and the regular teachers were graduates of

22. On the composition of the teaching staff, see n. 28.

23. E. Arie, Tripoli, to AIU, Paris, 18 October 1896, AAIU, IIE-5; ibid., 12 November 1899, AAIU, IIIE-6c; Ha-Cohen, *Higgid Mordecai,* p. 239. Bondy and Regignano were mentioned as teaching Hebrew.

24. E. Arie, Tripoli, to AIU, Paris, 20 January 1898, 14 May 1899, AAIU, IIE-5.

25. E. Arie, Tripoli, to AIU, Paris, 28 January 1897, 20 January 1898, AAIU, IIE-5.

the AIU teachers school in Paris (Ecole Normale Israélite Orientale [ENIO]). They were aided by assistants and instructors who were not professional teachers. These nonprofessionals were hired locally from among Jewish women and apparently were all European citizens.[26] They helped in the vocational courses, which were usually conducted in small groups.[27] Some of the assistants were merely monitors and helped keep some of the girls busy and quiet while the teacher was instructing another group. Many of these monitors had little education and could not teach even in the lower grades.[28] Some local assistance and supervision were also provided by the Jewish Women's Benevolent Society ('Ezrat Nashim) of Tripoli. During the first year of the school's operation, a volunteer from this society visited the school each day during the sewing and ironing classes and showed great interest in the school's activities and the progress of the pupils.[29]

When the director was on leave, it was customary for her husband, the director of the AIU boys school, to replace her temporarily.[30] Following the death of the second director, Claire Levy, her husband, Meir, taught an hour a day at the girls school and was assisted by three advanced female students. Later on, one of the teachers, Alegrine Benchimol, became more and more involved in teaching and actually performed the director's duties. Consequently, M. Levy recommended to the AIU center in Paris that her position as director be formalized so that her status and salary would reflect her actual work. This was done, and a year later they were also married.[31]

The impressions that the AIU staff had of their pupils were occasionally reported. These pronouncements reflect the different backgrounds and behavior patterns of the staff and pupils. The girls were often initially regarded by their teachers as "half savage," and it was deemed necessary to instruct them at first mainly in what were regarded by the Francophile teachers as "good manners."[32] This attitude caused some

26. On a failed attempt to dismiss a local teacher of Italian nationality, see D. Arie, Tripoli, to AIU, Paris, 30 November 1899, AAIU, IIIE-6c.

27. AIU, Paris, to E. Arie, Tripoli, 31 October 1899, AAIU, IIE-5; E. Arie, Tripoli, to AIU, Paris, 12 November 1899, AAIU, IIIE-6c.

28. E. Arie, Tripoli, to AIU, Paris, 1 May 1898, AAIU, IIE-5. On the teaching staff see also a report by E. Arie (E. Arie, Tripoli, to AIU, Paris, 12 November 1899, AAIU, IIIE-6c).

29. D. Arie, Tripoli, to AIU, Paris, 8 April 1897, AAIU, IIE-6b. On this society, see chap. 5.

30. D. Arie, Tripoli, to AIU, Paris, 8 April 1897, AAIU, IIE-6b.

31. M. Levy, Tripoli, to AIU, Paris, 15 June 1905, 25 November 1908, AAIU, IVE-22b.

32. E. Arie, Tripoli, to AIU, Paris, 28 January 1897, AAIU, IIE-5.

misunderstandings between the AIU and the girls' families. Some mothers complained that their daughters had been sent to school to learn academic subjects and professions, not to wash themselves. Instead, they found out that great emphasis was laid on cleanliness.[33]

Another difference of opinion concerned regular school attendance. Although there was strong competition with regard to registration in the AIU school, once pupils were enrolled, their attendance was not always regular. This was particularly the case among the girls, for whom going to school was something of a novelty. In addition, girls were expected to help at home, and quite often they had to remain there for this purpose, especially before the Sabbath and holidays. To encourage regular attendance, the director distributed inexpensive presents (e.g., bracelets and rings) at year's end among those girls whose attendance was satisfactory. In addition, punitive measures were taken to promote punctuality. Thus, penalties for arriving late helped to stop the phenomenon.[34]

Some staff members were at first quite critical of the girls' behavior, and they thought that the girls were not very intelligent. In the early stages of their work in Tripoli, most of the teachers complained about the character, behavior, physical appearance, and intellectual capacity of their pupils. The teachers claimed that the girls were quite lazy, were accustomed to idleness, and wanted others to think for them. They further stated that it was difficult to keep order in class and that the girls preferred singing to studying. It did not take the teachers long to realize that the girls were not stupid or lazy but simply had no tradition of learning in an academic setting. Following various unsuccessful attempts to use regular European teaching procedures in school, some teachers decided to employ methods better suited to the conditions in Tripoli and to the behavior of the girls. It was decided to attract the girls' attention through more dramatic means in a cheerful and playful atmosphere and to introduce them gradually to serious studying. Thus, since the girls liked to play and sing, the teachers began to incorporate songs, games, and performances in their instruction. The girls also enjoyed listening to stories, and consequently, historical material was often read in class. Some subjects that the girls particularly liked, such as history, were also used for the study of writing. Some teachers accused

33. Ibid., 27 December 1896, AAIU, IIE-5.
34. Ibid., 28 November 1899, AAIU, IIE-5; A. Benchimol, Tripoli, to AIU, Paris, 20 January 1908, AAIU, IIIE-10.

the girls of constant cheating and of being astonished when they were accused. The girls were also said to be quite happy to inform on one another and to see others punished. On a different level, the teachers maintained that their pupils were dirty and persisted in wearing jewelry in school, which was prohibited. These teachers were soon to realize that these characteristics resulted from socioeconomic conditions and were not due to character faults. The teachers noticed that both poverty and the lack of a regular water supply made it difficult for many Tripolitans to wash or to keep their clothes clean, especially since most Tripolitans had only one set of garments, which they wore until the clothes were old and torn.[35]

On a very limited scale the AIU girls school served as a means of integrating the various socioeconomic groups of the community. Although most of the pupils were poor, a few were not, among them graduates of the Italian school. These daughters of rich families were not accustomed to associating with the lower classes, and it was their first daily contact with members of a different class. Some rich girls were quite astonished to realize that the poor could learn and in some fields were even more advanced than themselves.[36]

The AIU institutions in Tripoli were under Ottoman jurisdiction. As such, any dispute concerning the schools (e.g., dismissal of a teacher) had to be resolved by an Ottoman court of law.[37] It appears, however, that no actual cases were referred to an Ottoman court. Ottoman involvement in the AIU school curriculum was, however, felt. Although the AIU center in Paris laid down the principles upon which the program of studies was based, the schools were also under the supervision of the Ottoman educational authorities. From 1901 onward, every school in Tripoli had to submit its curriculum and information on its pupils and staff to the authorities for approval. As part of this supervision, the municipal inspector of education visited the girls school in 1911. He entered all classes, asked questions, and was impressed by the achievements of the pupils. The management's desire to be on good terms with the authorities and to help the community to be more

---

35. M. Avigdor, Tripoli, to AIU, Paris, 4 January 1903, 16 March 1903, 11 January 1904, AAIU, IIIE-8; M. Levy, Tripoli, to AIU, Paris, 12 January 1906, AAIU, IVE-22b; A. Benchimol, Tripoli, to AIU, Paris, 6 January 1905, March 1905, 15 June 1905, 20 January 1908, AAIU, IIIE-10.

36. A. Benchimol, Tripoli, to AIU, Paris, 9 January 1907, AAIU, IIIE-10.

37. D. Arie, Tripoli, to AIU, Paris, 30 November 1899, AAIU, IIIE-6c.

involved citizens came to the fore during this visit. They told the Otto-man official of their wish to teach the girls Turkish, and he promised to pass the request to his minister.[38] This request came at a time when the authorities were very interested in Turkifying all segments of the popula-tion in order to strengthen Turkish-Ottoman national identity. Conse-quently, the AIU request served to further improve the relations between the school and the administration. Being under Ottoman jurisdiction could also carry financial benefits. In 1906, the director of the education department in Tripoli organized a charity bazaar and distributed the revenues among a number of schools, including the two AIU institu-tions, each of which received 800.15 francs.[39]

CONCLUDING REMARKS FOR THE OTTOMAN PERIOD

During the first fifteen years of its existence, the AIU girls school in Tripoli had a number of significant achievements. The AIU was the main force behind the spread of education for females among the Jewish lower classes. A growing number of families wanted their daughters to study and were even ready to make a financial sacrifice to that end. Even though the primary aim of sending the girls to school was to provide them with a profitable profession, many parents soon approved of aca-demic studies even without much vocational training. As a result, a few hundred girls were educated primarily in general studies and to a lesser degree in Jewish studies. In addition, numerous girls were trained in Western crafts, mainly connected with needlework. The AIU also ar-ranged musical and dramatic performances, set up exhibitions, and opened a library. As a result of all these activities, the Jewish community and some gentiles (primarily the Ottoman administration) became ex-posed to European (mainly French) culture. Furthermore, Jewish women became better equipped to get involved in public cultural, so-cial, and economic life. Nevertheless, the fact that numerous women made considerable cultural and professional progress did not in itself improve their social status, because the society at large did not change its basic concepts regarding women's role in society.

The non-community-sponsored educational networks in Libya had a significant influence over the Jewish community as a whole. A growing

38. M. Levy, Tripoli, to AIU, Paris, 10 July 1911, AAIU, IVE-22c.
39. Ibid., 24 April 1906, IVE-22b.

number of students opted for non-community-sponsored education. Thus, in 1910, out of a thousand male students, five hundred attended the traditional community school, and the rest studied in the Italian and AIU institutions, as well as with private tutors. The Tripolitan Jewish leadership felt obliged to improve the facilities and the level of teaching in its own educational institutions, and although academic secular studies were not introduced, vocational training was. Many of those who attended the Italian schools were from the upper socioeconomic strata and thus would become influential members of the Jewish community. The Westernizing influence of the school was enhanced by the increasing European (mainly Italian) presence in Libya.

As a result of these developments, toward the end of the Ottoman period, more of the Tripolitan Jewish youth were educated, and a growing number of them were educated in Western non-community-sponsored institutions. These institutions, however, were careful to maintain some degree of traditional Jewish atmosphere, taking into account how important this issue was for the local Jews. A higher number of Jewish boys than Jewish girls had some sort of schooling, but whereas more than half these boys had traditional education (in school or with private tutors), all the girls received Western education, mixed with some Jewish studies and vocational training. Although most of the Libyan Jewish youth studied for only a few years (usually not more than four), the education they received had some impact on cultural and social developments during the Italian and British periods.

EDUCATION UNDER ITALIAN RULE

The advent of Italian rule (1911–42) in Libya brought about several immediate changes in educational policy and practice. The Italian educational system became the state system and replaced the Ottoman network. Although private educational institutions were allowed to operate, state education had a far stronger impact on the population. This was especially so after 1922, when the Fascist party came to power in Italy and emphasized the centrality of the state and its interests in all internal and foreign affairs.

The relatively small Italian educational network that developed in Libya during the Ottoman period became after 1911 the cornerstone of a widespread state educational system. The Italian schools in Libya had a tradition of Christian and Jewish enrollment, with very little Muslim participation. This pattern changed following the Italian invasion, and especially after Arab resistance to Italian rule was suppressed during the 1920s and early 1930s. There were two main state educational systems in Libya during the Italian period. The first was a "metropolitan" one, similar to the one operating in Italy. The second was the "Libyan" system for the indigenous population.[40]

Jews frequented the state schools in increasing numbers, and they usually joined the metropolitan system. Due to the concentration of Jews in certain neighborhoods (such as the old city of Tripoli), some state schools had a majority of Jewish students. As a result of the mandatory elementary education, in these elementary schools a Jewish atmosphere prevailed, and studies were not conducted on the Sabbath and Jewish holidays. A growing number of Jews, and especially Jewish girls, went to these schools.

The AIU educational network in Libya did not grow during the twentieth century and remained confined to Tripoli. It continued to be a private European-style system geared toward Jewish children and providing them with French and Jewish education.

These developments enabled all Libyan Jewish boys and girls to study in Western-style schools. The boys also had the option of taking traditional Jewish courses at the community schools, and many Jewish boys attended an Italian school in the morning and a Jewish Talmud Torah school in the afternoon. This option was not available for girls, for whom there was no community-sponsored education during the Italian period.

During the Italian period, full-scale education for Jewish girls was provided only by the state Italian schools and to a lesser degree by the AIU.[41] Whereas most of the Jewish boys of school age received some kind of education for at least a few years in a variety of public institutions or from private tutors, the percentage of Jewish girls who studied was much lower. This was the case especially in the countryside, where until the 1940s hardly any Jewish girls attended school. For example, in 1929 in Tripoli, there were about 3,000 Jews of elementary school age—

40. For a discussion of Italian education in Libya, see Steele-Grieg, *History of Education,* pp. 17–28 and his tables; R. R. De Marco, *The Italianization of African Natives: Government Native Education in the Italian Colonies* (New York: Columbia University Teachers' College, 1943).

41. De Felice, *Jews in an Arab Land,* pp. 85–86.

2,000 boys and 1,000(!) girls. Although all the boys studied, only 500 girls went to Italian schools and about 150 to the AIU schools.[42]

The main attraction of the AIU school during the Italian period, in addition to its curriculum, was the Jewish atmosphere that prevailed there. Because Libya was under the rule of another European state, the AIU did not feel free to act aggressively to widen its educational network there. In addition, enlightening the local Jews became the responsibility of Italy, which as a European state was regarded by the AIU as capable of the task. Thus, whoever wanted to receive private French-Jewish education was asked to pay for it, and the AIU directors were very successful in collecting tuition fees.[43]

Due to the long period of time during which growing numbers of Jews were exposed to Italian culture and education, more and more Jews, especially men, knew Italian. According to the 1931 census, more Jews knew Italian than Arabs did (table 8). More Benghazi Jews knew Italian than Tripolitan Jews, apparently because of the greater Jewish participation in trade at the state level in Benghazi compared with Tripoli. In Tripoli many Jews continued to live in the Jewish quarter in the old city and to interact primarily among themselves.

During the early Italian period, it was very rare for the European schools to employ women to teach Jewish subjects, including the Hebrew language. One exception to the rule was Miriam Arari, who taught at the AIU school in 1919. She did not, however, stay in her position long, because the AIU was dissatisfied with her qualifications as a teacher and even more with her political activity. The management claimed that after Arari was hired, they realized that she was less proficient in both Hebrew and French than was previously thought. Consequently, her contract was not renewed despite the fact that she had been a very dedicated and energetic teacher. She was also very active in propagating Zionist ideas in Tripoli, to the chagrin of the AIU management. Due to the AIU's opposition at the time to Zionist activity, it is quite probable that Arari's involvement in Zionist circles in Tripoli contributed to her dismissal. She was not, however, representative of

42. Ibid., p. 321, n. 15. According to the report quoted by De Felice, there were twice as many boys as girls. Since the number of boys seems to be accurate, it is probable that "elementary school age" was defined differently for each sex, and this puts the percentage of girls who studied even lower.

43. L. Loubaton, Tripoli, to AIU, Paris, 7 June 1923, AAIU, IC-25. According to this report, 154 girls attended the AIU school in 1923/24.

Table 8. Knowledge of Italian among Non-Italians in Libya in 1931

PLACE	JEWS		ARABS		INDIGENOUS POPULATION
	Males	*Females*	*Males*	*Females*	
Benghazi	67.1%	40.8%	34.5%	1.6%	
Tripoli	43.8%	29.7%	29.2%	2.6%	
All Libya					4.6%

SOURCE: De Felice, *Jews in an Arab Land,* p. 69. Only the percentages were provided.

contemporary Libyan Jewish women, because she grew up and studied in Salonica and Jerusalem and stayed in Tripoli for less than a year.[44]

Community funding during the Italian period was only for male education—formal and informal alike. In 1929, for example, the community funded the education of 1,650 boys, who studied in the various traditional religious schools in Tripoli.[45] The communal expenditure on education for the period January–September 1931 was 134,920.85 Italian lire (out of a total expenditure of 502,085.95 Italian lire). More than half of this sum was for the salaries of Talmud Torah teachers, and the rest was used for food, clothing, and other assistance to poor male students as well as to support male students who went to Italy to continue their studies in higher religious institutions.[46] During the same year, the community of Tripoli also took advantage of the government's program and arranged for two groups of 200 Talmud Torah male students to attend a summer day camp on the beach for twenty-five days.[47] Nothing similar was organized by the community for girls.

During the Italian period, increasing numbers of Jewish girls acquired European education in the Italian schools. Others received European and some Jewish education in the AIU school. The Jewish component in their education was usually provided by local rabbinical scholars, whose knowledge and teaching qualifications were often quite poor. Consequently, the pupils attending these courses did not acquire a high level of knowledge in Jewish studies. During the 1920s, the Tripolitan Jewish leadership continued to ignore female education, in spite of the growing numbers of Jewish girls who attended non-Jewish schools and despite

44. Ibid., 16 December 1919, AAIU, IG-2. For more details, see chap. 5.
45. De Felice, *Jews in an Arab Land,* p. 321, n. 15.
46. Ibid., p. 335.
47. Ibid., p. 112.

external attempts to change this situation. Some leaders of the Board of Italian Jewish Communities (to which Libya belonged during the Italian period) who were sent on various missions to Libya tried to establish Jewish community–based female education (both academic and vocational) but to no avail. One of these persons was the vice chief rabbi of Torino, Dario Disegni, who was in Libya during 1930–31 and whose efforts in this direction bore no fruit.[48] It is possible that the community leaders, who had resisted changes to their educational system already during the Ottoman period, were especially opposed to external initiatives. This might be the reason why despite European competition and attempts at foreign cultural intervention, those educational initiatives that did succeed were launched by indigenous Jews, who attempted gradual change without completely abandoning traditional Jewish values. Thus, despite initial resistance and fear by the traditional leadership, a new Hebrew educational system was introduced that supplemented the existing one. The new system advocated and accommodated female education, which in the 1940s became part of the regular community services.

In Benghazi, Hebrew education, mostly by teachers from Palestine, was institutionalized within the local Talmud Torah school as early as 1915. It was, however, only for boys. In Tripoli, the acceptance of Hebrew education was slower than in Benghazi, and it faced more opposition from the Jewish leadership.

The teaching of modern Hebrew in Tripoli was initiated by a few individuals who were inspired by Zionist ideas.[49] In 1931, a group of young Tripolitan Jewish men who were interested in Zionism and the developments in Palestine taught themselves Hebrew in order to be able to read Hebrew publications from Palestine. As more Jews became interested in learning modern Hebrew, the activities of the initiators of this project grew, and they established a cultural society—Ben Yehudah (named after Eli'ezer Ben Yehudah, one of the main advocates of reviving the Hebrew language). Later the same year, regular courses (at first, only for the Hebrew language) were offered, including special classes for women. The first female pupils were adults who could not attend regular day classes because of their household tasks. For that reason,

---

48. Ibid., p. 90.
49. For a detailed discussion of the Hebrew revival in Libya, see R. Simon, "Ha-Tenu'ah ha-'Ivrit be-Luv," *Shorashim ba-Mizraḥ* 2 (1989): 173–209.

their classes were scheduled for the early morning (between seven and eight). Some of these women were members of important families in the community (e.g., Mazal-Ṭov Castelbolognesi, the wife of the chief rabbi of Tripoli), and their presence must have increased the prestige of this new enterprise.[50]

Because Jewish women in Libya did not have other alternatives for learning the Hebrew language and studying Jewish subjects, more women enrolled in these classes than men. For the same reason, it is quite probable that the number of female pupils who participated in these courses roughly equals the number of Tripolitan women who knew Hebrew during the 1930s and early 1940s.

Toward the end of 1931, an afternoon school, ha-Tiqvah, was established by the Ben Yehudah society. Its purpose was to teach Hebrew and Jewish studies to those Jews who had not had the opportunity to study them previously. At first, the school provided courses only for boys, but soon special classes for girls were added. Boys and girls studied separately for two hours in the afternoons of alternating days. Since girls had fewer opportunities than boys to study these subjects elsewhere, their enrollment in ha-Tiqvah school was higher than that of the boys (table 9).

Until the opening of ha-Tiqvah, most girls stayed at home or studied in the mornings in Italian schools and helped their mothers in various household tasks in the afternoon. Consequently, female participation in the new Hebrew school brought about changes in daily life at home and in the role of women in the family, in addition to the cultural implications it had.

All the teachers in ha-Tiqvah were volunteers. During the first three years, all the teachers were men, because few indigenous women knew Hebrew. However, by 1934/35, there were seven women in the sixteen-member teaching staff (four schoolteachers—one even teaching a boys' class—and three kindergarten teachers). At least five of these teachers had studied at the same school, including four who taught while they were still attending their final classes, which they finished with honors.[51] Despite the fact that the number of female teachers was constantly

50. Zuarez et al., *Yahadut Luv*, p. 143.

51. It is quite possible that the other two teachers also graduated from ha-Tiqvah, but not with honors, and thus their names were not mentioned in the special list. See ha-Tiqvah, *Ḥoveret Zikaron* (Tripoli: Teciuba, 5633 [1932]); idem, *Mazkeret le-Yom Ḥaluqat ha-Perasim la-Shanah ha-Revi'it* (Tripoli: Teciuba, 5636 [1935]).

Table 9. Student Distribution in ha-Tiqvah School in Tripoli

	GIRLS		BOYS		TOTAL	
YEAR	*Pupils*	*Classes*	*Pupils*	*Classes*	*Pupils*	*Classes*
1931/32	378	3—9	134	4	512	7—11
1932/33	352	8	221	4	573	12
1933/34	324	8	266	7	590	15
1934/35	440	10	316	9	756	19
1935/36	498		369		867	
1936/37					?	
1937/38					1,200	

SOURCE: Annual reports and sporadic school publications.

growing, the board of the Ben Yehudah society, which was responsible for directing ha-Tiqvah, was composed solely of men during the whole period under review. This is another indication that advances in the cultural and economic spheres notwithstanding, changes in the social and political spheres were much slower to follow.

Ha-Tiqvah had dedicated instructors who used modern teaching methods. They were very satisfied with the diligence and the achievements of their pupils, especially with those of the girls. The teachers believed that the girls had progressed even quicker than the boys, because they did not possess any previous knowledge of Hebrew and thus did not have to overcome previously learned mistakes. As a result of all this, the achievements of the pupils during the nine-month school year of 1931/32 were such that in the following year some pupils of both sexes were passed immediately to the third grade.[52]

Although the teaching of boys and girls took place on alternating days, both sexes participated in joint social and cultural school activities. This, too, was an innovation. On several occasions during the year, the school organized parties for the whole student body. Parents, community leaders, and public figures were also invited. At these parties, pupils of both sexes cooperated in staging performances, reading poetry, singing, and so on. The ideological commitment of the school was emphasized in another sort of activity, which took place during the festival of Purim. On that holiday, all the pupils (who could easily be identified as

52. Ha-Tiqvah, *Ḥoveret Zikaron*, p. 2.

such by their official school uniform of blue and white) made the rounds among the community members to collect contributions for the Jewish National Fund (JNF).[53] Thus, although instruction was segregated according to sex, some social and cultural contact between Jewish children of both sexes took place, and they were encouraged to act in support of their Zionist national identity.

The teaching staff treated the pupils of both sexes equally. Thus, for example, when it was realized that due to poverty some pupils lacked proper clothing, especially during the cold winter months, the school, together with the help of some community members, provided garments for all those in need.[54] Furthermore, in order to encourage the pupils in their studies, it was decided to distribute medals and certificates of honor to the best pupils. At the conclusion of the first school year (1931/32), 5.8 percent of the girls (22 out of 378) and 8.9 percent of the boys (12 out of 134) received these honors. Quite a few girls were not eligible for these prizes because they enrolled after the school year had already started, and therefore, they did not finish the whole year's program; otherwise, the number of girls in the honors list might have been higher.[55]

Another innovation of ha-Tiqvah was the inclusion of gymnastics—for both boys and girls—in its curriculum. It was clearly stated among the declared goals of the school that physical education was part of the curriculum because "it gives the pupils special powers, lightness, and agility, which will be of help to the pupils throughout their lives."[56] Gymnastics were performed not only in class but also for public events. Thus, for example, at the ceremony marking the conclusion of the second school year, physical exercises were performed by separate groups of boys and girls.[57] This was something Jewish children, and especially girls, were not accustomed to doing.[58] In introducing this subject, ha-Tiqvah might have been influenced by Maccabi (see chap. 5).

When the Hebrew school entered its second year, its curriculum and extracurricular programs became more diversified. Teaching became

53. Ibid., p. 4. On the JNF, see *Encyclopaedia Judaica*, s.v. "Jewish National Fund"; on Purim, see ibid., s.v. "Purim."

54. Ha-Tiqvah, *Hoveret Zikaron*, p. 3.

55. Ibid., pp. 5–7.

56. My translation, ha-Tiqvah, *Mazkeret* [no pagination].

57. Ibid.

58. The Maccabi sports association began its activities in Libya in 1920, but for a long period of time it had an all-male membership. For more details, see chap. 5.

based more and more on high-quality textbooks, many of which were adopted from the Hebrew school network in Palestine. Another change was that in addition to Hebrew and Jewish studies, a daily two-hour sewing course for girls was given by two female instructors. The school's management stated that this subject was added because it could be of great economic assistance to the girls during their youth and adult life alike. Furthermore, in order to complement the regular courses, day trips and lectures for all the pupils were organized.[59] These innovations increased the role of modern Hebrew education in the community and gradually changed the character of traditional Jewish education.

The management of ha-Tiqvah regarded female education to be of particular importance and elaborated both the reasons for its position and what should be done in this area:

And the girls? Can we continue any further in our frightening disregard of the education of our daughters? Brothers! Let us not forget that the girl of today is the mother of tomorrow! She, and she alone, is the one who builds the future of our sons, and the future of the nation. The Hebrews of tomorrow will be educated by the mother and not by the father! To prepare the mothers of Israel is the only means, the huge fence, the rock on which all the waves of assimilation will storm and break loose, without leaving any impression.

Let us insert into the hearts of our daughters a pure Hebrew spirit, and only then will we fulfill our obligation toward our nation and our God. In our school we do whatever is possible for this purpose. But let us not be running after the wind! The resources of the night school are not sufficient to perform this wide-ranging task. It is absolutely necessary to have a day school for girls, in which women and not men will teach, because it is impossible for a male teacher to provide a comprehensive education for a girl.

Brothers! Particularly nowadays we must stand guard. The new generation that is being revived is not similar to the previous generation! These times pressingly demand that the boy and the girl of today should know well, from a tender age, their religion, language, and the history of their nation, from which and only from which they can understand what it means to be a Jew and what is the meaning of Judaism, and if they do not understand this,

59. Ha-Tiqvah, *Ḥoveret Zikaron*, p. 5; idem, *Mazkeret;* Zuarez et al., *Yahadut Luv,* p. 149.

they may be harmed. . . . The leadership of the community must organize a school for boys and girls, and the teachers should be totally dedicated to the youth entrusted in their hands. All the community must help in general, and financially in particular, as needed. A Hebrew day school for girls should immediately be established.[60]

These remarks were addressed to the male members of the Tripolitan community by one of the board members of ha-Tiqyah (who were all men). From these statements it is quite clear that it was not deemed necessary to explain why boys should be educated. When it came to girls, the reasoning that was put forward was not that they as human beings should be given equal opportunities to develop spiritually; the emphasis was on their role with regard to the next male generation. It was stressed that it was important to prepare the mothers of the forthcoming generation, singling out its male component, so that the boys would not be negatively influenced by external trends and assimilation but would remain within the framework of Judaism. Similarly, the inclusion of women in the teaching profession was not advocated as a necessary part of opening all economic, cultural, and social fields to women. The justification for this move was that women are better qualified to teach girls than men are. From these statements and from the absence of women on the school's board during the whole period of its existence, one can conclude that the innovations of the Ben Yehudah society with regard to women were geared toward the interests of men. However, inadvertently, they contributed to the advancement of Libyan Jewish women.

Ha-Tiqyah had remarkable success in teaching children modern Hebrew and Jewish subjects. As a result of these achievements, the Jewish leadership decided to make the Ben Yehudah society responsible for the community's education department. Consequently, its ideas gradually became the official educational policy of the community, although their widespread implementation had to wait until the 1940s. The school continued to operate until 1939, when it was forced to close down because of the Italian anti-Semitic racial legislation.[61]

Ha-Tiqyah was an innovative enterprise due to its goals, approach,

60. My translation, ha-Tiqyah, *Hoveret Zikaron*, pp. 11–12.
61. For more details on the Ben Yehudah society and ha-Tiqyah, see the anniversary brochures for 1932 and 1936 cited in n. 51, as well as Zuarez et al., *Yahadut Luv*, pp. 148–52; De Felice, *Jews in an Arab Land*, p. 98; Simon, "Ha-Tenu'ah ha-'Ivrit."

and methods. In contrast to the traditional Jewish education provided by the community, the Ben Yehudah society emphasized the study of modern Hebrew as a living language, and the pupils became proficient in reading, writing, and speaking it. The study of Hebrew was complemented by other subjects, such as Jewish history, the geography of Palestine, crafts, and gymnastics. The purpose of the whole program was in essence a national one: to prepare a sound intellectual and ideological foundation for future Zionists and to provide them with the necessary tools to fight assimilation and to survive physically and economically.

Until ha-Tiqvah opened, the community's leadership and the various indigenous Jewish cultural groups (with the exception of the women's organizations, and even there to a very limited degree) did not attempt to educate females. The Ben Yehudah society, however, regarded the education of females as indispensable for the future of the nation as a whole (even though men still played the central role in the society's activities and in the community at large). Nevertheless, through this channel Jewish girls in Tripoli received a Jewish education. The number of women who became proficient in the subjects offered grew, and indigenous Jewish women became teachers of the courses provided by the Ben Yehudah society. Once this society became responsible for the Jewish community's education, the way was open for enrolling girls in day schools run by the community. This goal was realized only in the 1940s, following additional cultural, social, and political changes in the region.

Most of these developments came to an end with the implementation of the anti-Semitic racial legislation, which took place in Italy and Libya in 1938. Jews—pupils and teachers of all levels—had to leave government schools, and foreign "enemy" schools and some private organizations and schools were closed down. The AIU had to stop its activities in Libya in 1939 and renewed them only in 1947. The Ben Yehudah society, too, had to close down in 1939. When Italy entered the war in mid-1940, all state schools closed down.[62] During World War II, regular Jewish community schools also suffered because of political and economic restrictions on several categories of Jews, especially when they were located in fighting zones. Although the communities tried to continue their educational activities, it became increasingly difficult to do so, due to military operations, deportations, expulsions, and economic prob-

62. Steele-Grieg, *History of Education*, p. 27.

lems.[63] As a result, during World War II, almost all the girls and many boys were deprived of any kind of education for up to five years. Despite the fact that a growing number of Jewish girls were educated during the Italian period, the principle of female education was not yet accepted by the traditional Jewish community leadership. Consequently, whereas the Jewish communities made special efforts to find solutions to continue male education during the war, nothing of the kind was done with regard to the girls.

Because much of the educational infrastructure was destroyed during the war, it was easier to restructure certain parts after the war. In many cases the new formations were quite different from the old ones in both structure and content. Furthermore, the innovative core faculty members who were nurtured during the 1930s by the Ben Yehudah society were eager and able to implement educational changes for the benefit of the new generation, including their own children. Another important factor in the 1940s was the presence in Libya of educators who were accepted by the community and who had the knowledge and the means to implement changes in education.

EDUCATION UNDER THE BMA AND ARAB RULE

The most important change in Jewish education in Libya following the British occupation in 1942–43 was the establishment of Hebrew schools for both sexes as the core of the Jewish communal educational system.[64] This innovation was made possible by the desperate condition of some communities at the end of the war, the change in political trends in the community, the presence of Palestinian Jewish soldiers in the British army stationed in Libya, and the de facto abrogation of the anti-Semitic racial legislation. Although in most small communities Italian and traditional religious education for boys continued to exist and to absorb Jewish students, the Hebrew schools had the most influence on Jewish youth.

63. On the Libyan Jewish community during the war, see Simon, "Yehudey Luv 'al Saf Sho'ah."

64. In the beginning, funding for these Hebrew schools was provided by both British and Jewish sources (local and Jewish Agency and AJDC). Later on, the British decided that the Jews should be integrated into the local Arab school system, and at that point, the British stopped funding the Hebrew schools, with the exception of Arab teachers for Arabic.

Benghazi

In November 1942 Benghazi became the first major Libyan town to be occupied by the British army. When the British entered the town, it was badly damaged by bombings. Most of the Jewish community had been deported to Jado and nearby villages in the center of the Tripolitanian mountains. The few hundred Jews who remained in Benghazi were demoralized by the upheavals of the previous two years. They were also impoverished as a result of the war and the racial legislation. The few Jewish children who remained in town were scattered in the streets, were shabby and undernourished, and had been without regular schooling for about four years. The remnants of the community were in no position to handle the numerous social, cultural, and economic problems that faced them. The initiative passed to the Jewish soldiers, who launched an emergency program to collect the Jewish children from the streets and bring them back to school. At that point, the British authorities approved of their actions and did not consider the political implications, because the BMA was interested primarily in getting the children into some kind of an educational framework under the supervision of responsible adults. As a result of the small number of Jewish children in Benghazi when this operation started, and because of the confused state of mind of the leadership-deprived community, the soldiers could run the school according to their customs and understanding. Most of the founders of the Benghazi Hebrew school were not qualified teachers, and they relied heavily on the only model they knew: the Hebrew school network in Palestine. As a result, the curriculum was strongly influenced by that model and so were the learning environment and teaching methods. One of the major innovations of the Hebrew school system in Benghazi was the introduction of coeducation, and when the Hebrew school was opened in Benghazi, both sexes participated in the same classes.[65]

The teaching in the Benghazi Talmud Torah Hebrew School, as the new school was named, was conducted at first by volunteers from among the Jewish soldiers and some veteran indigenous male teachers.

65. On the Hebrew school in Benghazi see Simon, "Ha-Tenu'ah ha-'Ivrit"; *Darkenu*, 5 April 1945; "Yehudey Tripoli be-Yamim Eleh," *Milḥamtenu* (September 1943): 26; report by A. Yellin, 30 April 1943, quoting a letter from E. Za'if, Benghazi, CZA, J17/8064; Yehoshafaṭ [Harkabi], Benghazi, to Prof. S. H. Bergman, Jerusalem, 18 November 1943, CZA, S25/5217; Y. Ben-'Ami, Benghazi, 17 December 1944, CZA, S6/1984; J. Guetta, Benghazi, 12 July 1945, CZA, J17/8064.

Although the first soldier-teachers lacked teaching experience, they were very enthusiastic and dedicated to their mission. One of their main objectives was to keep the children off the streets, and they tried to teach their pupils some Hebrew, mainly through songs and games. More proper schooling came later, when experienced teachers were located among the soldiers, and the latter began to teach together with three Talmud Torah teachers. One of the soldiers prepared the school's syllabus, based on the curriculum of the Hebrew schools in Palestine complemented with Italian textbooks that he found in Benghazi. The soldiers translated parts of the Italian textbooks into Hebrew, omitting inappropriate (e.g., praises of Fascism) sections.

In 1945, after all the deportees and the exiled had returned to Benghazi, the Hebrew school had 426 pupils (146 girls and 280 boys, aged six to seventeen years). No detailed breakdown of the student body was provided, but it seems probable that the number of older boys who attended school was higher than the number of older girls. The reason for this was that due to religious obligations, it was traditionally regarded to be more important for men—but not women—to be educated. Consequently, every effort was made to ensure that all Jewish males, even if past elementary-school age, received a basic Jewish education, so that they would not remain illiterate and unable to participate in Jewish religious and communal life. This was not the case with regard to female education. Nevertheless, some efforts were taken to educate illiterate female adults. For this purpose, evening coeducational classes for Hebrew were also started, and some hundred adults, most of them women, attended.

During the school year of 1942/43, most of the teaching in the Hebrew school in Benghazi was done by indigenous men and soldier-teachers. The latter knew that their stay in Cyrenaica might be interrupted at short notice because of troop movements or the growing opposition of the military command to their educational activities.[66] Consequently, soon after the consolidation of the Hebrew school, the most experienced soldier-teachers started to train indigenous candidates who had no teaching experience. Twelve young Jews, four of whom were women aged sixteen to seventeen years, attended the first teacher-training course. They were instructed intensively for two months each

66. This opposition was primarily political. The British wanted to develop an Arab school system for all the indigenous population. For the time being, the British allowed the Italian schools to operate, but they opposed the addition of Hebrew schools as part of the state educational system.

day from 1.30 to 5.30 P.M. and continued their studies with written materials. After their graduation, four women and one man were added to the teaching staff of the Hebrew school in Benghazi. Each new teacher was assisted and supervised by a soldier-teacher. The role of the female teachers was regarded as especially important mainly with the little children, who knew only Italian or Judeo-Arabic (but no Hebrew), whereas most of the soldiers knew Hebrew and some English (but only a few knew Italian or Judeo-Arabic). Gradually, the new teachers became more independent, but as long as the soldiers were around, the soldiers thoroughly coached the novices before each lesson. The four female teachers were also instructed in hygiene, and together with eight female relatives of the pupils, who came on shifts each day, they washed the pupils and cut their fingernails, in the hope that their mothers would carry on this treatment at home.

After the soldiers had to leave during late 1944–early 1945, the Hebrew school in Benghazi was operated solely by indigenous teachers. Most of these instructors (four women and three men) were new to their profession. In keeping with the old social concepts, and despite the role women had begun to play in education, the director of the school was one of the new male teachers. One could witness similar phenomena elsewhere, and only the Italian-Jewish school in Tripoli had a Jewish female director. The teachers had a very heavy teaching load, and each one of them taught two shifts (in the morning and in the afternoon). The director, however, due to his administrative obligations, taught only during the second shift.

Most of the credit for the modern, Palestinian-Jewish atmosphere in the Benghazi school was given to the female teachers, who had received all their training from the soldiers and thus were not bound by old habits. The appointment of women as teachers was regarded by the soldiers as an important social achievement, because of their usual lower status in comparison to men.[67] It is, however, evident from a comparison of the salaries of the teaching staff in Benghazi that the female teachers were paid less than their male colleagues. It seems that this gap did not reflect only experience and tenure, because some of the male teachers were new too (see chap. 3).

---

67. The soldiers were particularly impressed by the custom of segregation of the sexes during meals (Zamir and Yariv, Tripoli, to Yosifon and Ben-Yehudah, 7 November 1943, CZA, S25/5217).

No objection was raised in the community with regard to Jewish men teaching girls. When, however, the issue of opening an Arab government school for the Jews of Benghazi was discussed with the authorities, the community would not allow Arab men to teach their children and especially their daughters.[68]

In addition to Hebrew, Jewish studies, and the geography of Palestine, other subjects, such as arithmetic, crafts, drawing, and music, were also introduced in the Hebrew school in Benghazi. Exhibitions were arranged, a choir was formed, and performances focusing on national topics were staged, usually in connection with the various Jewish holidays. The Jewish community was the main audience for these events, which, together with the accomplishments of the pupils, raised the prestige of the Hebrew school and its teaching staff. This, of course, was also very important for improving the status of women, who formed the majority of the regular teaching staff throughout the period. The school continued to operate in this manner until late 1949, when the Jews of Benghazi moved to Tripoli in preparation for their emigration to Israel.

Tripoli

The developments in education in Tripoli were somewhat different from those in Benghazi. The reason for this apparently was that during World War II the community of Tripoli as a whole suffered less than that of Benghazi, and most of the Tripolitan Jews remained in town. Therefore, the Palestinian Jewish soldiers did not temporarily replace the local leadership and could not start a new educational system from scratch but had to deal with existing communal and Italian institutions.[69]

Tripoli was occupied by the British army in January 1943, but the new Hebrew school was not opened until the following school year (1943/44). In Tripoli, in contrast to Benghazi, there were no social conditions that necessitated the establishment of an institution to take care of the children, because the former traditional network had not collapsed completely. Since the education system in Tripoli was much

68. Report from Benghazi, 25 April 1944, CZA, J17/8064.
69. On the educational activities in Tripoli during this period, see Simon, "Ha-Tenu'ah ha-'Ivrit"; *Hed ha-Ḥinukh* 249–51 (Nisan–Siyan 5704 [April–June 1944]); Zuarez et al., *Yahadut Luv,* pp. 171–77; Zamir and Yariv, Tripoli, to Yosifon and Ben Yehudah, 7 November 1943, CZA, S25/5217; report on the educational activity in Tripoli, 9 November 1943, CZA, S25/1984.

less harmed during the war than that in Benghazi, its structure underwent fewer changes. Thus, a Hebrew system was established, but a traditional Talmud Torah school for boys continued to operate. In addition, although women entered the system both as pupils and as teachers, the classes remained separated according to sex, and women usually taught only girls and little boys. The Hebrew educational system in Tripoli was organized during the spring and summer of 1943 in a more methodical manner than in Benghazi. Another difference between Tripoli and Benghazi was that when Hebrew education was being planned in Tripoli, the soldiers knew that the British army was gradually departing from Libya. As a result, the main contribution of the Jewish soldiers in Tripoli was educational planning and training new teachers, and not actual teaching. Some of the new trainees were graduates of the courses offered by the Ben Yehudah society in the 1930s. They became experts in Hebrew and used modern pedagogic methods as well as a curriculum based on that of the Hebrew schools in Palestine. Due to the size of the Tripolitan community, the number of teachers—both veteran and new—was much higher in Tripoli than in Benghazi, and there were more schools to choose from.

Shortly after Tripoli was occupied by the British army in 1943, Talmud Torah renewed its activities in the central synagogue in the old city, where some hundred male pupils recited the scriptures and the prayers. During the spring of 1943, planning for the Hebrew school was initiated by previous members of the Ben Yehudah society (which officially renewed its activities on 11 July 1943) and a group of Jewish soldiers headed by the chief military rabbi of Tripoli, Dr. Efraim Urbach from Jerusalem. Because of the limited number of qualified teachers for the new enterprise, and because special Italian schools for Jewish children continued to operate, it was decided to divide the Jewish student body into two. All children aged seven years and above were to go to the Italian Jewish schools, and the community took upon itself the task of complementing their general education with Hebrew and Jewish studies. The other group included all the six-year-olds, who were to attend only the new Hebrew school, which was to provide comprehensive Hebrew, Jewish, and general education. It was further decided that each year a higher grade would be added to the Hebrew school, and those who started in this school would receive all their education there.

The main contribution of the Jewish soldiers in Tripoli was in planning the operation and the curriculum of the school as well as

training new and veteran teachers in order to answer the needs of the
new program. Four soldiers started the teachers' training program.
They divided their students into two groups, according to sex and
experience. One group included women aged nineteen to twenty-two
who had little previous knowledge of Hebrew and no teaching experience. It was planned that these women would teach the younger children. Their studies included general subjects, Hebrew, pedagogy, singing, crafts, and drawing. During their studies and later on, they
showed great dedication to their mission. The other group was composed of men who were somewhat older than the women. Some of
these men had previous teaching experience, especially in traditional
Jewish studies. They would teach the older children in the Italian
Jewish schools.

When the new Hebrew school was opened in Tripoli in September
1943, it had about 360 pupils and 11 teachers—10 of whom were female
graduates of the special teachers' course. Each subsequent year, a few
hundred new pupils were enrolled in this school. The highest enrollment was in 1949, at the beginning of the mass emigration to Israel,
when there were about 2,530 pupils and 40 teachers.[70] In addition to the
female teachers in the regular Hebrew school, there were also four
female instructors (two teachers and two assistants) in the kindergarten,
which was operated by the community for 150 children of both sexes
aged four and a half to six years.

In addition to those children who studied in the Jewish school system in Tripoli, there were about 2,000 Jewish pupils in the local Italian
Jewish schools. The community provided these children with special
courses in Hebrew and Jewish studies. The girls attended these lessons
in the mornings in their Italian Jewish school, and the boys were taught
by twelve male teachers in the afternoons, usually in the Talmud Torah
building. The curriculum of all these Jewish pupils included gymnastics,
and they participated in municipal field days in the stadium of Tripoli,
together with pupils of other Tripolitan schools.[71] It appears that boys
participated in extracurricular activities more than girls. Thus, for example, in the summer of 1949, the AJDC organized a day camp at the beach

70. The reports did not provide a breakdown according to sex.
71. *Qol ha-Moreh* 2 (Nisan 5706 [Spring 1946]), reporting on an event on 12 May 1946
in which 700 pupils from various schools participated. The Jews were instructed by Emma
Polacco, the director of the Italian-Jewish school.

for Jewish schoolchildren. Out of the 1,290 participants, 900 were boys and only 390 were girls.[72]

The teachers at the Hebrew school of Tripoli were very dedicated to their work. However, because of their limited education (most of the teaching staff had left school after the fifth grade) and the short duration of their training, their academic qualifications were not very high. As the years passed, and higher grades were created in the Hebrew school, this problem became more acute. The supervisors of the Hebrew school were not much more learned themselves and could not help the staff very much. The teachers tried to improve their knowledge through reading, and they asked Jewish educators in Palestine for guidance and textbooks. Furthermore, in many cases the enthusiasm and dedication of the teachers compensated for numerous flaws in their knowledge and teaching.

Because of the short training period undergone by the new teachers, because innovative teaching methods were used (including songs and games), and apparently also because most of the initial teaching staff were women, the community at first viewed the Hebrew school with low esteem. When, however, the achievements of the new school started to become apparent, it became increasingly more respected by the community. Still, the teachers themselves felt the need for further improvement and repeatedly asked the Department of Education of the Jewish Agency in Jerusalem to reinforce the Tripoli Hebrew school with teachers and inspectors from the Hebrew network in Palestine, who could further train the Tripolitan teachers. Until 1947 this request remained unfulfilled.

The arrival in August 1946 of the new chief rabbi of Tripoli, Shelomoh Yelloz, from Palestine triggered some developments in the Jewish educational network. He was very critical of the existing educational system in Tripoli. As a result, he initiated three major projects, two of which were relevant for both sexes: vocational education, high-level teacher training, and a yeshiva.

In April 1947, a vocational school for Jewish girls was opened in Tripoli, where some four hundred girls learned sewing, cutting, embroidery, and knitting, as well as some Italian, Hebrew, and arithmetic. The

---

72. *Ḥayenu,* 9 September 1949. Some of these children were staying temporarily in Tripoli, waiting to emigrate to Israel.

school aimed to provide Jewish girls with a profitable profession, "so that they will not have to become servants in places which are below the dignity of Jewish girls."[73] It is not clear, though, how long this enterprise lasted, how many groups were trained there, and for what period of time each.

The second important operation initiated by Rabbi Yelloz was improved teacher training. During the second half of 1947, Dr. Moshe Auerbach and his son Shemu'el arrived in Tripoli. Both of them were experienced educators in the Hebrew religious network in Palestine. Their mission was to inspect and improve the Jewish educational system in Tripoli. They became responsible for the development of the Hebrew school in Tripoli and organized a teacher-training course in which several indigenous teachers of both sexes studied for about three hours each evening after their eight-hour work day (composed of two four-hour shifts).[74]

Rabbi Yelloz's third educational initiative was geared only for boys and reflected the prevailing attitude toward education. During the summer of 1947 a yeshiva was established in Tripoli with the assistance of Jewish religious organizations abroad. Approximately eighty boys studied religious studies supplemented by some secular courses (e.g., Italian and Arabic). A while later, evening classes for an additional two hundred working-class men were offered in Tripoli to teach Jewish religious studies.

Rabbi Yelloz emphasized the need for poor Jewish women to learn a profitable profession in order to prevent them from working as servants in unsuitable places. On the other hand, he paid much more attention to the scholarly education of men. He stressed the importance of education for those men who had not studied for several years because of the war. He did not refer, however, to the fact that an even larger number of women were also deprived of education for the very same reason. His attitudes influenced the educational programs that he initiated: vocational training for girls, supplemented by a few academic courses, versus a higher religious institution and evening religious courses for men, supplemented by foreign language study. No academic programs for

---

73. *Nitzanim* 24 (Elul 5707 [Summer 1947]): 5; A. Guetta, Tripoli, to the Youth Department/Religious Division, 23 July 1947, CZA, S32/123; Zuarez and Tayyar, *Ḥokhmat Nashim*, p. 16. See also chap. 3, this volume.
74. Zuarez et al., *Yahadut Luv*, p. 172.

illiterate, working, or unemployed women were established, and although some academic courses were incorporated into the female vocational school, the emphasis there was on vocational training.

As a result of the mass emigration of Jews from Libya to Israel
during 1949–51, many teachers left the country, sometimes at an even
quicker rate than the community as a whole.[75] As a result, experienced
teachers were in short supply, and teacher training continued to be in
high demand. This need was answered by some of the Israeli immigration emissaries who operated in Tripoli and were veteran educators. In
1949 they established a coeducational teachers' course (headed by
Zalman Bugaṭin) for veteran and new teachers.[76] During 1950, another
teacher-training course was given in Tripoli under the same management; its students included about twenty Jewish women from well-to-
do families who studied primarily the Bible and Hebrew.[77] In addition,
a course for youth movement instructors (*madrikhim*) was offered in
Tripoli at the same time. Most of the students in the latter were also
schoolteachers, and many of them were women. Thus, during this period of mass emigration, there were in Tripoli and its vicinity three
courses for Jewish teachers and instructors in both the regular Hebrew
school system and the extracurricular educational-social network. Some
of these teachers stayed in Libya after the mass emigration ended and
for a while continued to provide Jewish-Hebrew education to the youth
that remained in Tripoli. Due, however, to obstacles put forward by the
new independent Arab regime, the Jewish character of the education
provided for Jewish children decreased, and eventually Jewish schools
ceased to exist.

During the preparations for emigration to Israel, more evening
courses in the Hebrew language were offered in Tripoli in both the old
and the new parts of town. Women were very eager to study, and some
of them even left their babies and husbands alone at home in order to
learn Hebrew. Their daring, however, had its limitations, and in mixed
company they bowed to social conventions: "There was a constant
shortage of space, and the few chairs were always taken by the stronger

75. On the mass emigration, see R. Simon, "Me-Ḥug Tziyon le-Tziyonut Magshima:
Ha-ʿAliyah mi-Luv le-Yisraʾel," *Shorashim ba-Mizraḥ* 3 (1991): 295–351.

76. Annual Report on Tripolitania, 1949, PRO, FO 371/80864.

77. A. Nadad, Department of Middle Eastern Jews, to Dr. Y. Benshalom, 3 May
1950, CZA, S32/1069; M. Vardi, Tripoli, to N. Bar Giyora and Y. Elitzur, 30 May 1951,
CZA, S32/124.

students, and of course the 'stronger sex' always had the upper hand."[78] Although exact data on this project were not provided, it is clear from the description that many women participated in these courses, even to the extent of "neglecting" what was considered to be their main mission in life—taking care of their babies and husbands. These women were stubborn enough to leave their traditional chores in order to study, but in the presence of men, their status remained inferior, and it was taken for granted that men had priority over the few privileges that were offered, such as the use of chairs.

The main innovation in the education of Jewish females in Tripoli during the 1940s was the incorporation of females into the Jewish community's educational system as pupils and teachers. Although the classes in Tripoli were separated according to sex, some extracurricular activities at school were performed by both sexes together, and teacher training was in part coeducational. On the whole, however, there was still a stronger emphasis on the academic accomplishments of men, whereas the vocational aspect of female education was stressed. Many Jewish women in Tripoli reached a stage in which they felt themselves to be ready to opt for education over some of their traditional household tasks, but in mixed company, and especially in a less-educated environment, their status remained low and they received fewer privileges than men did.

According to British data on private Jewish schools in Tripoli in 1949–50, the number of pupils and teachers decreased as a result of the mass emigration to Israel (table 10). This trend was even stronger with regard to girls, whose numbers dropped much faster than those of boys, despite the fact that more boys left Libya earlier through the Organization for Youth Immigration (on Youth Immigration, see chap. 5). The data might reflect the presence in Tripoli of Jews from the hinterland, who were less accustomed than urban Jews to sending their daughters to school.

Between 1947 and 1960, Tripolitan Jewish girls were able once again to study at the AIU school, which renewed its activities in Tripoli in 1947, after it had been closed down during World War II. In the second phase of its operation, the AIU school acquired a strong Hebrew and Zionist character, contrary to its first period in Tripoli. This was in keeping with developments in other AIU schools resulting from events

78. My translation, *Ḥayenu*, 10 August 1950.

Table 10. Population in Private Jewish Schools in Tripoli

		PUPILS			
YEAR	SCHOOLS	*Female*	*Male*	*Total*	TEACHERS
1949	3	898	867	1,765	25
1950	2	487	632	1,119	20

SOURCES: Annual Reports on Tripolitania, 1949, PRO, FO 371/80864, and 1950, FO 371/90314. No data on the distribution according to sex and religion in the public schools were provided. It appears that the annual reports give this information only about the communal and AIU institutions.

during the war, when many Jews were disappointed with the behavior of France toward the Jews. Consequently, many Jewish communities opted for Jewish national revival and Zionism instead of becoming part of European civilization and society. The AIU understood that in order to be able to operate in these communities, it, too, had to change its policies, including its national identification, and come out in favor of Zionism. Most of the teaching in the new AIU school in Tripoli was conducted in Hebrew (and not in French, as in the past), and it was based on educational programs and textbooks from Israel. The French language, culture, and history continued to be taught, but there was much less emphasis given to those subjects. The change in the role of the AIU school vis-à-vis the well-developed Hebrew schools brought about a decrease in the former's student body and teaching staff. The teaching staff consisted of four members (including only one woman, a sewing teacher, though the kindergarten, too, was run by a woman).

Following Libyan independence, French once again became the language of instruction in the AIU school, due to the changing political conditions in Libya and the opposition of the Arab authorities to any demonstration of Hebrew and Zionist national feelings. In 1953, the AIU school included fifty-seven pupils (thirty-six girls and twenty-one boys) in a kindergarten and three grades. The number of pupils in the AIU school increased following demographic changes in Tripoli. As a result of the mass Jewish emigration from Libya, most of the remaining Jews were well-to-do families who were concentrated in the newer parts of Tripoli and not in the old city, which previously had been the center of Jewish life. Thus, the number of Jewish pupils decreased in the former Italian Jewish schools in the old city, and Arab pupils became the majority there. Jewish parents preferred their children, and especially their daughters, to study in a Jewish environment, and consequently, many Jewish children were transferred to the AIU school. This situation did not last long, because the Libyan authorities closed down the AIU school in April 1960 for political reasons that had nothing to do with the Jewish community (i.e., opposition to France in identification with the Algerian revolution). This brought to an end Jewish education in Libya.[79]

Few women attained senior positions in the Jewish educational system in Libya, and those who did so were concentrated in Tripoli. Only one became a member of the community's education department (1943–44),[80] and three were on the board of the Jewish teachers' association, with one of them reaching the rank of vice-president in 1946.[81] In addition, there was one female school director, and all Jewish kindergartens were run by females.

The Countryside

In the countryside, females received less education than in Tripoli and Benghazi. Although in several small towns and villages there were Italian schools for girls, it seems that only a few Jewish girls attended them. The education of Jewish boys in most of these places was confined to religious studies, especially reading the Bible and prayers, "and the girls, of course, did not study at all."[82] This continued to be the case in several small communities until the emigration to Israel.[83] In some places, however, Hebrew and new teaching programs and methods were introduced and in turn brought about a change in the attitude toward female education.

In Khoms, Rabbi Frigia Zuarez established a Hebrew school in 1928. Fifteen years later, the community had 157 Jewish children of school age

79. Reports by H. Khalfon, Tripoli, to the Youth Department, Jerusalem, during 1947–48, CZA, S32/123, S32/1069; H. L. Levy to Dr. J. J. Shapiro, Paris, 16 December 1953, AJDC, Geneva, Box 10C, C-56.502; De Felice, *Jews in an Arab Land,* p. 269. On female Muslim education in Libya from the 1950s to the 1970s, see Attir, "Ideology," pp. 123–26.

80. J. Fargion, Tripoli, to the Youth Department, Jerusalem, 8 Tammuz 5704 (29 June 1944), CZA, S32/1068.

81. P. Shakir, Zliten, to the Youth Department/Religious Division, Jerusalem, 23 Ḥeshvan 5707 (1 November 1946), CZA, S32/123; *Ḥayenu,* 9 September 1949. For more details, see chap. 5.

82. My translation, Zuarez et al., *Yahadut Luv,* p. 174.

83. De Felice, *Jews in an Arab Land,* p. 374, n. 56, quoting a letter from U. Nahon to R. Cantoni, 2 April 1948, with regard to 'Amrus: "girls, naturally, remain illiterate."

(97 boys and 60[!] girls). It was reported that "for the time being, he [i.e., Zuarez] teaches only the boys, because in their condition today [1943] he cannot do anything for the girls, and they do not study." Later on, however, girls were included in this school, but exact data on their enrollment and studies were not provided.[84]

In Zliten (east of Khoms), too, the inclusion of girls was connected with innovation in teaching in the Hebrew school. In 1943, Tzuri'el Shaked, one of Zuarez's students, established a Hebrew school for both sexes in Zliten. Local Jewish girls, who until then could not read or write Hebrew, studied Hebrew and Jewish studies in school for the first time. The girls studied separately from the boys, and their classes took place in the evening because of the lack of teachers. The director was assisted in his educational activities by his wife, Esther. She had graduated from the teachers' course that had been organized by the Jewish soldiers in Tripoli and became a teacher in the Hebrew school there before moving to Zliten.[85]

A Hebrew school was also established in Barce, with the active participation of the Jewish soldiers in the initial stages. In 1945, this school included seventy pupils of both sexes, but no details were provided on their distribution according to sex and age or on the indigenous teachers.[86]

In 1947, there were seventy-five Jewish children of both sexes in the local government Italian-language school in Zawiya. In the afternoon, these children complemented their studies with Hebrew and Jewish subjects in the local synagogue.[87]

CONCLUDING REMARKS

The major development in Jewish female education during the time of the BMA was their incorporation into the community-based education system. This was in large part due to the modernization process of the community, which was manifested by the establishment of the Hebrew

---

84. "Yoman Ṭripoliṭani," *Milḥamtenu* 8 (July 1943): 26; Zuarez et al., *Yahadut Luv*, p. 178 (my translation).

85. Zuarez et al., *Yahadut Luv*, p. 180.

86. Masaud Bugattus, Barce, to the Youth Department/Religious Division, Jerusalem, 22 Av 5705 (31 July 1945), CZA, S32/952.

87. S. Bukris, Zawiya, to the Histadrut [Association of Jewish Workers in Palestine], 22 May 1947, CZA, S32/123.

schools, which operated according to pedagogic principles and curriculum of the Hebrew schools in Palestine. These operations increased the number of Jewish girls who went to school in the urban centers and in the countryside, where very few Jewish girls had attended school before. Furthermore, the teaching staff of the new system was trained by educators from Palestine and consisted mainly of indigenous women. As a result, women had a greater role in shaping the character of the future generation. They also strengthened their position in the community organization, although their representation in the decision-making process was still not in proportion to their participation. Nonetheless, in some organizations where the role of women was dominant, such as in the Jewish teachers' association, it became impossible to ignore them when the time came to fill leadership positions.

As a result of the mass emigration of Libyan Jews in the middle of the twentieth century and the establishment of an independent Arab kingdom in Libya, there was a steady decline in Jewish education in the region. Following the departure of the community leaders and teachers, community services, including education, were virtually nonexistent, and with the closure of the AIU school in 1960, comprehensive Jewish education in Libya came to an end. The only Jewish education that remained was the preparation of boys for their Bar Mitzvah ceremony by private tutors. Thus, Jewish education in the second half of the twentieth century became even more uncommon than it had been during the Ottoman period. This does not mean that the cultural level of the Libyan Jews deteriorated, but their culture became less Jewish. The rich Italianized families who remained in Libya made sure that their children—boys and girls alike—were educated in Italian schools in Libya and in Italy, but the emphasis shifted from Jewish to general studies.

One can observe some dramatic developments in Jewish female education in Libya during the nineteenth–twentieth centuries. From a state of being barely educated, Jewish females were trained in Western crafts, received Western education, and later made up most of the teaching staff of the Hebrew educational network. During all these phases, female education was connected with Western and modern educational trends. Thus, because women were deprived of Jewish education during most of the period under discussion, all those females who studied participated only in Western and Zionist education, namely, in the most advanced educational systems existing in Libya at the time with regard to cultural context, pedagogic principles and methods, and social and political ideas. Jewish priorities and the status of the individual in the family and in the society at large continued to be male oriented, but the growing identification of women with modernizing trends gradually modified these traditional attitudes.

❖ FIVE ❖

Participation in Public Life

❖

The involvement of Jewish women in public life in Libya was limited and was usually restricted to Jewish society. Despite their
improved education and their growing economic role, the social and
political status of Libyan Jewish women changed only slightly within
the family circle and even less outside it. Women's participation in
public life did, however, witness some gradual changes during the nineteenth and twentieth centuries. The areas and the amount of their involvement, the types of activities undertaken, and the number of
women involved all grew.

RELIGIOUS LIFE

According to Jewish rabbinic law, women are not required to participate in the service in the synagogue. As a result, during most of the
Ottoman period, Jewish women in Libya did not participate in public
prayer in the synagogue. For that reason, most of the synagogues in the
villages and those built before the nineteenth century did not have a
special section for women (*'ezrat nashim*). Women did, however, attend
the services at the synagogue, especially on the Sabbath and holidays,

and watched the Torah scroll when it was publicly displayed. Where there was no women's section, they had to observe the proceedings from outside, peering in through the windows or doors. Women also helped to found synagogues and were very active in their maintenance. In addition, they participated in religious activities outside the synagogue and often expressed their feelings and devotion through wailing and fasting.

Many synagogues in Libya built or renovated since the nineteenth century had a separate section for women. This section was usually separated from the main hall by windows through which women could observe the service and watch the Torah scroll.[1] Women used to go to the synagogue not only on Saturdays and holidays but also on the first day of each month. On these days they would spread their arms toward the scroll in supplication for long life and sustenance for themselves and their families.

It was repeatedly pointed out that the reason for women's religious behavior was that they did not know how to read and pray properly from a book.[2] The customs of Dar Barukh synagogue (established in Tripoli in 1830) were an exception. It had an *'ezrat nashim* in which European women read prayers from books, in contrast to the local women, who just used gestures and customary sayings as their way of praying. When the indigenous women saw their European counterparts praying from books, they mocked and insulted them.[3]

It was customary to bring all Jewish children—sons as well as young daughters—to the synagogue for the closing ceremony of the Day of Atonement (Yom Kippur) for the "priests' blessing" (*birkat kohanim*). According to the reports, people assembled in extended-family groups, with the eldest man surrounded by his sons and they by theirs, each putting his hands on the prayer shawl (*talit*) on his children's heads. Adult sons participated, but only small girls (probably only those who had not reached puberty). They stayed like this until the end of the

---

1. In Khoms and in Benghazi during the Ottoman period, a special section in the attic from which the women could observe the service was used for this purpose (see Ha-Cohen, *Higgid Mordecai*, pp. 325, 337).

2. Ibid., pp. 192, 248, 253. It was not customary for the Jewish women of Libya to listen to the reading of the Scroll of Esther during Purim in the synagogue, and instead they heard it only at home at night while they were fasting (ibid., p. 159).

3. Ibid., pp. 248–49. It is quite possible that this behavior, which was observed during the late Ottoman period, gradually stopped during the twentieth century, when the educational level of the Tripolitan women had improved.

recital of the blessing. During that event, mothers and grandmothers observed the ceremony from their special section in the synagogue or from outside and whispered blessings toward their children.[4]

Jewish women were quite active in religious life outside the synagogue. During funerals, they would wail and hit themselves, often exposing their hair. Quite a few rabbis complained that women mixed with men during the excitement of a funeral.[5] At the end of the seven days of mourning, it was customary for everyone in the deceased's family to wash in cold water and to put on newly laundered clothing. A similar custom was performed on the Ninth of Av (the day commemorating the destruction of the Temple in Jerusalem), but then they would wash in warm water. Women, however, washed their hair in warm water even after mourning, because it was impossible to comb if it was washed in cold water. Consequently, women had to continue their mourning if the last day of mourning occurred on the Sabbath, because they could not wash their hair in warm water on that day, even if the water was preheated the day before.[6] In Mislata, Jewish women used to gather on the eve of the Ninth of Av to wail for the dead and to seek their help.[7]

Most references to the Tripolitan Jewish burial society, the Ḥevrah Qadisha (Holy Society), concerned its male members. Women also participated in the activities of this society, but details on their numbers and organization have not been provided. The female members of the burial society participated in a limited number of its activities, and only in those that demanded close handling of the corpses of women. Thus, women alone dealt with the "purification" (*ṭohorah*) of deceased women.

Twice a year, on the last day of Sukkot and the last day of Passover, the community of Tripoli prepared a special festive meal, referred to as "the meal of Rabbi Gershon," for the members of the burial society. The members received food and liquor (*'araq*) and enjoyed themselves for several hours, eating, drinking, and singing. Some liquor was also sent to their homes—of males and females alike—and their neighbors (of both sexes) used to taste it, believing that this would help to ensure

4. Zuarez et al., *Yahadut Luv*, p. 370.

5. Ha-Cohen, *Ḥiggid Mordecai*, pp. 218–19; Abravanel, "Les Juifs," pp. 24–25.

6. Ha-Cohen, *Ḥiggid Mordecai*, pp. 219–20; T. Sutton, "La mort chez les Israélites tripolitains," *Revue des Ecoles de l'Alliance Israélite Universelle* 4 (1902): 263–64.

7. Slousch, *Travels*, p. 60.

longevity.[8] Since even men and women of the same family usually did not eat together at home, it seems unlikely that women participated in "the meal of Rabbi Gershon" with nonrelated males; they probably had to content themselves with the liquor that was sent to their homes.

Another custom connected with burial ceremonies was that during the funeral processions of old and pious Jewish men (but apparently not women), the women would pick up small pieces of the shrouds and take some of the *ḥumus* (chick-peas) and liquor that had been distributed during the funeral. These souvenirs were believed to be omens for long and healthy life, and mothers used to give these objects to their sons (but apparently not to their daughters) for that reason.[9]

Many ceremonies in Libya were connected with the dead and their graves. Jewish women visited the graves of relatives regularly, usually on Fridays. They would place lime on the grave, decorate and whitewash the gravestone, plant flowers around it, and keep the vicinity clean and tidy.[10] In addition to family gatherings around the tombs of relatives, there were also tombs whose occupants were worshiped by most of the Jews and often also by the Muslims. Among these graves were the ones attributed to two followers of the seventeenth-century false messiah, Shabetai Zevi.[11] Libyan Jews used to light candles in Shabetai Zevi's honor in the synagogue, and women often pledged oil for this purpose. Furthermore, many mothers named their sons after him. According to Rabbi Zion Vaturi (died 1911), there was a candle in honor of "Shabetai, the son of Tziva" in the old Tripolitan synagogue al-Thalithah. Women would light the candle and sing from the "Song of the Book" (Ghina ha-Sefer), referring to Shabetai Zevi: "Ḥanūn yā Raḥmān, jib al-Mashiyāḥ wa-maʿahu Natan. / Wa-yarūḥ kull ahwān, nuwallihu naḥkamu maʿa sulṭān" ("You are the Merciful and Forgiver, send the Messiah together with Natan. / And the sorrows of the time will pass, and we will return and rule with the sultan"). Rabbis were opposed to this and other instances of saint worship and tried to stop it or at least alter it. Thus, in 1860 the rabbinical judge Abraham Adadi (died 1864) changed some words of the song, and instead of "wa-maʿahu Natan" he inserted "wa-

---

8. Zuarez et al., *Yahadut Luv*, p. 397. On the role of the burial society in general, see *Encyclopaedia Judaica*, s.v. "Ḥevra Kaddisha."

9. Zuarez et al., *Yahadut Luv*, p. 398.

10. Tully, *Ten Years*, p. 121.

11. On Shabetai Zevi (1626–76) in general, see *Encyclopaedia Judaica*, s.v. "Shabbetai Zevi."

Livyātān" ("and Leviathan").[12] These worship activities, however, did not cease, and when Rabbi Khmus Fallaḥ (died 1941) heard the women sing in praise of "Shabetai, the son of Tziva," he broke the candle and reproached them.[13] It seems that despite the attempts of renowned rabbis to stop the worship of Shabetai Zevi in Tripoli, Jews—and women in particular—continued to worship him.

Another way in which Jewish women demonstrated their deep devotion was through their involvement in the celebration of religious holidays. Women had an important role in ceremonies that were held at home in connection with these festivals. Their main contribution was in the preparation of special dishes and sending portions of them as gifts to relatives, friends, and the poor. There were special foods that mothers used to send to their married daughters on the festivals of Hanukka, Purim, and Shavu'ot. Jewish women were also very active, even more so than men, in sending gifts during the festival of Purim, including donations to the poor and for the Land of Israel funds.[14] These ceremonies, dishes, and presents usually had symbolic meanings, which transformed the physical action into a spiritual one.

Women were seldom involved in the establishment of synagogues in Tripoli and in the countryside due to their inferior position in economic affairs. Nevertheless, the fact that a few women did establish synagogues proves that some of them were able to dispense their money as they pleased. It seems that all of those involved were widows. Thus, for example, the Dar Shweykah synagogue in Tripoli was established by a woman named Shweykah of the Guetta family, which stemmed from Yefren. She gave her house as an endowment, and in 1816 it became a permanent praying place. Later, it was officially established as a synagogue.[15] This case is unique in that the synagogue was named after a woman. Two other synagogues were established by widows: in Tripoli, the Ṭayyar synagogue was founded by the widow of Rabbi Ḥizqiyah

12. Leviathan is the name of a legendary monster often connected with the otherworld. Natan ha-ʿAzati (of Ghaza) was one of the main followers of Shabetai Zevi. Substituting "Leviathan" for "Natan" made the verse more general and not specific to a certain messiah (in this case, Shabetai Zevi).

13. Ha-Cohen, *Higgid Mordecai,* p. 93; Zuarez et al., *Yahadut Luv,* p. 389.

14. Ha-Cohen, *Higgid Mordecai,* p. 198; Zuarez et al., *Yahadut Luv,* pp. 372–74. The latter source includes a description of the celebration of the "Night of the Bsisa" (a dish of wheat, barley, honey, etc.) on the eve of the month of Nisan and the woman's role in it.

15. Ha-Cohen, *Higgid Mordecai,* p. 248; Zuarez et al., *Yahadut Luv,* p. 115. By gathering to pray at a private home, Jews could circumvent the Muslim prohibition on the establishment of new synagogues.

Ṭayyar,[16] and in Zliten, a synagogue was established in 1892 with a contribution of 600 francs by Ḥidriyah, the widow of Eliyahu Khalfon.[17]

The adoration of the Torah scroll and other holy scriptures as well as objects connected with them played a very important role in the religious life of the Jewish women of Libya well into the twentieth century. This attitude was observed not only in the synagogue but also in daily life, especially in connection with childbirth and childrearing. Thus, in Tripoli an ancient Torah scroll from Yefren served as a talisman for women who had difficulties in giving birth.[18] When a baby began teething, the mother would rush to the nearest synagogue and borrow the "Silver Hand" with which the reader of the Torah points at the words during the service. The mother would rub the pointer over the baby's gums, trusting that this action would soften them so that the teeth would grow out without causing any pain. On other occasions, when the baby was asleep in its cradle and the mother had to leave it alone for a while, she would put a Pentateuch, a prayer book, or a prayer shawl and phylacteries (*tefilin*) next to the baby's head.[19] Mothers believed that this would protect the baby while they were away. When a boy reached school age, his mother took him and a hard-boiled first-laid chicken egg to the rabbi. The rabbi wrote on the egg the first letters of the words of the sentence starting "Moses ordered us the Torah." The boy recited the sentence word for word after the rabbi and ate the egg. The rabbi then took a Pentateuch and hit the boy lightly on the head with it. This act was repeated by the other pupils, so that "the Torah will enter his head."

Religious fasting and "self-tormenting" (*'inuyim,* i.e., self-denial such as abstaining from washing themselves, sex, etc.) were very popular among Libyan Jews, and especially among women. In addition to the customary days of fasting, women also usually fasted during the two days of the New Year and for one day at the beginning of every month (New Month); some also fasted and "tormented" themselves on the evenings prior to the New Year, the Day of Atonement, the Ninth of Av, and New Month. Sometimes they also fasted on Mondays, Thurs-

16. Zuarez et al., *Yahadut Luv,* p. 121.
17. Ha-Cohen, *Higgid Mordecai,* p. 327.
18. Ibid., p. 266.
19. Zuarez et al., *Yahadut Luv,* p. 391. For an interpretation of the giving of the Torah pointer to a teething male baby as a symbolic phallic (male reproductive) oral transmission, see H. E. Goldberg, "Torah and Children: Symbolic Aspects of the Reproduction of Jews and Judaism," in *Judaism Viewed from Within and from Without,* edited by H. E. Goldberg (Albany: State University of New York Press, 1987), pp. 114–15.

days, and even for a whole week at a time, especially during the first week of the month of Elul.[20] Thus, although Jewish women did not participate in the more scholarly aspects of religious life, they were very active in expressing their beliefs through physical manifestations, either bodily or verbal.

Synagogue maintenance was mainly in the hands of women. On the eves of the Sabbath and holidays, Jewish women, often elderly ones, would sweep and wash the synagogue floors, clean the candles, prepare the wicks, and burn them with donated olive oil. Women who lived in the neighborhood of a synagogue brought the workers some samples of the food that they had prepared for the Sabbath or the holiday, together with some coffee and even brandy. All these women would celebrate in front of the closed cupboard (*heykhal*) in which the Torah scroll was kept by singing special hymns composed by women in honor of the Torah from the "Song of the Book."[21] On this and on other occasions, women would light candles and burn incense in honor of the Torah.[22] This was the closest women ever came to the Torah scroll. They believed, however, that the Torah scroll would protect them and their families, thanks to their closeness to it, their maintenance activities in the holy place surrounding this sacred object, and their numerous blessings, requests, and songs relating to the Torah. Honoring the Torah scroll was also manifested through adoration of those people who devoted their lives to its study. Thus, for example, in some privately funded yeshivot, female members of the donor families used to welcome the students who studied there and occasionally also provided them with food and drink.[23]

Most of these religious practices were customary throughout the period under study. It appears that although Jewish women did not participate in the official religious activities, which were organized by the community and took place in the synagogue, they were very much involved in nonformal and popular religious events inside and outside the synagogue. At the center of most of their religious acts was the veneration of sacred objects or the men closely related to those objects.

20. Ha-Cohen, *Higgid Mordecai*, pp. 191, 253, 287; Zuarez et al., *Yahadut Luv*, pp. 368–70, 373. See Tully, *Ten Years*, pp. 48–49, for an account of a Jewish maid in Tripoli in 1783 who fainted after three days of her attempt to conceal a week-long fast.

21. Ha-Cohen, *Higgid Mordecai*, p. 254; Zuarez et al., *Yahadut Luv*, pp. 387–88.

22. Tully, *Ten Years*, p. 279.

23. Zuarez et al., *Yahadut Luv*, pp. 99, 102.

First and foremost was the Torah scroll, followed by other objects (e.g., the Silver Hand and prayer books) and people (e.g., saints and rabbinic scholars) related to it. Jewish women and the whole society (Jewish and Muslim alike) believed that these objects and people had supernatural powers, which could be invoked for a general purpose (longevity, happiness, prosperity, etc.) and for specific cases (illness, infertility, etc.). Women's worship involved physical and verbal, but not scholarly, expressions and was manifested through fasting and self-torment; maintaining holy places and objects; blessing, praising, and singing in honor of holy objects and thus invoking their supernatural powers; participating in ceremonies; and preparing special dishes for these events and holidays. Although women were prevented from a scholarly expression of their beliefs, most Jewish men were in effect in a similar situation. The men participated in the service at the synagogue, but many of them did not understand the meaning of the Hebrew and Aramaic texts, and thus, their worship only appeared to be more scholarly than that of women; in reality it was not.

WELFARE ACTIVITIES AND WOMEN'S ORGANIZATIONS

Until the 1830s, charity (*tzedaqah*) was a matter of voluntary almsgiving by individuals (some of whom were quite poor themselves). The occasions for giving were usually special events in the donor's family or religious holidays.[24] This type of traditional welfare continued into the twentieth century parallel in Tripoli and some other places to centralized, institutionalized welfare.

In 1832, numerous Tripolitan Jews fled to the island of Jerba because of hostilities back home. Being in severe economic straits and excluded from the Jerban community services, the Tripolitans decided to adopt the system used by the Jerban Jews to help the Jerban poor. They established a welfare fund based on a special tax (*qabilah*) on kosher-slaughtered meat and on donations for reciting the Torah at the synagogue. They brought this system with them when they returned to Tripoli, and it was adopted by other communities (e.g., 'Amrus and Khoms). In the course of time, additional sources of income were found, and taxation was systematized. Thus, during the 1850s, it was

24. Ha-Cohen, *Higgid Mordecai*, pp. 190–93, 197–99, 215, 219, 274. On welfare practices in Judaism in general, see *Encyclopaedia Judaica*, s.v. "Charity."

customary for a special tax collector to check the accounts of the Tripolitan merchants and take 5 percent of their weekly revenues for the welfare fund, and in the 1870s, Tripolitans paid one thousandth of the money involved in each business transaction to the welfare fund. In some more remote communities (e.g., Gharyan and Yefren), however, an institutionalized welfare system did not develop, because it was considered shameful to rely on the public for aid.[25]

The participation of Libyan Jewish women in social and cultural women's organizations was not very common, and their involvement in mixed associations or in paid welfare activity was even more limited. Mainly upper-class and upper-middle-class women were members of women's organizations, but many other Jews, including men, benefited from their services. Participation in these organizations and in the more loosely operated traditional projects was totally voluntary.[26] To a certain degree this restricted the membership of the modern organizations to the wealthier women, who could spend more money and time for the benefit of others. On the other hand, the whole community used to participate in the older, more traditional welfare funds (*qupot tzedaqah, gemilut ḥasadim*, etc.).

Jewish women in the urban and rural regions of Libya were active throughout the period in the traditional collection of donations for welfare activities. They did this for causes related to the general public and for particular groups (e.g., women, students, inhabitants of specific towns in Libya or Palestine). Some of the traditional funds were run almost exclusively by women. Thus, for example, mainly women donated to Our Mother Rachel Treasury, which financed Sephardic yeshivot in Jerusalem. Female collectors regarded it as a special honor to be responsible for this operation, and even old and fragile women did not let this opportunity be wasted. These women went out to collect contributions on the eve of every New Month, believing that it would protect them in their daily life. The money thus collected was considered sacred, and it was forbidden to take any of it except for special cases

25. Ha-Cohen, *Higgid Mordecai,* pp. 148–49, 241–42, 288, 320, 324; Benjamin, *Eight Years,* pp. 286–87; Rae, *The Country of the Moors,* p. 98; S. Mendelssohn, *The Jews of Africa* (London: Kegan Paul, 1920), p. 77.

26. Only a few details were provided on the size and socioeconomic breakdown of their membership. On the absence of paid communal operators (*'asqanim*) of both sexes and its implication for the leadership of the community and for welfare and educational activities, see "Yehudey Tripoli," p. 25. Women's organizations among the Libyan Muslims were established only in the 1960s (Attir, "Ideology," p. 124).

of great need, when one could get a "loan" from it.[27] Rabbinical emissaries (*shadarim*) from the yeshivot in Palestine came to collect the money. No record was kept of the donations or their distribution, and everything was based on complete trust.

In many cases donors did not even know to whom the contribution went (such a donation was called *matan ba-seter,* "secret donation") and trusted the collector that it was for a just cause, because no one dared to cheat in this matter. The readiness of community members to volunteer to run these collections and to donate to them was not dependent on wealth, and as a matter of fact, most of the people who were involved in these operations were poor.[28]

Women also were involved in collecting donations for dowries for poor women. The most common instrument for this was a special society caring for poor maidens, Mohar ha-Betulot (Bride-Price for the Virgins).[29] Among the women who were especially noted for their role in these collections was Esther Gian (often referred to as Immi Esther, "My Mother Esther"). She also became responsible for Our Mother Rachel Treasury following a dream she had and she continued in this task for more than forty years, at first in her home town of Misrata and later in Ashdod, after she emigrated to Israel. Women used to come to her in both places and bring her their donations.[30]

During World War I, the economic condition of the Tripolitan community deteriorated due to the war activities and the isolation of the Italian-held areas. In addition, numerous Jewish refugees fled from the countryside, which was under Arab and Berber control. Many of these Jews poured into Tripoli, and many were destitute. The Tripolitan Jewish leadership as well as the women—as individuals and organizations— took it upon themselves to look after all the needs (food, clothing, housing, education, etc.) of these refugees, and especially of the children. One of the women who was particularly involved in this activity was Turkiyah Ḥaddad. She brought dozens of children into her home,

27. On taking "loans" for worthy causes from the collection until the arrival of the Shadar, see Zuarez and Tayyar, *Ḥokhmat Nashim,* pp. 9–11.

28. Zuarez et al., *Yahadut Luv,* pp. 399, 420; F. Zuarez, *Anshey Emunah* (Tel-Aviv: Va'ad Qehilot Luv be-Yisra'el, 1983).

29. See chap. 2 on marriage. *Hakhnasat Kallah* was a rabbinic commandment to provide dowries for brides and to rejoice at their weddings. The term is popularly applied to the provision of dowries for poor brides. On the traditional Jewish custom of "Bringing in the Bride," see *Encyclopaedia Judaica,* s.v. "Hakhnasat Kallah."

30. Zuarez and Tayyar, *Ḥokhmat Nashim,* pp. 12–13.

took care of all their needs, and found a teacher for them. She made sure that these boys (no mention of girls was made) did not have to work and could study full time.[31]

A new sort of organization, based on a European model, began to emerge in the mid-1890s among Jews with cultural, social, and economic ties with Europe. In late 1895, following the outbreak of a severe plague, a Women's Benevolent Society, 'Ezrat Nashim, was established by several well-to-do Jewish women in Tripoli.[32] Its immediate aim was to fight the plague, and its operations were geared to the community as a whole. A clinic was set up and equipped with all the required medical personnel, equipment, and facilities. The society also arranged for shipments of medicine and physicians from Europe. The physicians worked at the society's clinic and visited the sick in their homes. The needy sick were treated for free, and the expenses were covered by 'Ezrat Nashim. In addition, the members of this society participated in person in the health care activities. They set up daily shifts and visited the houses of the sick. In this they resembled the traditional Jewish institution that took care of the sick and visited them in their homes, Bikkur Ḥolim. However, with 'Ezrat Nashim, the interclass interaction was more evident. Unlike the members of Bikkur Ḥolim, who were from all social classes, the members of 'Ezrat Nashim were from the upper classes and did not otherwise have much contact with the poor elements of Tripolitan Jewry. Therefore, their participation brought them into closer relations with hitherto lesser known segments of the community. Due to the extreme severity of the plague and the scarcity of modern medical facilities in Tripoli, the activities of 'Ezrat Nashim were of great importance to the community, and many benefited.

Another project of 'Ezrat Nashim did not enjoy similar success. Their attempt to establish a hospital in 1899 failed because people were not accustomed to leaving their homes and staying in special places that

31. On Turkiyah Ḥaddad and on the welfare activities of Rachel Na'im, see Zuarez and Tayyar, *Ḥokhmat Nashim*, pp. 17, 20.

32. The name has a double meaning: (1) women's section in the synagogue and (2) women's help. There are several reports in the AIU archives on the activities of this society. See especially D. Arie, Tripoli, to AIU, Paris, 28 October 1895, AAIU, IIE-6a; the same, 8 March, 5 May, 22 November 1896 (Annual Report), 18 February 1897, AAIU, IIE-6b. On 22 November 1896 the board of the society included Esther Arie as president, Fortune Arbib as vice-president, Elisa Silva as secretary, Rachel Arbib as treasurer, and Rosina Hassan, Carolina Nunes Vais, Djara Guetta, Emilia Tayyar, and Emilia Arbib as board members.

treated sick people.[33] Whereas visiting the clinic might have been considered the same as visiting a physician, moving to stay in a house full of sick people was regarded as too risky and dangerous. For instance, quarantines were infamous in that those who were subjected to them very rarely survived. Similarly, the traditional Jewish institution of *heqdesh,* which accommodated and treated sick people, was mainly for the most destitute and transients, and thus it was shameful to have to go there.

Even in its early stages, the women's society participated in some activities that were geared specifically toward women. Thus, following the establishment of the AIU girls school in late 1896, a member of the society would visit the school every day during the vocational training classes to provide whatever assistance was needed and to supervise the progress of the pupils.[34] The initiative for this was apparently taken by the director of the AIU girls school, Esther Arie, who was also the first president of the society.

The forty women who joined the society tried to find other means of income in addition to their monthly dues of 1 franc. To this end, they organized a ball, which brought in 570 francs. They also tried to get money from rich Tripolitans at home and abroad but were not too successful in this venture. They also solicited grants from Jewish philanthropists, and they received 3,000 francs from the Baroness Hirsch.[35]

Most of the reports on ʿEzrat Nashim are from the second half of the 1890s, and it is difficult to assess its activities and impact after that period. From the reports at hand one can conclude that the membership of this organization was limited in number and from upper-class or upper-middle-class backgrounds. It appears that the membership did not grow much beyond the first forty members and had strong cultural connections with Europe. The last characteristic was best demonstrated by the society's first president, Esther Arie, the director of the AIU girls school, and the board member Carolina Nunes Vais, the director of the Italian girls school, both of whom grew up in Europe. It is interesting to note that despite the rivalry between the two foreign educational

33. Ha-Cohen, *Higgid Mordecai,* pp. 242–43. The attempt to establish a hospital also suffered from financial problems. See "Ha-Yehudim bi-Ṭripoli shel Afriqah," p. 204. See also *Encyclopaedia Judaica,* s.v. "Hekdesh."

34. D. Arie, Tripoli, to AIU, Paris, 8 April 1897, AAIU, IIE-6b.

35. Invoices of the society to the Baroness Hirsch for sums of 1,000 francs (17 November 1898) and 2,000 francs (5 November 1899), AAIU, IIE-6c; Ha-Cohen, *Higgid Mordecai,* pp. 242–43.

networks, senior figures from both parties cooperated in this society, whose goal was the welfare of the community as a whole.

The innovative approach of the ʿEzrat Nashim was demonstrated in its activities in the medical and educational fields. It was set up mainly to answer an immediate problem: the plague of 1895. The society's response to the plague was based on traditional grounds but developed in more modern directions. They used European medicine (both physicians and drugs) for fighting the plague and applied it in two ways. The more traditional method was visits by the physicians and society members to the patients' homes. In addition, a clinic was set up to which patients could come to receive treatment. In both cases, modern European medicine was used. It seems that after using this double system for a while, the society thought that the community was ready for a further step, namely, the opening of a hospital. This idea, however, did not find favor in Tripoli at the time.

The innovative nature of ʿEzrat Nashim was also manifested in its involvement in the vocational training at the AIU girls school. The society supported female education in general and vocational training in particular to improve the economic condition of the community as a whole and also to ameliorate the position of Jewish women.

Post-Ottoman Libya saw the establishment of several Jewish women's organizations. These societies were set up mainly in Tripoli, and their aim was to advance the position of Jewish women and to improve their economic, social, and cultural status. Whereas the influence of the AIU was strongly felt in ʿEzrat Nashim during the late Ottoman period, the Italian character of women's societies became dominant under Italian rule.

The first society to be mentioned during the Italian period was the Società Ebraica Femminile (SEF, Jewish Women's Society), which established a special institution, Lavoro e Virtù (Work and Virtue), on 7 May 1912 to provide special programs such as vocational training. The founders of Lavoro e Virtù included members of the Levy, Nunes Vais, Arbib, Nahum, Hajjaj, Silva, and Fresco families of Tripoli, which were among the more influential in the economic and social spheres.[36] The goals of

36. The first president of the society was Fortune Arbib (born 4 April 1856; died 19 March 1928); she was followed by Lidia Arbib Nahum. The secretary was Bianca Nunes Vais Arbib (born 18 December 1884), who was also active in the Italian committee organized by the newspaper *L'Eco di Tripoli* for the support of the air force. This is a rare example of a Jewish woman's involvement in a non-Jewish organization in Libya.

SEF were to support poor Jews in Tripoli, help women (including poor brides), and educate the youth. One of their projects was a sewing workshop for women. Despite its importance for the community, this enterprise suffered from inadequate economic support and had to close down in 1922, but the SEF was able to open a similar workshop somewhat later. The SEF collaborated with the AIU in these activities and acknowledged the important assistance of the latter to the poor and the youth of Tripoli. In 1941, three Jewish women's organizations were in existence in Tripoli, all of them headed by Lidia Arbib Nahum: the SEF, the sewing workshop, and the Associazione Donne Ebree d'Italia (ADEI, Association of Italian Jewish Women).[37] There was also an ADEI branch in Benghazi, which was headed by Jole Arbib.

From the scant descriptions of Jewish women's organizations during the Italian period, it seems that they tried to improve the economic condition of the community by establishing workshops for women to train them in European-style sewing. These activities were apparently not connected with attempts to combine vocational training with academic studies. It is, however, of interest to note that some of the leaders of these groups were also involved in broader activities within Italian society and tried to integrate the Libyan Jewish women into the organizational frameworks of Italian Jewish women. Just as the Jewish communities of Libya became part of the Board of Italian Jewish Communities, so were the Libyan Jewish women's organizations to become part of the wider ADEI. The membership of Jewish women's organizations in Libya during the Italian period consisted mainly of women with Italian background (through family connections and education). They were interested in strengthening their Italian identity as well as improving the condition of Jewish women in Libya. Those who used the services provided by these societies, mainly through the workshops, were mostly from the lower classes, whose cultural and social contacts with the Italian world were weaker and whose outlook was more traditional. Still, it is quite possible that by opting to go to these workshops, the more traditional Libyan Jewish women showed that they, too, wanted to become more involved in a modernized, Italianized environment.

37. The relations between the three Tripolitan groups and their respective activities are not clear. Levy, "Tripoli," p. 207; Raccah, *Lunario,* pp. 10–11, 15–16, 18; *Ḥayenu,* 25 January 1951; L. Nahum, Tripoli, to AIU, Paris, 24 August 1933, AAIU, IB-19; B. Nunes Vais Arbib, "Gli Ebrei di Tripoli," CAHJP, MS. P-66, pp. 9–10; De Felice, *Jews in an Arab Land,* pp. 361–62, n. 47.

During the BMA period in Libya, the Tripolitan women's organizations were in contact with the Women's International Zionist Organization (WIZO).[38] With the renewal of organizational activities in the Jewish communities of Libya after World War II, a branch of WIZO was established in Tripoli in mid-1944. It consisted of two divisions. The first was the "regular" WIZO, which had some preliminary operational difficulties due to personal conflicts among its members. The second was "Young WIZO," which included about thirty young women. It was apparently more active than the regular branch, and among its programs was the study of Hebrew.[39] Once the Zionist focus became dominant and emigration to Israel was imminent, the women's organizations became one of the tools to prepare the community for this comprehensive change. The local WIZO chapter also provided assistance to the members of the pioneering movement he-Ḥalutz, who established an agricultural training farm near Tripoli in the summer of 1944.[40] These activities were in marked contrast to those of the women's organizations during the Italian period, which wanted to become closer to the Italian world. This trend was in line with the general direction of the community at the time, which was characterized by increasing identity with Zionist ideas.

The members of WIZO apparently did not meet too often, but they participated in welfare operations for the community as a whole. Thus, for example, following the November 1945 riots, they received basic training in first aid each Saturday afternoon from Dr. Andrea Vitterbo and helped those Jews who were hospitalized because of their wounds.[41] Thus, the character of the Jewish women's organizations during the 1940s was basically Zionist, and their activities (e.g., studying Hebrew, helping he-Ḥalutz and Jews wounded in confrontations with the Arabs) were highly influenced by their national aspirations.

During the mass emigration to Israel in 1949–51, the activities of Libyan Jewish women's organizations decreased. Nonetheless, they con-

38. L. Nahum, Tripoli, to WIZO, London, 22 November 1945, CZA, S6/1984. It is not clear whether the term *WIZO* used by Jewish Palestinian soldiers and Libyan Jews alike to refer to women's organizations in Tripoli actually referred to one of the indigenous organizations or to a Libyan branch of WIZO. The term is found several times in the records after mid-1944.

39. Yariv, Summer 1944, CZA, S6/1984.

40. *Ḥayenu* (Tammuz 5704 [Summer 1944]), pp. 3–4. On he-Ḥalutz and female involvement in it, see next section.

41. E. ʿAzarya, Tripoli, to the Youth Department, Jerusalem, 28 December 1945, CZA, S32/1068.

tinued to support the JNF and communal issues until the establishment of the independent Arab kingdom of Libya (end of 1951),[42] when Zionist activities were outlawed. Because most of the leadership of the community left and those who remained were mainly the rich Italianized families, there was not much need for welfare projects (which were provided mostly by the AJDC) or much desire for Jewish cultural activities. As a result, activities organized by Libyan Jewish women virtually ceased in the 1950s.

Libyan Jewish women's organizations emphasized social and economic issues. The cultural and political nature of these organizations changed, however, over time, with the focus shifting from a French to an Italian and, finally, to a Hebrew-Zionist character. During most of the period the women's organizations assisted the sick and the poor by providing European medical treatment and instruction in profitable modern professions. Only in the late 1940s did the members themselves participate in cultural activities organized by these societies: until that time they essentially provided services for those who were at a lower economic level, and they did not deem it necessary to advance themselves culturally.

The main difference between traditional almsgiving and the newer charitable organizations was that the latter emphasized vocational training, academic education, and modern medicine as ways to ameliorate the economic and physical conditions of the poor and the sick, in addition to traditional almsgiving. The modern organizations attempted to provide long-term solutions to fundamental social and cultural problems, mainly through instruction. The traditional welfare system, on the other hand, contributed money or materials to a specific religious, social, or cultural institution or cause and answered the immediate needs of particular individuals. Consequently, the two systems differed in their organizational frameworks and the types of obligations they demanded from their members, in donations and volunteer work alike.

SPORT AND YOUTH MOVEMENTS

In the early 1920s, Libyan Jewish youth and young adults began to be involved in social and cultural clubs and associations that were based on European models. This was influenced mainly by the growing Italian

---

42. *Ḥayenu*, 25 January 1951.

presence in Libya following the 1911 occupation. Jewish recreational organizations for the youth were especially popular in Tripoli but were also established elsewhere in the 1930s and particularly during the 1940s. Along with the European-type youth organizations, the traditional societies geared for the youth continued to exist and new ones were founded. The main difference between these two types of organizations was that the traditional ones emphasized Jewish scholarship, ritual, and piety (e.g., reciting Psalms and singing in synagogue choirs), whereas the new organizations focused on recreational activities (e.g., sports and parties) and later also on Zionism and comprehensive preparation for immigration to Palestine. Gender also became a source of difference. The traditional youth organizations were solely masculine, whereas females played a growing role in the modern societies. When the new organizations were established, their first members were all males, but female relatives gradually joined the members for special events. During the 1930s, new cultural and social trends were connected with the study of Hebrew, the spread of Zionism, and the growing pioneering spirit. As a result, girls and young women became more involved in these organizations in their own right, and all the modern clubs eventually had female members. In keeping with the traditional character of the place, however, most organizations conducted separate activities according to sex, although some events, especially on the weekends, were for mixed groups. The leaders of these societies were usually male; in the 1940s a few organizations had one or two women on their boards, but they served mostly in the lower ranks.

Maccabi

The oldest Jewish sports organization in Libya was the Maccabi club, which was established in Tripoli in 1920.[43] During the 1920s and the 1930s membership included only males. Nevertheless, even in the early period, Maccabi did have performances and parties to which female relatives were invited, but they were guests at special events and not regular members. There were, apparently, some objections to the low involvement of women in Maccabi (for practical, not ideological, reasons). This resulted in a split in its ranks in 1926, and about a 100 of its 260 members left to establish another club: Gioventù Israelitica Tripolitana (GIT, Jewish Tripolitan Youth). The main reason for the break was

43. For a general survey of its activities, see Zuarez et al., *Yahadut Luv*, pp. 156–60.

the desire of those who left to have a stronger emphasis on entertainment (e.g., dancing, parties, and gambling), and at least some of these activities demanded the regular participation of women. The GIT operated for about four years but had to close down for financial reasons.[44]

From 1932 to 1938, Maccabi organized evening courses for the study of Hebrew, English, and French, in which "the members and their wives took part."[45] This statement appears to indicate that membership in Maccabi continued to be restricted to men although their wives could participate in some regular non-sports-related activities. It is quite possible that the offering of evening courses, and especially the inclusion of Hebrew in the curriculum, was influenced by the parallel activity of the Ben Yehudah society (see next section), which attracted a large portion of the youth who wanted to study Hebrew and Jewish subjects. By adding English and French to its program, Maccabi may have hoped to attract those people who were interested in studying European languages for economic or social reasons.

During this period, women also participated in performances that were staged by Maccabi in Judeo-Arabic and in Italian. This activity was quite new among Jewish adults in Tripoli. Although the European schools gave student performances from the late nineteenth century on, it was not customary for Libyan Jewish adults, and particularly not for Jewish women, to participate in the theater. Although these shows were intended primarily for club members, they became quite popular among the general Jewish public. Here, too, the example set by the Ben Yehudah society in this respect might have been of some influence, and other organizations, too, tried to strengthen their popularity by imitating them.

Due to the anti-Semitic racial legislation of late 1938, Maccabi ceased to operate in 1939. The club reopened in 1943 on a much larger scale than before the war. In 1944 it had about 500 members (with an additional 100 in the sports section), including some women. Membership later dropped, and in 1947 stood at 150 of both sexes. The reasons for the decline included the growing number of Jewish youth organizations in Tripoli in the late 1940s and the November 1945 riots (in which over a hundred people were killed and much property was destroyed). Because of their relatively small number and recent inclusion, female members

44. De Felice, *Jews in an Arab Land*, p. 327, n. 46.
45. Zuarez et al., *Yahadut Luv*, p. 159.

were, for the most part, not involved in the leadership of Maccabi; there was apparently only one female board member.[46]

During the second period of its operation, Maccabi laid great emphasis on activities involving both sexes. The main reason for this change was the desire to prevent assimilation and mixed marriages between Jews and Christians (Italian or British). In order to convince the youth not to look for entertainment elsewhere, various Jewish organizations tried to offer satisfactory alternatives. The Maccabi club organized various kinds of entertainment, which took place mainly on Sabbath and holiday evenings. Hundreds of young Jews attended these parties, which often lasted until the early hours of the morning. Quite a few of the more traditional members of the community did not view these activities with favor, because they feared a deterioration in morals. Nevertheless, they did not oppose this development openly, because they knew that its aim was to prevent a much less desired outcome. These parties resulted in quite a few weddings, and this was another sign of the changing times in a community in which fixed marriages were the rule. On Saturdays, Maccabi started to offer lectures on cultural, historical, and contemporary issues. This, too, was done in an attempt to attract Jews of both sexes to attend exclusively Jewish activities and prevent them as much as possible from mixing with the gentiles.[47] The club also tried to answer the religious needs of the youth, who were accustomed from infancy to participating in religious activities, especially on the Sabbath and holidays. To fulfill this need, the leadership of Maccabi organized Sabbath prayers with a male choir for an audience of both sexes.[48]

Maccabi emphasized recreational activities for the whole family in which cultural and religious events were included, whereas some other organizations were more ideologically motivated. The influence of these organizations, especially during the 1940s, caused the Maccabi club to add more scholarly activities to its program and to try to cooperate with the other Zionist groups. The latter, however, regarded

46. In 1944, one woman, Lucia Levy, occupied the tenth place in the thirteen-member executive committee of Maccabi, and she was responsible for instruction and Hebrew culture. The board that was elected in mid-1945 did not include any women. See Reports of Maccabi, Tripoli, October 1944 and 14 June 1945, CZA, S5/797.

47. Zuarez et al., *Yahadut Luv,* p. 160.

48. Maccabi, Tripoli, to the Youth Department/Religious Division, Jerusalem, 20 January 1947, CZA, S32/121.

Maccabi as less dedicated to Zionism and not a very serious organization: they claimed that it occupied itself first and foremost with sports and entertainment and that its membership and audiences were mainly the wealthier Jews who were more inclined to assimilation.[49] Because of these perceptions, competition and at times ill feelings between Maccabi and the other Zionist organizations existed.

During the more than thirty years of its experience in Tripoli, the Maccabi club played an important role in the community. It pioneered in sporting activities and also sponsored recreational events for the whole family. Although it focused on sports and entertainment, it also paid increasing attention to scholarly and religious issues. In addition, although it started as an all-male organization, it was the first Libyan Jewish society to gradually incorporate women into its activities. Consequently, when other groups were formed, activities involving mixed participants and audiences were not a novelty anymore. It was possible for them to start from a more advanced beginning in this respect and reach higher stages of intergender cooperation.

The Ben Yehudah Society
The Ben Yehudah society was an indigenous Tripolitan Jewish organization that played a major role in the 1930s in changing the cultural, social, and political aspirations and behavior of the Libyan Jews, especially their youth. The immediate goal of the Ben Yehudah society was the revival of the Hebrew language, because they regarded it as one of the most exigent measures for national Zionist revival. The ideology of the society also extended to social and economic issues, and as a result, its influence on the youth was all-embracing, including cultural, social, economic, and political aspects. During the first period of its operation (1931–39), the Ben Yehudah society focused on teaching, but it did sponsor recreational activities (e.g., performances and parties), and since its facilities served as a meeting place for a large part of the Tripolitan Jewish youth, it can also be regarded as an organization for the youth. During the 1930s, women participated in the activities of the Ben Yehudah society but did not attain leadership positions, and their status was lower than that of the male members.[50] Similar to other

49. "The Pioneering Youth Movement in Tripoli," early 5705 (Fall 1944), CZA, S6/1068.
50. "Matzav ha-Yehudim bi-Ṭripoli," *Yalquṭ ha-Mizraḥ ha-Tikhon* 6–7 (August 1935): 35.

organizations, the Ben Yehudah society had to cease operations during World War II due to the racial legislation.

A short while after the renewal of the Ben Yehudah society's activities in Tripoli (11 July 1943), a genuine youth movement emerged from it. By that time, a Hebrew day school was already being planned by the regular communal education system, with the active involvement of the Ben Yehudah society veterans. Consequently, it was decided to shift the society's focus from teaching to social and cultural activities, although Hebrew courses were still provided. As a result, numerous young Jews of both sexes who lived in the old Jewish neighborhoods and belonged to the lower socioeconomic strata came to the club each night for study and recreation. This change in the character of the organization came at the same time as attempts of Jewish emissaries from Palestine to organize the indigenous youth, including little children, in youth movements. In order to facilitate their activities, the emissaries wanted to operate through an existing organization that was ideologically close to their outlook. They preferred the Ben Yehudah society, with its stress on Zionism and culture, to Maccabi, which emphasized recreational activities. Another reason for the choice of the Ben Yehudah society was a practical one and was related to communication difficulties between the emissaries and the Tripolitan youth. The Ben Yehudah society's activists (in contrast to most of those in Maccabi) were fluent in Hebrew, and many of the local emissaries knew hardly any Italian, not to mention the local Judeo-Arabic, which were the main languages of the Tripolitan Jews. By cooperating with the Ben Yehudah society, the emissaries found an ideal intermediary from both the ideological and communication aspects.

Despite the obvious advantages that the Palestinian Jewish emissaries had from working through the Ben Yehudah society, they were critical of what they regarded as the organization's decadent idiosyncrasies. The emissaries complained that most of the men came to the Ben Yehudah club to meet girls, buy sweets and liquor, smoke, and play billiards—activities that the emissaries strongly condemned as signs of intellectual and physical degeneration. It was noted that on those nights when women came to attend their Hebrew classes, the number of male visitors was especially large, and they came there mainly to meet the women. The emissaries wanted to use the facilities and prestige of the Ben Yehudah society to create a youth movement on the model of those operating among the Jewish community in Palestine. However, they disapproved of the more frivolous activities of the society and did not want those characteristics to influence the youth movement. Consequently, after the Tripolitan youth movement had a large enough membership, the emissaries decided to separate it from the parent organization so that the "ailments" of the latter would not inflict the former.

In October 1943, after some searching for suitable youth, the emissaries were able to establish a youth movement with about seventy children of both sexes (table 11). The members were divided into three sections: Observers (*maqshivim*), Scouts (*tzofim*), and Seniors (*bogrim*). Graduates of the youth movement and others who planned to settle in a kibbutz in Palestine joined he-Ḥalutz (The Pioneer, see next section). The age-groups of the members in the three sections of the youth movement and he-Ḥalutz changed slightly during the period, but were roughly 11–13, 14–17, 17–20, and 25–30, respectively. Following a period of intensive work, membership in the movement rose, and they moved to separate premises. By this act, the movement established its independent identity, although it continued to carry the name of Ben Yehudah in its title (Tenuʿat ha-Noʿar Ben Yehudah, the Ben Yehudah Youth Movement) in order to continue to benefit from the prestige that the Ben Yehudah society enjoyed in the community.[51]

The Jewish emissaries from Palestine encountered quite a few difficulties introducing new patterns of behavior to the members of the Tripolitan youth movement. One of the concepts that was most difficult for the local community to accept was with regard to the change in the status of women. The youth movement stood for proper but free relations between the sexes, based on the model of Jewish youth movements in Palestine. Since this was in marked contrast to the traditional modes of behavior in Libya, especially in the urban sector, parents worried about the outcome. Rumors began to spread about the questionable morals of the members of the youth movement, and especially of some of their leaders.[52] These rumors and the desire of the Ben

51. The emissaries involved in the establishment of the pioneering youth movement in Tripoli were Yaʾir Duer ("Yariv"), Zeʾev Katz ("Zamir"), and Naftali Bar-Giyora (Rubin, *Luv*, pp. 51–57, 69–72). It seems that the leaders of the Ben Yehudah society who were elected on 5 November 1944 (i.e., after the separation) were more favorably inclined toward the youth movement than the previous leaders. For details, see n. 54 below.

52. Yaʾir [Duer], Summer 1944, CZA, S6/1984; Rubin, *Luv*, p. 69. On the embarrassment of an indigenous Jewish female member of the youth movement when her Palestinian guide tried to hug her in order to evade police surveillance, see ibid., p. 75. One cause of alarm was mixed *horah* dancing.

Table 11. Membership in the Ben Yehudah Youth Movement and
he-Ḥalutz

	SEX	SUMMER 1943	MARCH 1944	SEPTEMBER 1944	DECEMBER 1945	DECEMBER 1945
Ben Yehudah						
Observers	F	1 group	} 60	} 110[a]		1 group
	M	1 group				1 group
Scouts	F	1 group	} 60	{ 4 groups of 10 each		2 groups
	M	1 group				1 group
Seniors	F/M	1 group	10	20		
Total		70	130	170	200	150
He-Ḥalutz	F/M	30		150		
Total		100	130	320	200	150

SOURCE: Reports from Tripoli, 1944–45, CZA, S32/1068.
[a]Data are given for September 1944 for all other categories (including totals) except this one.

Yehudah society to keep the leadership of the youth movement under its control caused a lengthy quarrel between the traditional leadership of the Ben Yehudah society and the new and more daring leadership of the youth movement. One of the major issues of disagreement was the position of women in the movement. This dispute was resolved in 1947, when an understanding was reached regarding the level of independence and cooperation between the two organizations. The leadership of the youth movement was reorganized, and one woman was included.

Several circles in the community opposed the inclusion of girls in mixed activities in the youth movement. Nevertheless, the emissaries insisted that a healthy society is based on regular and equal participation of women in all spheres of life. It was difficult, however, especially in the early stages, to achieve real integration during the discussions and the lectures. These difficulties resulted in part from the general seclusion of girls in Tripoli and from the lower level of education of many of them. Nevertheless, a few girls knew Hebrew quite well, and some even initiated correspondence with Jews in Palestine. Difficulties also resulted from the traditional behavior patterns at home and in the public domain, where it was not customary for women to intervene in scholarly discourse. Even though the discussions in the youth movement were not on Jewish religious subjects, they dealt with Jewish history and destiny, ideological issues, and the like, concerning which girls were not accustomed to offering opinions. Furthermore, even those girls who studied in school had to perform numerous household tasks in the afternoon. This obligation interfered with their studies and left them with little spare time for social activities, including those of the youth movement. Stereotypes relating to occupations were not erased either. Despite the sense of equality that the emissaries tried to imbue in the youth, it was customary in the youth movement for the girls to sweep the floors every Friday. Another difficulty related mainly to the senior groups. It was still customary in Libya, even in the 1940s, to marry off girls at a young age. Consequently, it was regarded as strange and unnatural for adult females to stay single and, furthermore, waste their time in ideological debates with nonrelated bachelors.[53]

Although the youth movement advocated the equal status of women, its leadership until 1947 included only men.[54] During 1945, the activities of the youth movement were led mainly by Abraham Adadi and Tzurishaday Vittorio Fadlun. During the summer of that year, Adadi was responsible for supervision of the other guides, and he himself led three of the girl Scout groups (Alumah, Massadah, and Ḥanitah). Somewhat later, he transferred the guidance of these groups to a more veteran male guide. During this period, several mixed activities were arranged for the members of the movement (e.g., ceremonies to commemorate important events in Jewish history, games, and day trips in the vicinity of Tripoli).[55]

There was a short interruption in the activities of the youth movement due to the November 1945 riots, but it resumed its operations soon after. In December 1945, at the first meeting after this suspension,

53. "The Pioneering Youth Movement in Tripoli," early 5705 (Fall 1944), CZA, S32/1068; Rubin, *Luv*, pp. 56, 72, 92.

54. In early 1944 the indigenous leadership of the youth movement was composed of three men: Asher Messica, Elia 'Azaria, and Tzurishaday Vittorio Fadlun (A. Messica et al., Tripoli, to the Youth Department, Jerusalem, 1 Adar 5704 [24 February 1944], CZA, S32/1068). In the fall of 1944, five members of the Seniors group led the movement, but their names were not provided ("The Pioneering Youth Movement in Tripoli," early 5705 [Fall 1944], CZA, S32/1068). On 5 November 1944, the Ben Yehudah society elected an all-male seven-member board (*Ḥayenu*, Kislev 5705 [November–December 1944]; letters by J. Mimun, 11 Kislev 5705 [28 November 1944], J. Mimun, 17 Kislev 5705 [4 December 1944], and A. Adadi, 5 December 1944, Tripoli, to the Youth Department/Religious Division, CZA, S6/3847).

55. A. Adadi, Tripoli, to the Youth Department, Jerusalem, 28 February, 22 July 1945, CZA, S32/1068; Rubin, *Luv*, p. 72.

some 150 members were present, with the girls in the Scouts section outnumbering the boys. The movement held two weekly meetings (from 4:00 to 7:30 P.M.); on each day, boys and girls met separately. In addition, there were coeducational meetings on Saturdays, which were divided according to age-group.[56]

During 1946, complaints started to mount against Adadi from the more traditional members of the community. Some rabbinical students stated that they opposed his activity in the movement because of what they regarded as irreligious behavior, namely, hiking with girls on Saturdays. Adadi thought the criticism against him was ridiculous. He was, however, well acquainted with the sensitivities of the community and was aware of mounting opposition against him within the movement. As a result, he decided to step down from the leadership of the movement for a while. This move paved the way for some personnel and organizational changes in the leadership of the youth movement.

When Adadi realized that the leadership that replaced him would not allow free relations between the sexes, he incited four board members to create a new and rival youth movement. This split was assisted by Emma Polacco, the director of the Italian Jewish elementary school, who allowed the new movement to use the school's facilities. Adadi's rivals believed that his intent was contrary to the customs of the community, and they claimed to have aroused "all the youth" against him. The opponents of Adadi stated further that Dr. Andrea Vitterbo and Emma Polacco, who supported the establishment of the rival movement, were detached from the traditions of the community because they came from Italy and wanted to reshape the community according to a foreign model.

Veteran members of the youth movement, including some who were now in he-Ḥalutz, called the members to a general meeting and explained to the youth that the rift resulted from personal conflicts and the wish of the dissident members to establish a new movement that would allow more freedom in the relations between the sexes. They claimed further that this venture was under the influence of assimilated Italian Jews who were not sensitive to the customs of the Tripolitan Jews. Following these explanations, most of the members stayed with the older group, which soon thereafter renewed its contacts with the

56. E. ʿAzaria, Tripoli, to the Youth Department, Jerusalem, 28 December 1945, CZA, S32/1068. No details were provided on the Seniors.

Ben Yehudah society, although it remained independent. Those groups whose guides had moved to the new movement received new mentors, and a course for youth movement instructors renewed its operation on a larger scale.[57]

The lengthy disputes within the leadership of the youth movement and between the latter and the Ben Yehudah society were based not only on personal rivalries but also on issues of principle. One of the foremost of these issues was intergender relationships. The behavior of Adadi and his followers was apparently too daring even for many of the young people. This was despite the fact that the Adadi faction, too, was sensitive to the attitude of the community in these matters and often segregated groups according to sex. After the rift, the leadership of the older youth movement appointed Rachel Magnagi as its secretary. This was an important position, because the secretary dealt with other organizations, including the Jewish Agency, and handled most of the reports and the correspondence. Thus, although the veteran youth movement advocated somewhat limited and restricted contacts between the sexes, it was the first organization connected with the Ben Yehudah society to appoint a woman to its board.

By the end of 1947, the strife between the youth movements seems to have quieted down. During weekdays, the members of the Ben Yehudah youth movement participated in various activities in groups segregated according to sex, and on Saturdays there were mixed parties, which were organized each time by a different group. On Saturday evenings, prayer meetings were held "according to the spirit of the Land of Israel." Occasionally, day hikes out of town were organized on Saturdays. The youth movement also staged several performances, and the guides continued to receive instruction in their seminar.[58] From the archival descriptions it turns out that even under the more traditionalist leadership, activities involving both sexes took place on the organization's premises as well as during day hikes out of town. The community, however, did not protest these activities, apparently because the leaders of the movement were careful not to antagonize the spiritual heads of

57. A. Adadi, Tripoli, to the Youth Department, Jerusalem, 3 April 1946, CZA, S32/1068; V. Fadlun, Tripoli, to the Youth Department, Jerusalem, 15 June 1946, CZA, S32/1069; R. Magnagi, Tripoli, to the Youth Department, Jerusalem, 20 August 1947, CZA, S32/1069.
58. R. Magnagi, Tripoli, to the Youth Department/Religious Division, 9 December 1947, CZA S32/123.

the community. One of the expressions of this sensitivity was the keeping of many Jewish religious traditions, including public prayers, even if
in a more Israeli fashion. At that time many Tripolitan Jews contem-
plated emigrating to Israel, and therefore, adjusting to Israeli customs
was viewed with favor.

He-Ḥalutz

Among the socioeconomic innovations of the Palestinian Jewish emissaries was the emphasis on "pioneering," namely, directing the Jews
toward communal agricultural life. Although Jews lived in rural areas in
Libya, most of them were not farmers. Furthermore, agriculture was
not considered a respected profession among the urban Jews. The emissaries, however, wanted to share their beliefs and bring about a social,
economic, and cultural transformation of the Libyan Jewry, and especially of its youth. In order to realize this goal, in mid-1943 they established a local branch of he-Ḥalutz (The Pioneer).[59] The membership of
he-Ḥalutz included graduates of the youth movement and appropriate
people in their twenties who were willing to undergo special training
and change their life-styles in order to eventually settle in a kibbutz in
Palestine. During the summer of 1943, about thirty young Jews of both
sexes aged twenty-five to thirty years joined he-Ḥalutz (see table 11).
The prestige of he-Ḥalutz rose, and in a short time its membership
more than tripled. This resulted in part from a resolution passed by the
Immigration Committee (*va'adat 'aliyah*) of the Tripolitan community,
which distributed the certificates for immigration to Palestine, that only
members of he-Ḥalutz could immigrate to Palestine on the special certificates for pioneers.[60]

At this stage, he-Ḥalutz was headed by a board of active members
and was divided into five immigration groups (*qevutzot 'aliyah*). They
met every Saturday to discuss Zionist and settlement issues, the future
of the members, and the "self-realization of pioneering" (*hagshamah
ishit ḥalutzit*). In addition to these discussion groups, a general meeting
of all the members took place every Saturday.[61] However, they realized

---

59. On the international he-Ḥalutz movement, see *Encyclopaedia Judaica*, s.v. "he-
Ḥalutz."
60. On immigration to Palestine, including the different kinds of certificates, see
below, n. 98.
61. Ya'ir [Duer], Summer 1944, CZA, S6/1984.

that theoretical instruction did not suffice and that practical training for pioneering life in an agricultural commune was needed.

In June 1944, he-Ḥalutz started to train its members in agriculture in a farm located near Zawiya, some thirty miles west of Tripoli. The first group of trainees at the agricultural training farm (*ḥavat hakhsharah ḥaqla'it*) consisted of ten men. At this point it was still considered too bold to let a nonmarried mixed group who were not even related to live together out of town. This moral issue was in addition to the fact that the whole subject of agricultural training was strange to most members of the community, who opposed the idea that their children would live an "immoral life" in order to be trained in a "despicable" profession. The absence of women was regarded by the initiators of the enterprise as an acute problem, and they believed that it hindered the proper preparation of the members for communal life. When referring to this problem, the difficulties that were emphasized were those of atmosphere and keeping the kitchen in order. Thus, the Palestinian Jewish emissary who criticized the traditional outlook of the Tripolitan Jews did in fact reveal his own prejudices by implying that the place of the women was in the kitchen and not in agriculture, even in this new pioneering venture.[62] Somewhat later, however, thirteen men and one woman worked on the farm, but it is not clear whether they all actually lived there and whether the woman performed agricultural work rather than housework. Work at the farm ceased in December 1944 because the owner of the farm decided not to renew the contract with he-Ḥalutz.[63]

Following intensive search, a much bigger farm was located about six miles outside Tripoli, and in February 1945 it was leased for eight years from its Italian owner.[64] The second commune was at first also composed only of men. There was, however, some external female involve-

62. Yariv, Summer 1944, CZA, S6/1984; report from Tripoli, early 5705 (Fall 1944), CZA, S32/1068.

63. Some of the discussions prior to the establishment of the commune were conducted at the home of an Italian Jewish female teacher, Lucia Levy. The emissaries who were involved with the agricultural commune were Ya'ir Duer and Naftali Bar-Giyora (locally known as Moshe Cohen and Yeḥi'el ha-Levy). It was established at the end of the festival of Shavu'ot, and the group was consequently named Bikkurim. See Rubin, *Luv,* pp. 76, 79, 82–83, 125; Zuarez et al., *Yahadut Luv,* pp. 257–59; Yariv, Summer 1944, CZA, S6/1984; Yissakhar, Tiberias (*sic*), Adar–Tammuz 5704 (March–July 1944), CZA, S6/1984; J. Mimun, Tripoli, to the Youth Department/Religious Division, 6 Adar 5705 (19 March 1945), CZA, S32/1068.

64. Rubin, *Luv,* p. 125; Zuarez et al., *Yahadut Luv,* pp. 259–60; J. Mimun, Tripoli, to the Youth Department/Religious Division, 6 Adar 5705 (19 March 1945), CZA, S32/1068.

ment in the activities of the commune. The Tripolitan WIZO members helped see to the needs of the commune members (but these women did not actually work and live on the farm).[65] During 1945 the composition of the commune had changed, and it included females among its members.[66] Although it is not clear how many there were and what their occupations were, it is known that there was at least one woman who was a cook. This commune had to be evacuated during the riots of November 1945. All the members of the commune were saved, including the female cook, whose earrings were plucked from her ears by the mob. The Tripolitan agricultural commune did not renew its activities, and he-Ḥalutz, too, suspended its operations for a few months.

In March 1946 it was decided to renew the activities of he-Ḥalutz. The first meeting took place on 18 May 1946 and was attended by "numerous" members. By that date, the membership of the organization had reached about 150 Jews of both sexes, and the nine-member secretariat included one woman: the teacher Lucia Levy, who represented the Ben Yehudah society. He-Ḥalutz held general meetings for all its members on Saturdays, in which ideological and current issues were aired. During this phase of its operations, two groups of he-Ḥalutz were composed of female workers and pupils from two Jewish vocational schools. These girls, aged sixteen years and older, did not know Hebrew well, and as a result, their ideological instruction was conducted in Italian. They were enthusiastically led by two female students from the Italian high school who also knew no Hebrew. By early 1947, a third female group, guided by a young man, was organized. The girls started to learn Hebrew there and received ideological instruction and one month's training in nursing in the hospital.[67]

The leaders of he-Ḥalutz regarded it as highly important to have written materials for instructing working women, especially those of the "oriental sects" (*'edot ha-mizraḥ*), whose level of education was considered very low. The organization wanted to completely change the lifestyles and values of these girls and to direct them to productive work in Libya and later in Palestine. He-Ḥalutz leaders believed that books on

---

65. *Ḥayenu,* Tammuz 5704 (June–July 1944), pp. 3–4.

66. J. Mimun, Tripoli, to the Youth Department/Religious Division, 6 Adar 5705 (19 March 1944), CZA, S32/1068.

67. Reports sent from Tripoli to the Youth Department, Jerusalem, by V. Fadlun, 3 August 1946, L. Levy, 20 October 1946, [L. Levy], report on he-Ḥalutz, early 1947, CZA, S32/1069; A. Adadi, 23 May 1946, CZA, S32/1068; L. Serrusi, 8 May 1947, CZA, S32/122.

agricultural training for girls were essential for the education of these Tripolitan Jewesses. Due, however, to the limited knowledge of languages by the female instructors and members alike, the local leadership wanted the books to be in French or in English (Italian was not mentioned), and not in Hebrew. By mid-1947, at least one member of these groups was fluent enough in Hebrew to acknowledge the receipt of two Hebrew books and to emphasize the desire of these girls to become pioneers together with their "sisters" in Palestine.[68]

While the theoretical-ideological activity was going on, he-Ḥalutz and ha-Noʿar ha-Aḥid (the Unified Youth) established an urban training commune (*hakhsharah ʿironit*) of approximately twenty members on 24 November 1946. They were employed by various Tripolitan craftsmen and other individuals and deposited their salaries in a mutual treasury. This group lived together in a house belonging to Maccabi in the outskirts of Tripoli. In their spare time they tried to cultivate the small plot of land next to the house. All the needs of the commune were looked after by a secretariat. The original secretariat was composed of two men and one woman, but as time went on, references were made only to an all-male secretariat.[69] The inclusion of women continued to be problematic. In the first year of its existence, quite a few female members of he-Ḥalutz and other supporters from the community visited the commune, especially on the weekends and holidays, and some helped in the work, but none lived there. Only in January 1948 did some females join the commune, and at least one was brought there by her father; that is, she came with her family's blessing. In at least one case, the woman's brother was also a member. Before the breakup of the commune in mid-June 1948 due to Arab riots, there were six female members out of a total of fifteen. Numerous other candidates had to be turned down because of scarcity of funds. It seems, however, that female members did not go out to work but stayed "at home" performing traditional female tasks, such as cooking, cleaning, and doing some maintenance work.[70]

Despite several setbacks in its activity, he-Ḥalutz did contribute to the training of pioneers who wanted to immigrate to Palestine. When

68. Same sources as in n. 67.

69. V. Fadlun, Tripoli, to the Youth Department, Jerusalem, 16 November 1946, CZA, S32/1069; J. Serrusi, Tripoli, to the Youth Department, 20 February 1946, CZA, S32/1069; Rubin, *Luv,* pp. 86–87, 139–92.

70. A. Tayyar, Tripoli, to the Youth Department, Jerusalem, 9 Adar 5708 (17 February 1948), CZA, S32/123.

twenty certificates for the immigration of pioneers were distributed in Tripoli in August 1946, they were given to fifteen men and five women, most of whom were trained in the agricultural commune of he-Ḥalutz. This group (*garʿin,* "kernel"; this is the usual term for a group planning to settle in a kibbutz) faced numerous difficulties in Palestine, not because they were ill-prepared for agricultural communal life but rather because of the attempts of political elements in Palestine to intervene in the group's activities and introduce freer relations between the sexes. As a result of these pressures, the first group of pioneer emigrants from Tripoli disintegrated a few months after its arrival in Palestine.[71]

Other Youth Movements in Tripoli

Ha-Tzofim ha-Datiyyim (the Religious Scouts) was established on 16 February 1943 by five veteran members of the Ben Yehudah society. They started their operations in the Ben Yehudah club but later moved to a separate and bigger house and became somewhat detached from the Ben Yehudah society. The leaders of this movement claimed that their membership was in the hundreds and included children aged ten to eighteen years old from both sexes and from all ranks of life. The movement was active every weekday and also organized camps out of town that lasted from two to three days. The camping, hiking, and sports became a disguise for the members' paramilitary training, and several of them were active in the Haganah (the self-defense organization). The skills they acquired in these activities helped them plan and carry out illegal emigration and defend the community.[72] No specific details on female involvement in these activities were provided, but from the reports on the defense of the community and illegal emigration, it is obvious that women were involved.

There were several unification attempts among the youth movements in Tripoli. During 1949 they joined forces within the framework of Beney ʿAqiva.[73] The membership of the combined movement at that date included both boys and girls.[74]

---

71. J. Mimun, Tripoli, to ha-Ḳibbutz ha-Dati [the Religious Kibbutz Movement], 21 January 1947, CZA, S32/123; Rubin, *Luv,* pp. 86–87, 151, 153–54, 162, 166, 171–73, 176–77, 185, 187–88, 190–91.

72. Zuarez et al., *Yahadut Luv,* pp. 161–64. See below on self-defense and on emigration.

73. On this international Jewish religious youth movement, see *Encyclopaedia Judaica,* s.v. "Benei Akiva."

74. B. Berakhah, Tripoli, to the Youth Department/Religious Division, 17 Av 5709 (11 August 1949), CZA, S32/123.

The Israeli emissaries who were active in Tripoli during the mass emigration period (1949–51) tried to politicize the Libyan Jewish organizations, including the youth movements. The emissaries did this in order to strengthen their political parties, which had sent them to Libya.[75] Reacting against the political agendas of these emissaries, the director of the Talmud Torah school in Tripoli, Gabriel Arbib, established within the premises of his school a youth movement called Talmud Torah Leyli (Nocturnal Talmud Torah). The activities of this movement were supervised by seven male teachers and three seventh-grade Talmud Torah male pupils. These instructors were to be joined by two female teachers following their graduation from an English-language course. By the end of February 1951, the membership of Arbib's organization reached 450 boys and girls (including 45 girls in the third and fourth grades). The activities included courses in Hebrew, geography, history, and Zionism; singing and playing games; and helping those pupils who had difficulties with their homework.[76] It seems that this movement included mainly pupils of the Talmud Torah school and that its main purpose was to keep the school's pupils off the streets and away from undesired ideological influences.

In mid-1951 a group of thirteen females led by Pedahtzur Hacmun met three times a week to study Hebrew (including grammar) and the geography of Israel. On Saturdays, they had general discussions on Zionism, life in Israel, and the like. This group did not have a regular meeting place and used to convene in the home of one of the members. Because of the restricted meeting place, they had to limit their activities and the size of the group.[77] It is possible that similar groups that were not connected to any of the larger organizations met privately in other houses. Even if this was a unique case, it shows how eager some Libyan Jewish women were to learn Hebrew and to prepare themselves for their immigration to Israel.

Youth Movements outside Tripoli

During the 1940s, many Jewish communities in Libya arranged activities for the youth, quite often though the local Hebrew school or the

---

75. These factions belonged to the religious movement, the Center, and the Left (Y. Greenfeld, Tripoli, 23 August 1950, CZA, S20/224[1]).

76. G. Arbib and B. Berakhah, Tripoli, to the Youth Department/Religious Division, 15 and 26 February 1951, CZA, S32/124.

77. P. Hacmun, Tripoli, to the Youth Department, Jerusalem, 27 Iyyar 5711 (1 June 1951), CZA, S32/1069.

local branch of the Ben Yehudah society. There are very few details on these activities, especially on female involvement, with the exception of those that took place in Benghazi and in Zliten.

In Benghazi the Jewish youth movement started shortly after the final British occupation of Cyrenaica in late 1942, due mainly to the strong influence of the Palestinian Jewish soldiers on the local community. One of the main problems that the youth movement in Benghazi faced was the lack of an appropriate meeting place.[78] Following the departure of the Jewish soldiers from Benghazi in late 1944-early 1945, a local committee was elected to lead the youth movement. This seven-member committee included one woman, Rinah Na'im, who was elected in the sixth slot and acted as an assistant. The movement was divided into four groups: two of senior girls, one of senior boys, and one of junior girls, but only the last group was led by a woman (Rinah Na'im). All the groups studied Hebrew as part of their activities.[79]

Some eighty members of both sexes, divided into eight groups, were involved in the activities of he-Ḥalutz in Benghazi. The goal of this association was to establish an agricultural communal training farm, and an 8-dunam farm near Benghazi was selected. Although he-Ḥalutz included women, only men were mentioned in connection with this commune.[80]

In addition to these organizations, there was a youth club in Benghazi that previously had served as the Jewish soldiers club (Ge'ula Club). By early 1945, it had about 150 members, some of whom were females. The activities of this club included discussions and lectures, as well as entertainment, dancing, and card playing.[81] This club did not have an ideological orientation and focused on cultural and recreational activities.

In the autumn of 1946, the youth movement in Zliten included 100

78. They met at first in the Hebrew school and then moved to the Ge'ula Club (the Jewish soldiers club). After a while, the adults asked the youth to leave, and for some time they had to meet in the street, until they managed to find a permanent location (Y. Ben 'Ami, Benghazi, 17 December 1944, CZA, S6/1984).

79. K. Jenah and A. Tesceba, Benghazi, to the Zionist Organization, 25 Elul 5705 (4 September 1945), CZA, S32/952.

80. It is quite possible that this organization was identical with the Agudat Na'arey Benghazi (Association of Benghazi Boys) or derived from it. The latter was organized by the Palestinian soldier-teachers, and by early 1945 included about fifty permanent members (*Darkenu*, 5 April 1945; a report by Minkov, attached to a letter from J. Baratz to the Immigration Department, 23 November 1944, CZA, S6/3847).

81. *Darkenu*, 5 April 1945; Y. Ben 'Ami, Benghazi, 17 December 1944, CZA, S6/1984.

boys and 78 girls aged seven to sixteen years. Some fifth-grade students of both sexes assisted the adult guides. In December 1946 a seven-member board was elected that included two women: the secretary, Ruth Shtiyi, and the collector, Malo Salhub. In the opening ceremony of the movement no women addressed the audience, and donations were made only by men, but women participated later on in the singing and dancing.[82]

The Training of Youth Movement Guides
The guides (*madrikhim*) in the youth movement had an even more difficult task than the indigenous teachers in the Hebrew schools in Libya because although the character, methods, and curricula of the Hebrew schools were very different from those of the other schools in Libya at the time, schooling in itself was no innovation. Youth movements, on the other hand, were a new phenomenon in Libya, especially the ideologically oriented ones. Consequently, there was no tradition of youth movement guides in Libya, and most of the initial inspiration and training of the guides came from Palestinian Jews. As time passed, some veteran indigenous guides started to train new guides themselves. In 1947 a special seminar for guides was organized by the Ben Yehudah society in which approximately thirty members of both sexes participated. The instructors in this seminar were apparently all men. Later on, some Israeli emissaries who operated in Tripoli between 1949 and 1951 directed several training programs. One of these programs was for youth movement guides. It was headed by the Israeli immigration officer Meir Max Vardi, who was assisted by three Israelis and a Libyan Jew.[83] Thirty people (twenty women and ten men), most of whom were schoolteachers, participated.

One of the major vehicles for changing the cultural and social position of the Libyan Jewish female was the youth movement. It enhanced the

82. No further details on this movement were provided. See *Nitzanim* 16 (Ṭevet 5707 [December 1947/January 1948]): 10–11; P. Shakir, Zliten, to the Youth Department/ Religious Division, 23 Ḥeshvan 5707 (17 November 1946), CZA, S32/123.

83. The staff included Barukh Duvdevani (the outgoing immigration officer), Yonah Cohen (an Israeli journalist with *Ha-Tzofeh* [Israeli religious daily], who apparently directed the seminar part of the time), Zalman Bugaṭin, and the rabbi and teacher from Khoms, Frigia Zuarez. Details on the training program were not provided. See Zuarez et al., *Yahadut Luv,* p. 171; reports from Tripoli to the Youth Department/Religious Division, by R. Magnagi, 1947, CZA, S32/1069; B. Berakhah, 10 Kislev 5710 (2 December 1949), CZA, S32/123; M. Vardi, 30 May 1951, CZA, S32/124.

cultural level of Jewish women, facilitated their involvement in mixed society, and gradually allowed them to occupy leadership positions in mixed organizations. These improvements were mainly due to the fact that most of these organizations advocated a new socioeconomic order including equal rights for women. Simultaneously, they were sensitive to the traditions of the community and were careful not to antagonize its representatives with drastic social changes.

COMMUNAL SELF-DEFENSE

The Jews of Tripolitania were ill-prepared to defend themselves during the riots of November 1945. The situation drastically changed after the Jewish defense organization in Palestine, the Haganah, sent some of its members to Tripoli to provide the Jews there with paramilitary training, including the use of firearms.[84] The real identity of these emissaries was often concealed from the indigenous Jews, and the Haganah's covert activities were sometimes disguised as activities of the Jewish youth movements (e.g., ha-Tzofim ha-Datiyyim). The training and practice operations were generally conducted in small and detached cells, to prevent the leakage and spread of information, especially if someone got caught by the authorities.

There were only about 200 Haganah members in Tripoli (out of a Jewish population of about 20,000 in the mid-1940s). It was assumed that about 25 percent of these defenders were young women. Some of them participated in the regular training and were eventually convinced that they could not perform the required activities while wearing dresses but should change to pants.[85] Taking into account the innovative nature of this enterprise and the low level of female participation in most mixed voluntary activities, and especially in the politically oriented organizations, female participation in the self-defense organization seems to have been quite high. In addition to these members, the Haganah profited from the wide support of the community. Many Jews, including women and older people, did not participate in the fighting but contributed to the defense of the community by hiding reports, weapons, and ammunition, transferring them, and caring for the wounded.

---

84. Zuarez et al., *Yahadut Luv*, pp. 231–54. On the Haganah in Palestine and on its connections with Jewish communities in the diaspora, see *Encyclopaedia Judaica*, s.v. "Haganah."

85. Zuarez et al., *Yahadut Luv*, pp. 236–37; Rubin, *Luv*, p. 56.

During Arab attacks on the Jewish quarter in the old city of Tripoli, Jewish women often incited the men to defend the community. Furthermore, these women also frightened the rioters by their shouts and the fact that they, too, were carrying arms. Many of the weapons were bought from criminals, and ammunition was often prepared at home, usually by filling pipes or bottles with explosives. Women were involved in the production of ammunition, but as was to be expected, the information on these activities refers mainly to accidents. Thus, for example, two sisters from the Nhaisi family were severely injured, and one of them died from her wounds, following a failure in the production of ammunition at home. Women were also very active in distributing weapons and ammunition from central depots in private homes to members of the Haganah. They would hide the contraband in baskets underneath foodstuffs or on their bodies. Women were very helpful and resourceful in concealing forbidden military equipment and documents from police investigators. The Tripolitan women also cared for the wounded Jewish defenders, mostly men. When these men were in the hospital, the women attended to all their needs and also guarded them from threatening Arabs.[86]

During the Arab attack on the Jewish neighborhoods of Tripoli on 12 June 1948, there was an organized Jewish defense by men, women, and children in the Jewish quarter of the old city. This area was almost completely inhabited by Jews and could be sealed off. The Jews defended the quarter by throwing stones, hand grenades, and Molotov cocktails from windows, balconies, and roofs and attacking the rioters with firearms and sticks. The new neighborhoods of mixed population were far less defendable than the old Jewish quarter because of their population composition and physical structure. Consequently, most of the damage was done there, and many Jews moved back to the old city for security reasons and because their houses and belongings were destroyed.[87]

ZIONIST ACTIVITIES

Jewish women in Libya had a great attachment to the Land of Israel. This was expressed in a number of ways, some of which were more traditional than others. Starting by supporting existing institutions in

---

86. Zuarez et al., *Yahadut Luv,* pp. 234, 245, 252–54.
87. Ibid., pp. 231–32; De Felice, *Jews in an Arab Land,* pp. 223–24.

Palestine, they then became personally involved in the Jewish national revival there. Thus, for example, they were active in collecting money for funds to support traditional-learning and welfare institutions in Israel,[88] but later on they also donated to the JNF. Women also participated in the acquisition of land in Israel and were involved in Zionist activities, legal and illegal immigration to Israel, and the study of various subjects connected with Israel and Judaism (such as the Hebrew language, history, and geography). With the exception of the more traditional fund-raising activities, this participation did not occur until the 1930s.

At the beginning of the twentieth century in Libya, indigenous Jewish men became interested in modern political Zionism. Throughout the whole period of Zionist activity there, no women were on the boards of the mixed-gender Zionist organizations centered in Tripoli and Benghazi. This reflected a situation in which women were seldom involved in political activity and leadership. In the 1940s, however, some women were involved in local branches of WIZO. Women were interested in the development of Jewish settlement in Palestine. Thus, for example, when a representative of the JNF visited Tripoli in 1923 and gave a public lecture on Jewish life in Palestine, there were many women in the audience, which was very uncommon until then.[89]

Young Jewish women became increasingly involved in the operational level of the Zionist youth movements. This involvement was of great significance, because during the 1940s, the youth movements were one of the major channels for the spread of Zionism in Libya. Zionist activity, which was innovative both in content and in method, attracted mostly the young and those who were interested in a comprehensive change in their ideology and life-style. The whole operation was geared toward the creation of a new type of Jew, who would immigrate to Israel and lead a completely different way of life. Because very few young women participated in the agricultural commune and because women were not accustomed to being involved in scholarly and ideological discussions, very few of them reached leadership positions in the Zionist youth movements despite their high membership level.

Among the older adults, only a small number of women were involved in Zionist activity. Some of these activists came from other

---

88. See the section above on welfare activities.
89. A. Elmaleh, Tripoli, to the JNF, Jerusalem, 5 April 1923, CZA, KH1/216.

countries and on the whole were better educated than the majority of the Libyan Jewish female population. Miriam Arari was one of the first female Zionist activists in Libya; in fact, she was one of the first active political Zionists in Libya of either sex. Arari, who was originally from Salonica and had studied in Jerusalem, came to Tripoli in 1919 to teach French and Hebrew at the local AIU girls school. Her superiors in Tripoli did not think much of her teaching abilities but emphasized her involvement in Zionist propaganda. She held meetings accompanied by performances and singing in which AIU students were involved.[90] Her activities were quite exceptional for a Jewish woman in Libya, especially at that period. However, her mark on Libyan Zionism was not deep, because her contract with the AIU was not renewed and she did not remain in Tripoli long.

A more common way for Libyan women to be involved in Zionism in Libya was through donations to the JNF. During the twentieth century, the JNF began to occupy an important place among the various traditional funds that supported institutions in Palestine (e.g., Rabbi Me'ir the Miracle Maker, Rabbi Shim'on Bar Yoḥay, Our Mother Rachel) and was often operated in a similar manner. Collections for the JNF were made in synagogues and cultural-social clubs (such as Ben Yehudah), following speeches and performances. When the collection was conducted in a synagogue, the women threw money from their special section down to sheets held by the men downstairs, accompanying this with cries of joy.[91]

Female support of the JNF included donations for planting trees in Palestine,[92] mention in the Golden Book (*sefer ha-zahav*),[93] and the collection of donations from community members, which were then transferred to the regional representatives of the JNF in Tripoli (all of whom were men). Among the women who were mentioned as espe-

90. L. Loubaton, Tripoli, to AIU, Paris, 16 December 1919, AAIU, IG-2; *Israel,* 11 December 1919.

91. Zuarez and Tayyar, *Ḥokhmat Nashim,* pp. 13–15.

92. See *Ḥayenu,* Tishri, Ḥeshvan, Ṭevet 5705 (September–October 1944, January 1945), for donations made by women or in their honor. According to Rubin (*Luv,* p. 93), in 1945 special performances were staged before a female audience in Tripoli, and a few tens of thousands of MAL were collected to plant a forest in Israel in honor of the Tripolitan women.

93. *Ḥayenu,* Sivan 5705 (June 1945). One of the ways in which the JNF collected money was to have people honor other people by listing their names in the so-called Golden Book and donating money for this purpose. Most of the women honored in this way were written in the lower categories, for which 100 MAL was donated, although for some, like Emma Polacco, 500 MAL was donated.

cially active in collecting donations were Rachel Naʿim and Esther Berrebbi.[94] In addition, some female members of the youth movements participated in special drives to collect money for the JNF in the community. At times, and especially as a Jewish holiday approached, this activity was performed by the whole movement, boys and girls alike. A special case involved a semiclandestine drive in mid-1952, in which twelve pairs of girls visited the homes of approximately 300 of the Jews who remained in Tripoli following the mass emigration. At that time, the Jews were careful not to show any sign of their support for Zionism, and the emptying of their collection boxes[95] became urgent because of the change of the local currency following the declaration of Libyan independence. These girls did a very thorough job, and money was collected whether the family had a collection box or not. Since the organizers of the operation considered it improper to send out mixed couples for this task, only girls from respectable families were invited to participate.[96] In all of these operations, although much of the field work was conducted by women, the overall control and leadership was in the hands of men.

With the exception of female involvement in Hebrew and Jewish studies within the framework of the Ben Yehudah society, there were no other female activities geared toward Israel until the early 1940s. During World War II, Zionist activities were hardly feasible. Following the anti-Semitic racial legislation, World War II, and the encounter with Palestinian Jewish soldiers in the British army who were stationed in Libya, the longing for Zion had strengthened in many circles in Libya. In reaction to the events of the war and the 1945 riots, the attempts to immigrate to Palestine increased among Jewish men and women alike, especially among the younger generation.

Until the late 1940s, Jewish emigration from Libya to Palestine (ʿaliyah) was very limited mainly due to difficulties in entering Palestine but also because of weak motivation for leaving Libya.[97] Thus, during the 1930s, only a few Libyan Jews immigrated to Palestine, mostly with

94. Zuarez and Tayyar, *Ḥokhmat Nashim*, p. 20; *Ḥayenu*, Ḥeshvan 5705 (October 1944), pp. 13–14.

95. Having a collection box in the home was common, not only in Libya, and people donated weekly.

96. C. Solel, Tripoli, to JNF, Jerusalem, 7 July 1952, CZA, S86/180.

97. For a comprehensive study of Jewish emigration from Libya to Israel, see Simon, "Me-ḥug Tziyon."

certificates of "capitalists."[98] Many of these Jews settled in the Monte-fiori neighborhood in Tel Aviv, on lands that were bought by a Libyan Jewess, Buba Jwili, in whose honor they erected a synagogue.[99] Another Tripolitan woman, Rachel Naʿim, used to send money from Tripoli to the Tripolitan immigrants in Tel Aviv. She, too, was later commemorated by the establishment of a synagogue (Ohel Raḥel, Rachel's Tent) in Ramat Gan.[100] On the whole, Libyan Jews received only a few dozen immigration certificates to Palestine during the Mandate period.[101]

Legal emigration from Libya to Palestine was renewed on a limited scale after World War II. During the 1940s, legal immigration to Palestine was very restricted and based on small quotas, and Libyan Jews received few immigration certificates. Some of the certificates that were allocated to the community of Libya were given to families, and in that case, women emigrated in the traditional way as members of a family. Another kind of certificate was distributed to individual "pioneers," and a few of them were granted to women.

In July 1944, a group of twenty families (about ninety people) left Libya for Palestine. This group was headed by a woman, Clara Levy Haddad, together with her "husband," the engineer Moshe Haddad. To make maximum use of each family certificate, the organizers artificially increased the size of the families. Quite a few fictitious marriages and adoptions were arranged solely for this purpose. Such was the marriage of Clara Levy and Moshe Haddad, who were divorced after their arrival

98. During the British Mandate period in Palestine (1921–48), Jewish immigration was based on quotas set up by the British. There were several kinds of immigration certificates, the most important of which were for "capitalists" (those who had a certain sum, usually £1,000, in their possession), "pioneers" (young people who were ready to do any kind of physical work, but particularly in agriculture), and "students" (in high schools, vocational institutes, and universities). The total annual quota was divided by the Jewish Agency among the various countries from which Jews wanted to emigrate to Palestine. The country quotas were determined mainly by the number of candidates for immigration and the political condition in each country. Zionists in Middle Eastern and North African countries often complained that the Jewish Agency gave precedence to European Jews in the allocation of immigration certificates. On the Jewish Agency for Palestine, see *Encyclopaedia Judaica,* s.v. "Jewish Agency."

99. Zuarez et al., *Yahadut Luv,* p. 295.

100. Zuarez and Tayyar, *Ḥokhmat Nashim,* pp. 19–20.

101. It should, however, be remembered that the Zionist movement in Libya had only a few hundred registered members, and the demand for certificates became significant only in the 1940s. Furthermore, following World War II, the Jewish Agency regarded as its major mission the saving of those European Jews who were rescued from concentration camps or who lived in devastated regions in Europe, and consequently, most of the certificates were allocated to them.

in Palestine. Levy was renowned in Libya for her role as a teacher and a member of the Education Department of the community of Tripoli. Her involvement in public affairs can be deduced from the fact that her name was provided by the immigration representative in Tripoli to various Jewish institutions in Palestine. He recommended her as a reliable person who should be contacted whenever there was any problem concerning her group of immigrants. Her loyalty to "the movement" (*ha-tenu'ah,* namely, the Jewish religious movement) was also emphasized by people in Tripoli.[102] Two years later, in mid-1946, Clara Levy was once again one of the contact people (together with Elia Hacmun) for a group of Libyan "pioneer" immigrants to Palestine.[103] Most of these pioneers (five women and fifteen men) were graduates of the agricultural commune of he-Halutz and joined kibbutz Sedeh Eliyahu or family members who had immigrated earlier.[104]

The major change with regard to Jewish emigration from Libya during the 1940s was the spread of illegal immigration (*'aliyah bet*) to Palestine.[105] In some of these attempts, women participated as family members, but in others, the initiative was their own, and they acted as individuals, not as followers.

The earliest method of illegal emigration of Jewish women from Libya was by fictitious marriage. The Palestinian Jewish soldiers were eager to use any means to help the Libyan Jews leave for Palestine. Consequently, fictitious marriages were arranged between those soldiers who were planning to return to Palestine and those indigenous Jewish women who wanted to emigrate or who were threatened by Arab kidnappers. Although some couples stayed married, it was understood that after their arrival in Palestine, the couple would seek a di-

102. J. Fargion, Tripoli, to the Jewish Agency, Jerusalem, 29 June 1944, CZA, S6/3847; J. Fargion, Tripoli, to the Youth Department, Jerusalem, 8 Tammuz 5704 (29 June 1944), CZA, S32/1068; Rubin, *Luv,* pp. 76–77, 89, 99, 126, 129–30. For more details on Clara Levy, see Rubin, *Luv,* pp. 79, 114, 121, 123.

103. Y. Yerfel [Raphael], Youth Department/Religious Division, to J. Mimun, Tripoli, 14 July 1946, CZA, S32/123.

104. See the section on he-Halutz. For immigration purposes it was sufficient for females to be members of he-Halutz, because due to "family problems" (i.e., opposition on the part of the women's families) they were not allowed to join the commune at this period (Rubin, *Luv,* p. 76). For details on this group of immigrants and the reasons for its disintegration, see CZA, S6/1791, S6/3315, S6/3847, S32/123, L10/237(1).

105. *Bet* was an abbreviation for *bilti legalit,* "illegal." *'Aliyah bet* can also be interpreted as "second *'aliyah*" (*bet* is the second letter of the alphabet), in contrast to the first (legal) one. The term should not be confused with Second 'Aliyah (*ha-'aliyah ha-sheniyah*) referring to the 1904–14 emigration of young pioneers from Eastern Europe.

vorce, and the woman would live with relatives, family friends, or on her own. This behavior was quite unusual for Libyan Jewish women and was possible only because of the great desire of many Jews, including women and their families, to emigrate from Libya to Palestine.[106] There are no details on the extent of this phenomenon, which was characteristic of the early 1940s, but it has been estimated that a few dozen women took part.

The desire of the Libyan Jews to leave Libya increased following the growth of Libyan Arab nationalism in the 1940s. Jewish determination was further strengthened after the establishment of the state of Israel in May 1948. During a nine-month period (mid-May 1948 to early February 1949) although every Jew was allowed to enter Israel, departure from Libya was forbidden by the BMA, who did not want the forces of either of the belligerents in Palestine to be strengthened. Only following British recognition of Israel and the ending of most of the hostilities, was the prohibition on Jewish emigration from Libya removed. To facilitate smooth immigration to Israel, Israeli officials were allowed to operate openly in Libya and coordinate the emigration from all across the country directly to the Israeli port of Haifa via Israeli ships.

Before free Jewish emigration from Libya to Israel was allowed, women took part in several bold attempts at clandestine illegal emigration from Tripolitania. They left by the sea route to Sicily and Italy or took the land route to Tunisia and thence to France. Once in Europe, they were assisted in their escape to Palestine by ha-Mosad le-'Aliyah Bet (Organization for Illegal Immigration), which was a branch of the Jewish Agency and was set up by Palestinian Jews. These emigrants, many of whom belonged to the Zionist youth movements and he-Ḥalutz, were organized in secret and detached cells, usually without the knowledge or the approval of their families and the heads of the community. The women who participated were considered even more daring than the men, due to the obstacles that traditionally hindered the freedom of Libyan Jewish women. During their escape, these women had to stay for long periods of time with young non-related men and travel through remote areas vulnerable to attacks by robbers. Occasionally these women even dressed in men's clothing to

---

106. Zuarez et al., *Yahadut Luv*, pp. 264, 275; Zuarez, *Aḥat mini Rabot: Qorot Mishpaḥah Aḥat* (Tel-Aviv: Vaʿad Qehilot Luv be-Yisra'el, 1970), p. 5.

mislead potential assailants.[107] At that time, all this was atypical behavior but was accepted in the unique case of illegal immigration to Palestine.

Those illegal emigrants who took the sea route would hire freight or fishing boats (mainly from Italians). The Jews were smuggled during the night from remote Tripolitanian bays and jetties to Sicily or southern Italy, where representatives of the Jewish Agency took care of them. Most of these emigrants were men, but some groups included women as well. Thus, for example, more than seventy women departed illegally by this route during September 1948.[108]

Another escape route from Libya was through the desert between Tripolitania and Tunisia. This operation benefited from the numerous Muslim smugglers who roamed the area, and the planners of the illegal emigration collaborated with them. Among the organizers was a Tripolitan Jewish woman, Rachel Naʻim. She met the smugglers at her home in Tripoli, where many emigration operations were planned, without the knowledge of most of the emigrants. The Jews who left through the desert were often disguised as Arabs in order to cross the border safely. Local Jewish communities on the Tunisian side assisted the emigrants on their way to Tunis, from which they continued to Marseille, where they were met by representatives of the Jewish Agency.[109]

During the period of mass legal immigration (1949–51), most of the Libyan Jews went directly to Israel, some went to Italy, and approximately 5,000 remained in Libya. Families usually stayed together, but a few hundred young Jews of both sexes immigrated to Israel without their families through ha-Mosad la-ʻAliyat ha-Noʻar (the Organization

107. The references to these activities, from Libyan Jewish and British sources alike, relate only to Tripolitania.

108. According to British reports, 119 men and women left Tripoli for Syracuse on the *Dulcinea* during the night between 31 August and 1 September 1948; 70 women and 4 men left Tripoli for Italy on *Don Chisciotti* during the night between 1 and 2 September 1948. Both these groups reached their destination safely. During the same month, a group with 34 men and 6 women was caught by the British ("Jews," Monthly Political Intelligence Reports, Tripolitania, July–October 1948, PRO, WO, 230/130; Zuarez et al., *Yahadut Luv,* pp. 281, 285–86, 319).

109. One of the Jews who helped the emigrants in Tunisia was Victor Bramli. In early 1949, for example, he secured the release from arrest of approximately a hundred Tripolitan emigrants, including a few women who were dressed like men. He arranged for their accommodations for almost seven months, until they could continue on their trip (Zuarez et al., *Yahadut Luv,* pp. 278–83; Zuarez and Tayyar, *Ḥokhmat Nashim,* p. 23).

for Youth Immigration).[110] From the data on the distribution of male and female Libyan immigrants to Israel, it turns out that among the youth who came through the Organization for Youth Immigration there were more boys than girls, but when families came as a group, there were usually more females than males. This was apparently the result of the reluctance of families to let young women travel on their own, especially to a new country. Also, some of the young male family members had left separately earlier through the Organization for Youth Immigration, and some of the adult men stayed behind to look after their businesses or to oversee the orderly liquidation of their assets.

LEADERSHIP

During the 1940s, a Palestinian Jewish soldier noted that one of the characteristics of Jewish life in Tripoli was the absence of female full-time public servants (*'asqaniyot*).[111] Because all public service in the Jewish community in Libya was voluntary, those who participated in it were often well-to-do men or those who were willing to sacrifice material benefits to serve the public good. This left its mark on Jewish life in Libya, especially in the period immediately after World War II, when many men rushed to make easy money and were left with no spare time for public service. Women were prevented by law in some cases from assuming leadership positions over the community; in other cases, it was voluntary and reflected the structure and activity of the various organizations.

No women participated in leadership of the community during the period under discussion. The organization of the Jewish communities in Tripolitania and Cyrenaica was set down by law for the first time by the Italian legislation of 1916 and was slightly revised a number of times later on. According to this legislation, the right to vote for the leadership of the community was granted only to Libyan and Italian male Jews over twenty-one years old, and only they could be elected to

110. For statistics on emigration from Libya see the statistical reports for 1949–52 of the Immigration Department (CZA, S20/96) and of the Organization for Youth Immigration (CZA, S20/469). See also Zuarez et al., *Yahadut Luv*, pp. 297–321; *American Jewish Yearbook* 53 (1952): 426.

111. "Yehudey Tripoli be-Yamim Eleh," p. 25. As late as the 1960s, Libyan Muslim women still did not participate in mixed activities with men (Attir, "Ideology," p. 124).

office.[112] This was the only time in which Jewish women in Libya were prevented by state legislation from voting and from being elected to positions within the community.

Even without similar laws, most of the Libyan Jewish organizations, and in particular the more politically oriented ones, did not have women in their leadership.[113] This might be due to the fact that women were much less involved in political and ideological discussions than men, and even when they were active in political organizations, it was mainly on the operational level, and the leadership remained in male hands. Some women did become board members in mixed organizations, but they usually held the less senior posts. This occurred mainly during the 1940s, following the growing involvement of women in mixed organizations. Even so, female participation in leadership was not proportional to the size of the female membership in these organizations. Usually, there were more women leaders in the "progressive" and "revolutionary" organizations or in those which had high female membership.

As Jewish women became more involved in communal education, they started to participate in the governing bodies of the various educational institutions. Thus, in the mid-1940s, the Education Department of the community of Tripoli included the Italian-born teacher Clara Levy.[114] Furthermore, women reached high ranks in the Jewish Teachers' Association of Tripoli and Vicinity, which was founded in the 1940s. This achievement was apparently due to the fact that the establishment of the teachers' association was initiated by the teachers of the Hebrew school network, who advocated modern ideas and among whom women played an important role. Thus, in 1946 the seven-member board of this association included two women who came from Italy: the vice-president was Lucia Levy, a teacher and an activist in the Ben Yehudah society, and one of the board members was Emma Polacco,

---

112. There were also some educational and financial restrictions on the holding of public office. See Bengasi, Comunità Israelitica, *Norme per le comunità israelitiche della Libia* (Benghazi: Tipografia Cirenaica Nuova, 1929 VIII), p. 4 (#6, based on Royal Decree #611 of 6 May 1920); De Felice, *Jews in an Arab Land,* p. 128, relating to the Royal Decree of 1928.

113. For example, there were no women among the leaders of the Ben Yehudah society (1931–44), the Zionist Organization of Tripolitania (1916–51), the Zionist Circle in Benghazi (1916–49), the JNF Committee in Tripoli (1945), and even the Association of Libyan Immigrants in Palestine (1943).

114. J. Fargion, Tripoli, to the Youth Department, Jerusalem, 8 Tammuz 5704 (29 June 1944), CZA, S32/1068. See also n. 102.

who directed the elementary Italian Jewish school.[115] In 1949 the five-member board of the Religious Jewish Teachers of Tripolitania included one woman: the treasurer, Lina Serrusi, who won the fifth slot with nineteen votes.[116] The pioneering ideology of he-Ḥalutz, which advocated a comprehensive change in Jewish life-style, the transfer to communal agricultural life, and the equality of women, apparently had only a slight influence on the composition of its board. In 1946 the nine-member secretariat of he-Ḥalutz included only one woman: Lucia Levy.[117] It is not clear how many women were in the organization, but it is known that their full involvement in the experimental agricultural commune was problematic and apparently very low, and this seems to have had an impact on their representation.

With the organization of mass legal emigration from Libya to Israel, special committees were established in Tripoli to organize the flow of emigrants. In 1949 the Immigration Bureau in Tripoli was composed of a board of three men who were assisted by seven salaried clerks, including one woman in the fourth slot: Rachel Magnagi, the secretary of the Ben Yehudah Youth Movement.[118] A year later, the six-member committee for Youth Immigration included representatives of various Tripolitan bodies, and two of them were women: Emma Polacco represented the schools and Esther Ḥaddad was responsible for supplies and equipment.[119]

Although it is true that female representation in leadership was very low, it gradually became an accepted phenomenon. The female office-holders were young and educated, often had an Italian background, and were involved in the Zionist movement. Thus, in those organizations in which female participation was high or where modernist ideas were advocated, intellectual, young, and energetic women could reach leadership positions, although not in proportion to their true participation.

115. *Ha-Tzofeh,* 8 December 1946; P. Shakir, Zliten, to the Youth Department/Religious Division, 23 Ḥeshvan 5707 (18 November 1946), CZA, S32/123. See also n. 102.

116. *Ḥayenu,* 9 September 1949. Lina Serrusi had been a member of he-Ḥalutz in the Ḥanah Senesz group (L. Serrusi, Tripoli, to the Youth Department, 8 May 1947, CZA, S32/122).

117. V. Fadlun, Tripoli, to the Youth Department, Jerusalem, 3 August 1946, CZA, S32/1069.

118. Report No. 1 of the Immigration Bureau, Tripoli, to the Immigration Department, Jerusalem [May 1949], CZA, S20/555.

119. It was not mentioned whom Ḥaddad represented. See Committee for Youth Immigration, Tripoli, to the Youth Department/Religious Division, 28 March 1950, CZA, S86/180.

During the sixteenth to nineteenth centuries, an unknown number of Jewish women reached positions of influence due to their close relations with Muslims, especially with the ruling elite. Jewish sources are silent about this phenomenon, which was atypical of the behavior of Jewish women at the time. European sources occasionally refer to it, especially during the Qaramānlī period (1711–1835). During this era, there were Jewish women who became entertainers and even concubines of Muslim dignitaries. These women had freedom of movement within the rulers' courts, and quite often they were the only means of communication among the various women's quarters and between the latter and the outside world. As a result of their position they were able to spread rumors and intrigue, and sometimes served as tools of rival Muslim parties.[120]

There are hardly any details on the background and identities of these Jewish women. Two exceptions are Esther Arbib ("Queen Esther," d. 1800) and her daughter Mezeltobe (Mazalṭov), who were active in the late 1770s to the 1790s, during the reigns of ʿAlī and Yūsuf Qaramānlī, the autonomous rulers of Tripolitania. They did not live in the palace but had free access to it and visited it frequently.

Esther Arbib's family was an influential one in Tripoli. They were important merchants, and her husband, Yeshaʿyahu Arbib, served as the community's head (*qaʾid*) until 1778, when he was succeeded by their son-in-law, Abraham Khalfon. She reached her position through her wit and character, and not through sexual favors, even according to unflattering European sources: "She is not young, and so corpulent, that it is thought necessary for five or six men to walk always close to the animal she rides on, expressly for the purpose of assisting her in case of a fall."[121] She became acquainted with the ruler when he was ill and used to soothe him with her stories and put him to sleep. Gradually, her influence over him increased, and she conspired to secure the succession of his youngest son, Yūsuf, instead of his two other sons, whom she detested.

Also active in this plot was Mezeltobe, who was rumored to be Yūsuf's mistress. She used to move freely between the women's quar-

120. S. Dearden, *A Nest of Corsairs: The Fighting Karamanlis of Tripoli* (London: John Murray, 1976), pp. 114–15.

121. Tully, *Ten Years*, p. 180 (letter of 26 October 1787); Dearden, *A Nest of Corsairs*, p. 93, quoting a report of the British consul in Tripoli, Edward Cooke, from 12 May 1777.

ters of the ruling family and spread rumor and intrigue, trying to strengthen the position of Yūsuf. One method she used was to try to incriminate Ḥasan, the older prince, for having relations with the wife of Aḥmad, the middle brother. When Mezeltobe realized that her plot had failed and that Aḥmad had decided to punish her, she tried to escape the country. Aḥmad tried to prevent Mezeltobe from taking ship to Malta, but because of the great influence of her mother upon the ruler, she was allowed to leave in November 1790.[122]

The influence of Esther Arbib upon ʿAlī can also be seen from the fact that following the murder of Ḥasan by Yūsuf in July 1790, she managed to convince the ruler that he should not punish Yūsuf. Her reasoning was that ʿAlī was indebted to his younger son, who saved him from being a victim of the ambitious Ḥasan.[123] During the period of her great influence (late 1770s until 1793), Esther Arbib was "considered the head of the Jewish nation, as all favours or petitions granted to the Jews by the Bashaw are only obtained from the sovereign through her influence."[124] It was even rumored in 1786 that thanks to her influence over the ruler, the Jews managed to transfer the assets of Tripoli to Livorno.[125]

When ʿAlī Burghul al-Jazāʾirī seized control of Tripoli in the summer of 1793, all the indigenous population suffered greatly. Esther Arbib was punished not only because of her position in the court but also because of her family's fortunes. She was tightly chained and put in the castle's dungeon until her family ransomed her with 100,000 pataques (£5,000), "in specie or in jewels" but not in paper. The only concession the ruler granted was for her family to fetch an easier chain, and they brought one from the prison of the British consulate.[126] When the Qaramānlīs returned to power in 1795, Esther Arbib regained her influence and kept her position under both ʿAlī and Yūsuf until her death in 1800.[127] There are several other indications that influential Jewesses were active in the court of Tripoli well into the nineteenth century.

122. Tully, *Ten Years,* pp. 268–69 (letter of 10 November 1790); Dearden, *A Nest of Corsairs,* pp. 99–100, 102; Feraud, *Annales tripolitaines,* p. 202n.

123. Feraud, *Annales tripolitaines,* pp. 202, 284.

124. Tully, *Ten Years,* p. 180 (letter of 26 October 1787).

125. Feraud, *Annales tripolitaines,* p. 277 ([les Juifs] ont transporté à Livourne l'actif de Tripoli").

126. Tully, *Ten Years,* pp. 362–63 (letter of 17 August 1793).

127. Dearden, *A Nest of Corsairs,* p. 132. For further details, see Slousch, *Sefer ha-Masa'ot,* 2:57–58.

CONCLUDING REMARKS

Examining the involvement of Libyan Jewish women in public life, one sees that it was not a new phenomenon but that it was usually restricted to the Jewish community. The main change was with regard to the areas, quality, and depth of their involvement. Furthermore, there was a departure from closed female-only circles to mixed organizations and from case-based welfare to attempts at comprehensive changes in political, social, and economic life.

Until the end of the nineteenth century, women's involvement in public life was mainly limited to the practical, emotional, and popular aspects of religion (e.g., the maintenance of synagogues and holy places, preparation of special symbolic dishes for the festivals, saint worship, fasting, wailing) and charitable endeavors. Most of these activities were conducted within the family circle or in a closed female environment. Women had no part in the more intellectual activities of the community due to tradition and their lack of education. The growing involvement of women in education and economic life, the model put forward by the Italian colonialists and the Zionists, and the establishment of new social and cultural structures were the main reasons for the gradual change in the role of Jewish women in the public life of the community.

Hardly any change occurred in women's involvement in religious life. This was the most conservative aspect of life, and traditions were maintained zealously by the religious leaders. There were, however, changes regarding welfare activities. The new welfare societies tried to implement long-term remedies, through training and health care, to cure the social, cultural, and economic ailments of Libyan Jewry. Traditional individual charity did not cease but was no longer the only means of aid to those in need. Some of these operations were not geared only toward women, and consequently contacts between nonrelated males and females grew.

Jewish women also became more involved in recreational activities for both sexes. Although they started as guests of the full-fledged male members of various recreational organizations, they later became members in their own right. Once mixed recreational activities were no longer a novelty, the door was open for mixed cultural operations. These started with the revival of the Hebrew language, where cultural awakening was tied to social and political issues, including the demand for women's full participation in public life.

After World War II, the Zionist youth movements and the Hebrew schools (both of which were heavily influenced by Palestinian Jewish soldiers) not only advocated the equality of women, but numerous instructors were desperately needed, and there was no escape from hiring many women for these jobs. This trend was also manifested later in the activities connected with self-defense and emigration. Simultaneously, women continued to be active in traditional social roles, and many were involved in traditional and modern circles alike.

Holding leadership positions in mixed organizations was the last and most difficult phase for Libyan Jewish women to achieve. This necessitated not only a growing female involvement in mixed organizations but also a change of attitude regarding leadership by men and women alike. Because it was customary among the Jews and the Muslim majority that only men could hold leadership positions, men were reluctant to relinquish their power, and most women were not accustomed to demanding their rights. As a result, the few women in leadership positions were of the new generation, who were better educated, influenced by the European and Zionist models, and active in organizations that called for equal rights for women or that had high female memberships, where women could not be ignored any longer.

Conclusion

❖

In the process of change, the Jewish women of Libya occupied a middle position between the European and the Muslim women there. Many of the Europeans belonged to the veteran merchant Maltese community, which had strong connections with Malta, Italy, and England. Other Europeans included the growing numbers of Italian administrators, military, and settlers and, later, British administrators and military. Although many of the Italian settlers were from underdeveloped regions in their home country, their women were nonetheless better educated and more accustomed to involvement in a mixed society than the indigenous Libyan women. As for Muslim women, they embarked on a road similar to that taken by Libyan Jewish women only after Libya gained its independence, especially following the 1969 revolution. Although the process of change among the Libyan Jewish women did not spill over to the Muslim camp, it was a constant reminder to the Libyan population as a whole that a similar society can absorb changes and yet remain traditional in numerous aspects.

In examining the changes among the Libyan Jewish women, one sees manifested time and again that it was a clear case of change within tradition. Although there were changes in various aspects of life, mostly in the work force and in education, the community at large remained traditional in its interpersonal relations, social structure, and worldview. The principles upon which the community operated did not change drastically, and the power structure did not alter in either the private or the public domain. The basic position of women did not change, despite significant changes in several areas. The discrepancy is easier to understand if one realizes that the problem has two aspects: (1) personal changes based on qualifications and personal initiative; and (2) social concepts and images of one group with regard to itself and other groups, including the notion of equality in all spheres of life. It was one thing, and a difficult one at that, to let the discriminated group, in this case the women, develop and make use of their talents on an individual basis. It was a much more formidable task for the privileged group to fully accept as equals those whom they had regarded for generations as inferior and subordinate.

There were two main reasons for the changes experienced by the Jewish women of Libya: economic pressures and a shift in external role models. As a result of severe and repeated economic crises, families felt compelled to let females go out to work. This was followed by allowing the females to be trained professionally in order to secure a better job with a higher salary. Although the families were not interested at first in more than vocational training, this beginning paved the way for female academic education, which families began to appreciate for its own sake. Thus, a growing number of Libyan Jewish women became educated and went out to work, although there was not a complete correlation between the two processes: many working women remained illiterate, and not all educated women went to work. The gap between private and public position was manifested in this issue: despite the fact that many Jews approved of female education and work outside the household, the communal leadership did not alter its position on this subject, and until the early 1940s provided education only for males. Consequently, all educated Jewish females graduated from Western, nontraditional institutions.

One important source of social concepts and behavior is a group that serves as a model for identity and imitation. There can be more than one source of influence; two or more entities can have a strong impact on a community. This is often the case when dealing with a minority. For a long period of time, the spiritual and temporal leaderships of the Libyan Jews opposed any change in social interreligious and intergender interaction. Nonindigenous rabbis who were imposed on the community by the authorities faced strong resistance to their attempts to introduce changes, even when these were in line with Jewish religious law, because the local leaderships feared an erosion of their power. In contrast to this rigidity, the wealthier Jews were increasingly influenced in their ideas and behavior by Europe. Due to their economic status, the influence of these Jews was not limited to the economic field but was felt also in the political and social spheres. Many poor Jews who wanted to improve their economic condition viewed upward mobility as connected with changes in cultural and social behavior, taking the mercantile Jewish elite as their model.

Because they were a small minority, the Jews of Libya were strongly influenced by the culture and social behavior of the majority population—the Muslims—among whom they had lived for many centuries. With the absence of any other sizable and influential groups, the Muslims—the authorities and the general population—were for a long time the main external source of social influence on the Jews of Libya, including the attitude toward women. This situation started to change in the late nineteenth century, due to the reforms that took place in the Ottoman Empire and to growing European penetration of Libya, which culminated in the Italian military-political occupation. As a result of these developments a Western focus of identity grew in importance in Libya, with opposing reactions from the indigenous Muslims and Jews. The Muslim majority, forced from its position of dominance, regarded the Western influence as a deadly opponent with whom it preferred to have as little contact as possible and, in any case, refused to adopt its worldview. The attitude of the Jews was quite different. The Ottoman reforms and, to a greater extent, the Italian regime improved the status of the Jews by imposing equality among all the various segments of the indigenous population. Nonetheless, because many small Jewish communities lived among the Muslims with few if any Ottoman or Italian administrators close by, the Jews were careful not to antagonize their Muslim neighbors with excessive demands or unconventional behavior. A growing number of urban Jews, however, regarded Western cultural-social concepts, as embodied by the Italian regime and settlers, as their model of inspiration. The impact of this source grew further once Western Jews—first Europeans and later Zionists from Palestine—became dominant in this trend.

However, the Libyan Jews continued to be strongly attached to their internal focus of identity and did not want to lose their uniqueness. A study of social change must take such attitudes into account. Even though external influence in the process of change is important, it became repeatedly evident that successful changes were internally motivated. When foreigners, be they Jews or gentiles, tried to impose changes on the Jewish community of Libya, the leadership and the masses alike vehemently rejected the attempt. Changes were acceptable when individuals and groups felt the need for them and then searched for socially acceptable means to implement the changes. Even when using foreign tools, the community leadership and the majority of the Jews were careful not to cross certain boundaries that were regarded as the limits beyond which the self-identity and survival of the community would be fatally and irreversibly harmed. Thus, female education and paid work were gradually accepted, but free intergender relations and the involvement of women in leadership were not, because these were among the major characteristics of this male-dominated society. Whatever was deemed necessary for the physical survival of the community was approved of, as long as it did not impinge on the cultural-social character of the community.

In Israel, this process of change continued (mainly from the 1950s onward) under drastically different conditions. The barriers surrounding the Libyan Jews continued to exist, due to their settlement in Israel in small homogeneous villages and neighborhoods, but the difference between the various groups was no longer based on religion but on regional origin, and all the groups wanted to become part of the emerging Israeli society. Furthermore, mandatory education obliged all children to attend state school for at least eight years. In addition, economic necessity and custom brought increasing numbers of females of Libyan origin into the work force. The existence of veteran and active women's organizations in Israel also had an impact, as did the inclusion of the Libyan Jews among the "Oriental sects."

One can observe a sort of chain reaction in this process of change. Economic pressures bring greater occupational participation and variety. This has an impact in two spheres. Being an income producer increases the self-esteem of the individual and also the way others view that person. Furthermore, going out of the house, whether into the semiprivate domain, as was the case in the village, or into the public domain, increases the freedom of movement and choice of that individual. Going out to work also had educational and cultural implications, at first closely related to economic needs, namely, the acquisition of vocational training, but later widening into broad academic education. The changes in these fields caused transformations in the private and public domains with regard to intergender relations. The changes in the first two areas—the economy and education—were relatively quick, because they relied on personal initiative and noncommunity schools and businesses. This was not the case in other areas, because the acceptance of a hitherto-underprivileged element as equals was called for. Nonetheless, when the contributions of the formerly inferior group could not be denied, that group gradually reached positions of influence and leadership, although not immediately in proportion to its true involvement and achievements.

❖ BIBLIOGRAPHY ❖

ARCHIVES
Alliance Israélite Universelle (AIU), Paris.
Archivio Storico e Diplomatico (ASD), Rome.
Central Archives for the History of the Jewish People (CAHJP), Jerusalem.
Central Zionist Archives (CZA), Jerusalem.
Public Record Office (PRO), London.

MANUSCRIPTS
Arbib, B. Nunes Vais. "Gli Ebrei di Tripoli." CAHJP, MS. P-66.
Ḥevrat Mora Shamayim. "Sidur Hashkavah." Tripoli, 1949. CAHJP, MS. L-640.

PUBLICATIONS
Abravanel, H. "Les Juifs del'hinterland tripolitain." *Cahiers de l'Alliance Israélite Universelle* 90 (April–May 1955): 20–28.
———. "Shenat Ḥayim le-OSE bi-Ṭripoli (17.3.49–16.3.50)." *Yalquṭ ha-Mizraḥ ha-Tikhon* 2, nos. 5–6 (1950): 85–87.
Antoun, R. T. "On the Modesty of Women in Arab Muslim Villages: A Study in the Accommodation of Tradition." *American Anthropologist* 70 (1968): 671–97.
Attir, M. O. "Ideology, Value Changes, and Women's Social Position in Libyan Society." In *Women and the Family in the Middle East: New Voices of Change,* edited by E. W. Fernea, 121–33. Austin: University of Texas Press, 1985.
Ben-ʿAmi, I. *Haʿaratzat ha-Qedoshim be-Qerev Yehudey Maroqo.* Jerusalem: Magnes Press, 1984.
Bengasi. Comunità Israelitica. *Norme per le comunità israelitiche della Libia.* Benghazi: Tipografia Cirenaica Nuova, 1929 VIII.
Benjamin, I. J. *Eight Years in Asia and Africa from 1846–1855.* Hanover, Germany: The author, 1859.

Chouraqui, A. *L'Alliance Israélite Universelle et la renaissance juive contemporaine, 1860–1960.* Paris: Presses Universitaires de France, 1965.

Dearden, S. *A Nest of Corsairs: The Fighting Karamanlis of Tripoli.* London: John Murray, 1976.

De Felice, R. *Jews in an Arab Land: Libya, 1835–1970.* Austin: University of Texas Press, 1985.

De Marco, R. R. *The Italianization of African Natives: Government Native Education in the Italian Colonies.* New York: Columbia University Teachers' College, 1943.

Elmaleh, A. "'Arey ha-Pera'ot bi-Ṭripoliṭanyah." *Hed ha-Mizraḥ* 4, no. 28 (1945): 6–7; 4, no. 30 (1945): 6; 4, no. 31 (1945): 8–9; 4, no. 32 (1945): 8; 4, no. 33 (1945): 9.

———. "Beyn Shokhney ha-Me'arot bi-Ṭripoliṭanyah." *Hed ha-Mizraḥ* 2, no. 11 (1943): 5; 2, no. 12 (1943): 8–9.

Encyclopaedia Judaica. 16 vols. Jerusalem: Keter Publishing House, 1972.

Encyclopaedia of Islam. New ed. Leiden: E. J. Brill, 1960–.

Evans-Pritchard, E. E. *The Sanusi of Cyrenaica.* Oxford: Oxford University Press, 1969.

Feraud, L. C. *Annales tripolitaines.* Paris: Librairie Vuibert, 1927.

Franco, M. *Essai sur l'histoire des Israélites de l'Empire Ottoman.* Paris: A. Durlacher, 1897.

Goldberg, H. E. *The Book of Mordechai: A Study of the Jews of Libya.* Philadelphia: Institute for the Study of Human Issues, 1980.

———. "The Jewish Wedding in Tripolitania: A Study in Cultural Sources." *Maghreb Review* 3, no. 9 (1978): 1–6.

———. "Torah and Children: Symbolic Aspects of the Reproduction of the Jews and Judaism." In *Judaism Viewed from Within and from Without: Anthropological Studies,* edited by H. E. Goldberg, 107–30. Albany: State University of New York Press, 1987.

Ha-Cohen, M. *Higgid Mordecai.* Jerusalem: Ben-Zvi Institute, 1978.

Handlin, O. *A Continuing Task: American Joint Distribution Committee, 1914–1964.* New York: Random House, 1964.

Ḥazzan, E. *Ta'alumot Lev.* 4 vols. Livorno and Alexandria, 1879–1907.

Hirschberg, H. Z. *A History of the Jews in North Africa.* 2 vols. Leiden: E. J. Brill, 1981.

Italy. Istituto generale di statistica. *VIII Censimento generale della populazione, 1936.* Vol. 5. Rome, 1939.

Kahalon, Y. "Ha-Ma'avaq 'al Demuta ha-Ruḥanit shel ha-'Edah ha-Yehudit be-Luv ba-Me'ah ha-19 uva-'Asor ha-Ri'shon shel ha-Me'ah ha-20." In *Zakhor le-Avraham,* edited by H. Z. Hirschberg, 79–122. Jerusalem: Va'ad 'Adat ha-Ma'araviyyim bi-Yerushalayim, 1972.

Kleinlerer, D. "Cave Dwellers of North Africa: A Visit among the Picturesque Inhabitants of Djebel Garian." *Jewish Tribune* 94, no. 22 (1929): 1, 4.

Leven, N. *Cinquante ans d'histoire: L'Alliance Israélite Universelle, 1860–1910.* Vol. 2. Paris: Librairie F. Alcan, 1920.

Levy, A. "Tripoli." *Bulletin des Ecoles de l'Alliance Israélite Universelle* 44 (April 1914): 207.

Lewis, B. *The Jews of Islam*. Princeton: Princeton University Press, 1984.

Ludvig Salvator, Archduke of Austria. *Yacht-reise in den Syrten*. Prague: H. Mercy, 1874.

Lyon, G. F. *A Narrative of Travels in Northern Africa in the Years 1818, 19, and 20*. London: John Murray, 1966.

"Matzav ha-Yehudim bi-Ṭripoli." *Yalquṭ ha-Mizraḥ ha-Tikhon* 6–7 (1935): 35–36.

Mendelssohn, S. *The Jews of Africa*. London: Kegan Paul, 1920.

Nahon, S. U. "Yehudey Luv." *Yalquṭ ha-Mizraḥ ha-Tikhon* 1 (January 1949): 21–25.

Noy, D. *Shiv'im Sippurim ṿe-Sippur mi-Pi Yehudey Luv*. Jerusalem: Bi-Tefutzot ha-Golah, 1967.

Raccah, G. V. *Lunario ebraico libico 5698*. Tripoli: Zerd, 1938.

Rae, E. *The Country of the Moors: A Journey from Tripoli in Barbary to the City of Kairawan*. London: John Murray, 1877.

Rubin, B.-Z., ed. *Luv: Hedim min ha-Yoman*. Jerusalem: Ha-Agudah le-Moreshet Yehudey Luv, 1988.

Segrè, C. G. *Fourth Shore: The Italian Colonization of Libya*. Chicago: University of Chicago Press, 1974.

Simon, R. "Me-Ḥug Tziyon le-Tziyonut Magshimah: Ha-'Aliyah mi-Luv le-Yisra'el." *Shorashim ba-Mizraḥ* 3 (1991): 295–351.

———. "Ha-Tenu'ah ha-'Ivrit be-Luv." *Shorashim ba-Mizraḥ* 2 (1989): 173–209.

———. "The Trans-Saharan Trade and Its Impact on the Jewish Community of Libya in the Late Ottoman Period." *Proceedings of the American Historical Association, 1987*. Ann Arbor: University Microfilm International, 1988.

———. "Yehudey Luv 'al Saf Sho'ah." *Pe'amim* 28 (1986): 44–77.

———. "Yehudey Luv ṿeha-Sevivah ha-Nokhrit be-Shalhey ha-Tequfah ha-'Uthmanit." *Pe'amim* 3 (1979): 5–36.

Slousch, N. "Les Juifs en Tripolitaine." *Revue du Monde Musulman* 2 (1907): 28–34.

———. *Sefer ha-Masa'ot*. 2 vols. Tel-Aviv: Devir, 1938–43.

———. *Travels in North Africa*. Philadelphia: Jewish Publication Society of America, 1927.

Steele-Grieg, A. *The History of Education in Tripoli from the Time of the Ottoman Occupation to the Fifth Year under British Military Occupation*. Tripoli: British Military Administration, 1948.

Sutton, T. "Coutumes, croyances et légendes." *Revue des Ecoles de l'Alliance Israélite Universelle* 6 (1902): 421–28.

———. "Les Israélites tripolitains." *Revue des Ecoles de l'Alliance Israélite Universelle* 8 (1903): 62–63.

———. "La mort chez les Israélites tripolitains." *Revue des Ecoles de l'Alliance Israélite Universelle* 4 (1902): 263–64.

———. "Usages, moeurs et superstitions des Israélites tripolitains." *Revue des Ecoles de l'Alliance Israélite Universelle* 2 (1901): 153–57.

Ha-Tiqvah, *Hoveret Zikaron*. Tripoli: Teciuba, 5633 [1932].

―――. *Mazkeret le-Yom Haluqat ha-Perasim la-Shanah ha-Revi'it*. Tripoli: Teciuba, 5636 [1935].

Todd, M. L. *Tripoli the Mysterious*. Boston: Small, Maynard, and Co., 1912.

Tully, [Miss]. *Letters Written during a Ten Years' Residence at the Court of Tripoli*. Edited by S. Dearden. London: A. Barker, 1957.

Turkey. Maarif-i Umumiye Nezareti. *Salname-yi Nezaret-i Maarif-i Umumiye*. Istanbul: Asr Matbaası, H1321 (1903).

U.S. Congress. House. *Papers Relating to the Foreign Relations of the United States, 1875*. 44th Cong., 1st sess., 1875. Vol. 2.

"Yehudey Tripoli be-Yamim Eleh." *Milhamtenu* 10 (September 1943): 24–25.

"Ha-Yehudim be-Luv." *Yalqut ha-Mizrah ha-Tikhon* 1, nos. 7–8 (1949): 10–12.

"Ha-Yehudim bi-Tripoli shel Afriqah." *Ha-Mevasser* 13 (18 2d Adar 5670 [29 March 1910]): 203–5.

"Yoman Tripolitani." *Milhamtenu* 8 (July 1943): 24–29.

"Die Zahl der Juden in Tripolis." *Zeitschrift für Demographie und Statistik der Juden* 2 (1906): 176.

Za'if, E. "Mif'alenu ha-Hinukhi bi-Tzefon Afriqah." *Hed ha-Hinukh* 9 (1957): 58–61.

Ziadeh, N. *Sanusiah*. Leiden: E. J. Brill, 1950.

Zuarez, F. *Ahat mini Rabot: Qorot Mishpahah Ahat*. Tel-Aviv: Va'ad Qehilot Luv be-Yisra'el, 1970.

―――. *Anshey Emunah*. Tel-Aviv: Va'ad Qehilot Luv be-Yisra'el, 1983.

Zuarez, F., and F. Tayyar. *Hokhmat Nashim*. Tel-Aviv: Va'ad Qehilot Luv be-Yisra'el, 1982.

Zuarez, F., et al., eds. *Yahadut Luv*. Tel-Aviv: Va'ad Qehilot Luv be-Yisra'el, 1982.

PERIODICALS

American Jewish Yearbook (New York).

Daily Levant Herald (Istanbul).

Darkenu (Tel-Aviv).

Hayenu (Tripoli).

Hed ha-Hinukh (Tel-Aviv).

Hed ha-Mizrah (Tel-Aviv).

Israel (Rome).

Ha-Mevasser (Istanbul).

New York Times (New York).

Nitzanim (Tripoli).

Qol ha-Moreh (Tripoli).

Ha-Tzofeh (Tel-Aviv).

Ha-Yehudi (London).

Abu ʿAziz, Raphael, 80
Adadi, Abraham (Ben Yehudah Youth
    Movement guide), 177, 178–79
Adadi, Abraham (rabbi), 157
Adultery, 68, 70, 72, 73, 98
ʿaliyah, 4, 5, 7, 17, 18, 50, 77, 79, 147,
    148, 149, 152, 168, 180, 185, 190,
    192–97, 199, 203. See also Jews,
    Libyan: emigration of
ʿaliyah bet, 184, 190, 194–96
certificates for, 180, 184, 193
Mosad la-ʿAliyat ha-Noʿar (Organi-
    zation for Youth Immigra-
    tion), 148, 196–97, 199
Alliance Israélite Universelle (AIU),
    11, 17, 98, 110, 112, 114, 166, 167
girls school. See Schools, AIU girls
    school in Tripoli
American Joint Distribution Commit-
    tee (AJDC), 17, 98, 138, 144, 169
ʿAmrus, 6, 7, 46, 88, 93, 150, 161
Arab-Jewish relations, 4, 7, 8, 9, 16–18,
    33, 50, 67, 71–74, 82, 142, 149–
    50, 206. See also Kidnapping
riots, 74, 77, 78, 189
    in 1945, 18, 28, 105–6, 168, 171,
        177, 182, 188, 192
    in 1948, 183, 189
    in 1967, 3–4

Arab Libyan population. See Popula-
    tion
Arari, Miriam, 129–30, 191
Arbib, Bianca Nunes Vais, 166
Arbib, Emilia, 164
Arbib, Esther. See Esther, "Queen"
Arbib, Fortune, 164, 166
Arbib, Gabriel, 185
Arbib, Gustavo, 80
Arbib, Jole, 167
Arbib, Mezeltobe, 200–201
Arbib, Rachel, 164
Arbib, Yeshaʿyahu, 200
Arbib family, 166
Arie, David, 115, 116
Arie, Esther, 115, 116, 117, 121, 164, 165
Artom, Elia Samuele, 81
Association of Religious Jewish
    Teachers of Tripolitania, 199.
    See also Teachers
Associazione Donne Ebree d'Italia
    (ADEI), 167
Auerbach, Moshe, 146
Auerbach, Shemu'el, 146

Balbo, Italo, 65–66, 102
Barce, 78, 151
    Hebrew school in, 151
Bar-Giyora, Naftali, 25, 175, 181

Barda, Raḥamim, 72
Beautification, 32–33, 48, 49, 53, 54,
    55–57, 92. *See also* Cosmeticians
Beggars, 98, 100
Ben Yehudah society, 131–38, 143, 171,
    173–80, 182, 184, 187, 191, 192,
    198. *See also* Schools, ha-
    Tiqvah school
Ben Yehudah Youth Movement,
    174–80, 199. *See also* Youth
    movements
Benchimol, Alegrine, 123
Beney ʿAqiva, 184. *See also* Youth
    movements
Benghazi, 6, 7, 9, 13, 47, 62, 63, 64,
    68, 74, 76, 103–4, 106, 111, 113,
    131, 139–42, 155, 167, 186. *See
    also* Schools, Benghazi He-
    brew school
    youth movement in, 186. *See also*
    Youth movements
Berbers
    relations with Jews, 7, 50
Berrebbi, Esther, 192
Bikkur Ḥolim, 164. *See also* Health
    care
biryonim, 70, 72–73. *See also* Self-
    defense
Board of Italian Jewish Communi-
    ties, 81, 131, 167
Bride-price, 50–52
British army, Palestinian Jewish sol-
    diers' relations with Libyan
    Jews, 16, 44, 49–50, 103, 106,
    138–44, 151, 194, 203
British Military Administration. *See*
    Libya, British Military Admin-
    istration
Bugaṭin, Zalman, 147, 187

Capitulations Agreements, 5, 8–9
Castelbolognesi, Gustavo, 65–66
Castelbolognesi, Mazal-Ṭov, 132
Catholic girls school, Tripoli. *See*

Schools, Catholic girls school,
    Tripoli
Ceremonies, 27–28, 48–49, 52, 54, 55,
    56, 57, 61–62, 90, 94, 155–56,
    158, 159, 202
Charity. *See* Taxation, communal;
    Welfare
Cohen, Yonah, 187
Cooks, 106. *See also* Work, for wages
Cosmeticians, 85, 91, 92. *See also* Beau-
    tification; Work, for wages
Courtship, 47–50, 65–66, 80–82, 89,
    172
Crime, 97–98, 100
Cyrenaica, 6, 7, 16, 77–79, 105, 106

Dar Barukh. *See* Synagogues
Dar Shweykah. *See* Synagogues
Day of Atonement, 159
Derna, 6
Disegni, Dario, 131
Divorce, 26, 46, 58, 59, 64, 67–68, 70,
    193, 194
Dowry, 22, 30, 34, 50–52, 58–60, 63,
    86, 163
Dress, 23, 28–33, 37, 38, 39, 40, 41, 42,
    43, 44, 59, 88, 125, 188, 195, 196.
    See also Modesty
Duer, Yaʾir, 25, 175, 181
Duvdevani, Barukh, 187

Eating customs, 24–25, 29, 53, 87, 141,
    156–57
Education, 15, 108–10, 127–28, 152,
    205. *See also* Kindergartens;
    Schools; Vocational training
    coeducational, 103, 120, 139, 140,
    144, 147, 148
    community-sponsored
    for females, 15, 26–27, 109–10,
    116, 128, 130, 137, 138, 143, 146,
    150, 205
    funding for, 116, 127, 130
    state, 108, 110, 125–31, 138, 142, 149

Entertainers, 27, 48, 55, 91, 93–94, 200. *See also* Work, for wages
Entertainment, 27, 48, 49, 55, 56, 57, 61, 170, 171, 172, 173, 202
Esther, "Queen," 93, 200–201
'Ezrat Nashim (Women's Benevolent Society), 116, 123, 164–66. *See also* Women's organizations

Factory work, 102, 182. *See also* Work, for wages
Fadlun, Tzurishaday Vittorio, 177
Fallaḥ, Khmus, 158
Fasting, 90, 155, 159–160, 161, 202. *See also* Religious life
Fitusi, Ghebri, 65–66
Food, 25, 49, 52, 54, 55, 56, 57, 61–62, 87, 90, 156, 157, 158, 160, 161, 202. *See also* Eating customs
Forti, Abramo, 96
Fresco family, 166
Funeral customs, 27–28, 156, 157

Gebri, Meri, 65
Gershom Me'or ha-Golah, edicts of, 67. *See also* Divorce; Marriage, polygyny
Ge'ula Club, 186. *See also* Youth movements
Gharyan, 6, 7, 24, 29, 32, 47, 50, 52, 62, 67, 68, 89, 90, 96, 162
Gian, Esther, 163
Gioventù Israelitica Tripolitana (GIT), 170–71. *See also* Youth movements
Girls, attitude toward, 22, 25–26, 69, 155, 157, 164
Graves, visiting of, 157–58
Guetta, Djara, 164
Guetta family, 158

Hacmun, Elia, 194
Hacmun, Pedahtzur, 185
Ḥaddad, Esther, 199
Haddad, Moshe, 193
Ḥaddad, Turkiyah, 163–64

Haddad Levy, Clara. *See* Levy, Clara
Ḥag ha-Shoshanim, 47–48, 49. *See also* Courtship
Haganah, 184, 188–89. *See also* Self-defense
Hair, 30, 31, 54, 55, 57, 70, 156. *See also* Modesty
Hajjaj family, 166
Hajwal, Sol. *See* Solika del Maroc
Ḥalitzah, 68. *See also* Divorce; Widowhood
he-Ḥalutz, 175, 178, 180–84, 195. *See also* 'aliyah; Leadership; Youth movements
  cultural activities of, 180, 182, 183, 190
  and gar'in in Palestine, 184, 194
  leadership of, 182, 183, 190, 199
  membership of, 180, 182, 183
  training communes of
    agricultural, 168, 181–82, 184, 186, 190, 194, 199
    urban, 183
Hanukkah, 90, 158
Hassan, Gino, 65–66, 81
Hassan, Rosina, 164
Ḥazzan, Eliyahu, 64
Health care, 25, 92, 101–2, 124, 125, 141, 164–65, 168, 169, 182, 188, 189, 202
Hebrew language, revival of and implications for women, 14–16, 103, 121, 130–37, 147–48, 150–53, 168, 169, 170, 171, 174, 182, 185, 190, 192, 198–99, 202–3
Hebrew schools in Israel, and influence on Libyan Jewish schools, 16, 103, 131, 135, 139–48, 149, 152. *See also* Schools
Henna, 32, 33, 53, 54, 55, 56, 57. *See also* Beautification
Heqdesh, 165. *See also* Health care
Ḥevrah Qadisha, 156–57. *See also* Funeral customs
High Holidays, 53, 159. *See also* Holidays, Jewish

Hirsch, Baroness, 165
Hishavon, 59
Holidays, Jewish, 48, 53–54, 60, 62,
    87, 88, 90, 124, 128, 133–34, 142,
    154, 155, 156, 158, 159, 160, 161
Home industries, 43, 85, 86, 88, 91–
    92, 93. See also Work

Ididia, Issaco Nahum, 100
Illegitimate children, 70
Illiteracy, 34, 35, 109, 110, 140, 155, 205
Immi Esther. See Gian, Esther
Immigration to Israel. See 'aliyah;
    Jews, Libyan: immigration
Intergender contacts, 29, 31, 32, 47–
    50, 52, 65–66, 71–82, 89, 91–
    94, 103, 133–34, 142, 162, 170–
    74, 181, 184–88, 192, 202, 203,
    207
'inuyim, 159–60, 161
Islamization, 74, 75–76, 78–79
Israeli representatives, and activities
    in Libya, 17, 146, 147, 185, 187,
    195
Italian authorities, and involvement
    in Jewish affairs, 64–66, 80–
    81, 83
Italian language, knowledge of, 129,
    130
Italian schools. See Schools, Italian
Italians in Libya. See Population

Jado, concentration camp, 15, 16, 102,
    104, 105, 106, 139. See also Ra-
    cial legislation; World War II
Jazā'irī, 'Alī Burghul al-, 71, 201
Jerba, 161
Jewish Agency, 17, 138, 179, 193, 195,
    196
Jewish National Fund (JNF), 134,
    169, 190, 191–92
Jews, Libyan
    economic conditions of, 5, 7, 14, 17,
        19, 53, 91, 94–95, 98, 101, 104–
        6, 114, 116, 119, 125, 129, 134,

    139, 144, 161, 167, 169, 180, 197,
        200–201, 205, 206
    emigration of, 3–4, 5, 7, 18, 77, 79,
        142, 147, 149, 152, 168, 170. See
        also 'aliyah
    and contacts with Europe, 5, 11–18,
        24, 33–35, 80, 94–95, 111, 164,
        206
    as European citizens, 4, 5, 9, 12, 13,
        65, 67, 76, 80–81, 112–13, 155
    immigration of, 4–5, 67
    and implications of Muslim rule, 4,
        8–10, 13–14. See also Arab-
        Jewish relations
    and contacts with Palestinian Jews,
        14–17, 50, 103, 180, 187, 188–89
    settlement patterns of, 4, 5, 7, 18,
        50–51, 95, 98, 129, 149, 189
Jwili, Buba, 193

Katz, Ze'ev, 175
Ketubbah, 51, 58–59, 68, 83. See also
    Weddings
Khalfon, Abraham, 200
Khalfon, 'Azizah, 30
Khalfon, Eliyahu, 159
Khalfon, Ḥidriyah, 159
Khalfon, Shelomoh, 30
Khalfon synagogue, Zliten. See Syna-
    gogues
Khoms, 6, 32, 64, 74, 75, 78, 111, 113,
    150–51, 155, 161
    Hebrew school in, 150–51
Kidnapping, 74–79, 194
Kindergartens, 120, 132, 144, 149, 150

Language, foreign, and social mobil-
    ity, 112, 122, 171. See also He-
    brew language, revival of; Ital-
    ian language, knowledge of
Laundresses, 106. See also Work, for
    wages
Lavi, Shim'on, 4
Lavoro e Virtù (Work and Virtue),
    166

Leadership, 23, 34, 133, 136, 137, 141,
150, 152, 169, 170, 171–72, 173,
176, 177, 182, 183, 186, 187, 190,
194, 197–201, 203, 207
communal, 27–28, 197–98
of teacher associations, 150, 152, 198
Zionist, 190, 198
Levy, Claire, 123
Levy, Clara, 193–94, 198
Levy, Lucia, 172, 181, 182, 198, 199
Levy, Meir, 123
Levy family, 166
Libya
and Arab nationalism, 16, 17, 77–
79, 195
Arab state of, 16, 147, 149–50, 169,
192, 204
and British Military Administration (BMA), 16–18, 77–79,
105–6, 138, 139, 195
economic conditions in, 12, 15, 17,
19, 91, 94–95, 98–99, 101, 104–
6, 114, 119, 192, 197, 201, 205
Italian rule of, 13–15, 34, 101, 105, 127
attitude of Jews toward, 13, 64–
66, 76–77, 80–81, 83. *See also*
Racial legislation
Muslim society in, 7–9, 13, 14, 18,
33, 78
Ottoman rule in, 4, 5, 8–10, 64, 71–
76, 108
European penetration during, 9,
10, 91, 94–95, 110
French cultural penetration during, 11–12, 91, 95, 99, 110, 114–
26. *See also* Alliance Israélite
Universelle
Italian penetration during, 10–
12, 91, 95, 110–14, 116. *See also*
Schools, Italian
and conflict with United States,
73

Maccabi, 170–73, 183. *See also* Physical
education; Youth movements

Madrikhim, 147, 177, 178, 179, 182, 183,
185, 186–87. *See also* Teacher
training; Youth movements
Magnagi, Rachel, 179, 199
Maids, 73, 86, 91, 95–97, 100. *See also*
Work, for wages
Majority, age of, 65–66, 74, 75–76, 79,
81
Male guardians of women, 22–23, 28,
34, 64, 65–66, 71, 73, 79, 81, 83,
89, 96, 183, 197
Marriage. *See also* Kidnapping; Weddings
age at, 46–47, 64, 65–66, 74, 79,
177
attitude toward, 45–46, 49, 50, 62–
66, 70
fictitious, 49–50, 193, 194–95
mixed, 46, 49, 70, 71
Jewish-Christian, 26, 80–82, 172
Jewish-Muslim, 74–79
mock, 64
polygyny, 4–5, 26, 46, 67
Mercatelli, Luigi, 80–81
Merchants, 29, 91, 92–93. *See also*
Work, for wages
Midwives, 85, 91, 92. *See also* Health
care; Work, for wages
Miqveh, 54, 56, 68–69
Mislata, 6, 32, 53, 60, 76–77, 87, 88,
90, 92, 156
Misrata, 6, 7, 68, 75, 78, 163
Modesty, 28–33, 49, 50, 52, 54, 60, 62,
70, 72–73, 85, 89, 91, 92–94,
96–97, 146
Mohar. *See* Bride-price
Mohar ha-Betulot, 62–63, 163
Mosad la-'Aliyat ha-No'ar. *See* 'aliyah
Motta, Ricardo, 116
Mourning, 28, 156. *See also* Funeral
customs
Mussolini, Benito, 102

Nahum, Lidia Arbib, 166, 167
Nahum family, 166

Naʿim, Rachel, 164, 192, 193, 196
Naʿim, Rinah, 186
Nedunyah. See Dowry
Nemni, Linda, 65–66, 81
Nemni, Raffaelo, 65–66
New Month of the Girls, 90
New Year, 53, 159
Nhaisi, Elia, 81
Nhaisi family, 189
ha-Noʿar ha-Aḥid, 183. See also Youth
    movements
Nunes Vais, Carolina, 111, 164, 165
Nunes Vais, Mario, 80–81
Nunes Vais family, 166
Nurses, 101–2, 103, 104, 168, 182, 188,
    189. See also Health care;
    Work, for wages

Organization for Youth Immigration.
    See ʿaliyah
Ostrich feather processing, 98–99. See
    also Work, for wages
Ottoman Empire
    education in, 108, 126
    European penetration of, 9, 10, 110
    attitude toward non-Muslims, 8–9

Palestine, land acquisition in, 190, 193
Palestinian Jewish institutions, sup-
    port by Libyan Jews, 158, 162–
    63, 189–90, 191
Passover, 48, 53, 87, 88, 90, 156
Physical education, 134, 137, 144, 169–
    73. See also Schools, extracur-
    ricular activities; Maccabi
Poetry, oral, 86, 157, 160
Polacco, Emma, 144, 150, 178, 191,
    198–200
Polygyny. See Marriage, polygyny
Population
    Arab, 5, 14
    Christian, 5, 9, 80, 109, 204
    Italian, 11, 13–14, 34, 65, 80, 101,
        204
    Jewish, 4–7, 50–51, 188, 196

Press, 13, 15, 131
Purim, 90, 133–34, 155, 158
Purity, 54, 56, 68–69

Qabilah tax. See Welfare, funding for
Qadhdhāfī, Muʿammar al-, 7, 204
Qaramānlī, Aḥmad, 201
Qaramānlī, ʿAlī, 200–201
Qaramānlī, Ḥasan, 93, 201
Qaramānlī, Yūsuf, 72, 93, 200–201

Rabbinic students, support of by
    women, 160, 161, 163–64
Racial legislation, Italian, 15, 102, 104,
    136, 137, 138, 139, 171, 174, 192
Religious life, 34, 110, 154–61, 172,
    202. See also Fasting; Saint
    worship; Synagogues
Religious Scouts movement. See ha-
    Tzofim ha-Datiyyim
Rosh ha-Shanah. See New Year

Saint worship, 17, 33, 63, 157–58, 161,
    202. See also Religious life
Salhub, Malo, 187
Sanūsī, Idris al-, 78
Schools
    Alliance Israélite Universelle girls
        school in Tripoli, 11–12, 110,
        112, 114–27, 128, 129, 137, 148–
        50, 165. See also Teachers; Voca-
        tional training
    attendance in, 124
    and relations with communal
        leadership, 114, 115–16, 121
    curriculum of, 114, 120–26, 129,
        148–49, 152, 191
    enrollment in, 117, 120, 149
    extracurricular activities in, 126
    kindergarten, 120, 149
    and relations with Ottoman au-
        thorities, 12, 125–26
    and social integration, 122, 125
    and socioeconomic characteris-

tics of student body, 12, 115,
117, 125
teachers in, 121–22, 123–25, 129–
30, 149, 191
teaching methods in, 124–26
tuition fees of, 113, 115, 117–20,
129
vocational training in, 99, 114–15,
116, 117, 119, 120–23, 149
Barce Hebrew school, 151
Benghazi Hebrew school, 139–42.
See also Education; Hebrew language; Teachers, training of
and attitude of BMA, 138, 139,
140
coeducation in, 139
curriculum of, 139, 140, 142
extracurricular activities in, 142
and involvement of Palestinian
Jews, 139–41
student body of, 140
teachers in, 103–4, 139–44
Catholic girls school, Tripoli, 109–
10, 111
extracurricular activities, 110, 126,
130, 133–35, 142, 144–45, 147,
148, 171
Italian, 11, 12, 14, 111–14, 127–31, 144
curriculum of, 112–14, 115, 144
and socioeconomic characteristics of student body, 12, 111,
112–13, 127–28, 144
teachers in, 112
Khoms Hebrew school, 150–51
Talmud Torah, Tripoli, 109, 143
ha-Tiqvah school, 132–37. *See also*
Education; Hebrew language,
revival of and implications for
women; Teachers; Vocational
training
and attitude toward female education, 133–37
curriculum of, 132, 134–37
extracurricular activities in, 133–
35

student body of, 132, 133
teachers in, 132, 133, 135, 136, 137
vocational training in, 100
Tripoli Hebrew school, 142–45. *See
also* Education; Hebrew language, revival of and implications for women; Kindergartens; Teachers; Vocational
training
curriculum of, 143, 144
extracurricular activities in, 144–
45
kindergarten, 144
student body of, 144, 148, 149
teachers in, 143, 144, 145, 146, 151
Vocational school, Tripoli (1947),
145–47
Zawiya government school, 151
Zliten Hebrew school, 151
Sedeh Eliyahu (kibbutz), 194
Segregation of sexes, 22, 23–25, 26,
29, 32, 33, 47, 71, 82, 84–85, 94,
98, 134, 151
Self-defense, 72–73, 102, 184, 188–89,
203
Serrusi, Lina, 199
Shabetai Zevi, 157–58. *See also* Saint
worship
Shaked, Esther, 151
Shaked, Tzuri'el, 151
Shavu'ot, 158
shidukhin. See Weddings
shosvinin (shawwash). See Weddings
Shtiyi, Ruth, 187
Silva, Elisa, 164
Silva family, 166
Sirt, 6
Società Ebraica Femminile (SEF),
166–67. *See also* Women's orga-
nizations
Solika del Maroc, 63
Song of the Book. *See* Poetry, oral;
Torah scroll, adoration of
Strikes, 106. *See also* Work, for wages
Strongmen. *See biryonim*

Students, school age of Jewish, 116, 127, 128–29,
Sukkot, 53–54, 60, 62, 156
Sūq al-Jum'ah. *See* 'Amrus
Surfir, Giulia, 79
Synagogues
 Dar Barukh, 110, 155
 Dar Shweykah, 158
 establishment of, 34, 155, 158–59
 Khalfon, 159
 maintenance of, 34, 155, 160, 161, 202
 Ṭayyar, 158
 al-Thalithah, 157
 women's participation in service of, 34, 109, 110, 154–56, 191

Tajura, 6
Talmud Torah, Tripoli, 109, 143. *See also* Schools
Talmud Torah Leyli, 185. *See also* Youth movements
Tarhuna, 6, 74, 78
Taxation, communal, 62–64, 94, 95, 161–62. *See also* Welfare, funding for
Tayyar, Emilia, 164
Ṭayyar, Ḥizqiyah, 158–59
Ṭayyar synagogue. *See* Synagogues
Teachers, 102–4, 112, 129, 132–33, 135–37, 147–48, 151–52, 182, 187, 194, 198–99, 203. *See also* Schools; Work, for wages
 associations of, 106, 150, 152, 198, 199
 foreign, 102–3, 112, 122–25, 129
 salaries of, 103–4, 122, 123, 141
 training of, 103, 112, 121, 122–23, 132, 140–41, 146, 147, 148, 151, 152
Teachers' Association of Tripoli and Vicinity, 198. *See also* Teachers
al-Thalithah synagogue. *See* Synagogues
ha-Tiqvah school. *See* Schools, ha-Tiqvah school
Tito, Shalom, 109

Torah scroll, adoration of, 155, 159, 160–61
Tripoli. *See* Arab-Jewish relations; British army; Jews, Libyan; Libya; Ottoman Empire; Population; Schools; Women, Libyan Jewish; Women, Libyan Muslim
Tripoli Hebrew school. *See* Schools, Tripoli Hebrew school
Tubruq, 6
ha-Tzofim ha-Datiyyim (Religious Scouts), 184, 188. *See also* Youth movements

Urbach, Efraim, 143
Urfella, 6

Vardi, Meir Max, 187
Vaturi, Zion, 157
Veil of shame, 50, 52. *See also* Weddings
Veiling, 22, 29–59 passim. *See also* Modesty
Vitterbo, Andrea, 102, 168, 178
Vocational school, Tripoli (1947), 145–47. *See also* Vocational training
Vocational training, 12, 91, 94–97, 99–100, 112–23 passim, 126, 135, 145–47, 148, 149, 152, 165, 166, 167, 169, 202, 205, 207–8

Waitresses, 97, 100, 146. *See also* Work, for wages
Weddings. *See also* Marriage
 customs, 30, 32, 33, 40, 49–60, 61–62, 65–66
 private, 65–66
Welfare, 62–63, 98, 134, 161–69, 202. *See also* Taxation, communal
 funding for, 63, 94, 95, 98, 118–19, 161–63

Widowhood, 27, 58, 59, 71. *See also*
  Halitzah
Women, Libyan Jewish. *See also* Arab-
  Jewish relations; Kidnapping
  economic condition of, 15, 19, 22–
    23, 29, 31, 34, 51, 58–60, 83, 87,
    88, 91, 94, 134, 158, 191
  status of, 19, 21–35, 73, 81–82, 87,
    147–48, 153, 154, 177
  and position vs. men, 22, 25–29,
    147–48, 157, 176, 205
Women, Libyan Muslim, 22, 23, 24,
  28–33 passim, 70, 86, 91, 93,
  101, 102, 110, 130, 150, 162, 197,
  204
Women's Benevolent Society. *See*
  'Ezrat Nashim
Women's International Zionist Organization (WIZO), 168, 182, 190
Women's organizations, 100, 162, 163,
  164–69, 207. *See also* 'Ezrat
  Nashim; Women's International Zionist Organization
Work
  attitude toward, 85, 86, 87, 89, 95
  household, 23, 26, 27, 29, 30, 31, 33,
    43, 47, 50, 54, 84–90, 109, 111,
    124, 132, 148, 177, 181, 183, 207
  rest from, 90
  for wages, 15, 22, 73, 84–86, 91–107,
    121, 146, 182, 205, 207. See also
    Entertainers; Home indus-
    tries; Merchants; Nurses;
    Schools; Teachers
World War II. *See also* Jado; Racial
  legislation, Italian

effects on education, 15–16, 137–38,
  142, 146, 174
effects on work, 15, 97, 102, 104–5

Yefren, 6, 7, 24, 29, 32, 50, 51, 53, 54,
  56, 58, 60, 62, 69, 86–90, 93,
  158, 159, 162
Yelloz, Shelomo, 79, 100, 145–46
Yom Kippur, 159
Youth immigration. *See* 'aliyah
Youth movements, 16, 49, 147, 169–
  88, 190, 195. *See also* Ben
  Yehudah Youth Movement;
  He Halutz; Madrikhim

Zanzur, 6, 69
Zawiya, 6, 7, 25, 32, 52, 151, 181
  government school in, 151. *See also*
    Schools
Zionism, 13–15, 77, 129–30, 173–99
  passim. *See also* Hebrew lan-
    guage, revival of and implica-
    tions for women
  fund drives for, 190, 191–92
  and implications for women, 14–
    16, 133–34, 137, 168, 170, 176,
    180–83, 185, 187–97, 199, 202–3
Zliten, 6, 32, 151, 159, 186–87
  Hebrew school in, 151. *See also*
    Schools
  youth movement in, 186–87. *See
    also* Youth movements
Zu'ara, 6, 7, 32
Zuarez, Frigia, 150–51, 187